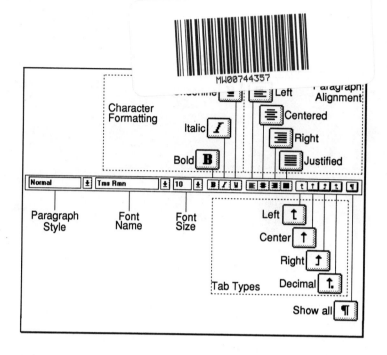

The MS LineDraw Character Set

	0	1	2	3	4	5	6	7	8	9
170+										
180+										
190+										
200+										
210+										
220+										

The SYBEX Instant Reference Series

Instant References are available on these topics:

AutoCAD Release 11

dBASE

dBASE III PLUS Programming

dBASE IV Programming

dBASE IV 1.1

DESQview

DOS

DOS 5

Harvard Graphics

Harvard Graphics 3

Harvard Graphics for Windows

Lotus 1-2-3 Release 2.2

Lotus 1-2-3 Release 2.3

Lotus 1-2-3 for Windows

Macintosh Software

Microsoft Word for the Macintosh

Microsoft Word for the PC

Norton Desktop for Windows

Norton Utilities 6

PageMaker 4.0 for the Macintosh

Paradox 3.5

PC Tools 7.1

Quattro Pro 3

Windows 3.0

WordPerfect 5

WordPerfect 5.1

WordPerfect 5.1 for Windows

Computer users are not all alike.
Neither are SYBEX books.

We know our customers have a variety of needs. They've told us so. And because we've listened, we've developed several distinct types of books to meet the needs of each of our customers. What are you looking for in computer help?

If you're looking for the basics, try the **ABC's** series, or for a more visual approach, select **Teach Yourself.**

Mastering and **Understanding** titles offer you a step-by-step introduction, plus an in-depth examination of intermediate-level features, to use as you progress.

Our **Up & Running** series is designed for computer-literate consumers who want a no-nonsense overview of new programs. Just 20 basic lessons, and you're on your way.

SYBEX **Encyclopedias** and **Desktop References** provide a *comprehensive reference* and explanation of all of the commands, features, and functions of the subject software.

Sometimes a subject requires a special treatment that our standard series don't provide. So you'll find we have titles like **Advanced Techniques, Handbooks, Tips & Tricks,** and others that are specifically tailored to satisfy a unique need.

You'll find SYBEX publishes a variety of books on every popular software package. Looking for computer help? Help Yourself to SYBEX.

For a complete catalog of our publications:

SYBEX Inc.
2021 Challenger Drive, Alameda, CA 94501
Tel: (510) 523-8233/(800) 227-2346 Telex: 336311
Fax: (510) 523-2373

SYBEX is committed to using natural resources wisely to preserve and improve our environment. This is why we have been printing the text of books like this one on recycled paper since 1982.

This year our use of recycled paper will result in the saving of more than 15,300 trees. We will lower air pollution effluents by 54,000 pounds, save 6,300,000 gallons of water, and reduce landfill by 2,700 cubic yards.

In choosing a SYBEX book you are not only making a choice for the best in skills and information, you are also choosing to enhance the quality of life for all of us.

Microsoft® Word for Windows,™
Version 2.0
Instant Reference

Robert Shepherd

SYBEX®

San Francisco • Paris • Düsseldorf • Soest

Acquisitions Editor: Dianne King
Series Editor: James A. Compton
Developmental Editor: Doug Robert
Editor: Savitha Varadan
Technical Editor: Bruce Gendron
Production: Robert Shepherd
Cover Designer: Archer Design

Library of Congress Card Number: 91-68450

ISBN: 0-7821-1054-1

Manufactured in the United States of America

20 19 18 17 16 15 14 13 12 11
10 9 8

For Jana

Tho, we are not now that strength that in old days
Moved earth and heaven; that which we are we are;
One equal temper of heroic hearts,
Made weak by time and fate, but strong in will
To strive, to seek, to find, and not to yield.

—Alfred, Lord Tennyson (*Ulysses*)

Acknowledgments

A lot of people contributed to this book. The author gets his name on the cover, but there would be no book to tickle the author's ego without the help of many others.

Savitha Varadan of SYBEX edited this book, and contributed a great deal to it. Every writer has multiple blind spots, and Savitha illuminated mine —she moved most of my commas to better locations, showed me how to treat parenthetical sentences, pointed out when my prose was more than a little windy, and generally untangled my fingers from my keyboard. Savitha allowed me my occasional forays into what some might call humor, and pulled me back from the precipice when I was in danger of making a fool of myself. Thanks, Savitha!

The unsung hero of many a computer book is the technical editor. Mine was Bruce Gendron, who tested *everything* diligently, pointing out not only my mistakes, but also my assumptions that would have left the reader baffled and bewildered. I've come to the conclusion that the more a technical editor aggravates me, the better the job that he or she is doing. It's not easy having your shortcomings brought into sharp focus on a Post-It! Thanks to you too, Bruce.

Throughout this project I've also had a daytime job, and I owe a debt of gratitude to the people at Ungermann-Bass, for whom I produce a magazine every month, for their compassion during the rough spots, and their tolerance of the time I had to devote to this book. Merra Lee Moffitt is one of those, and deserves thanks also for reviewing parts of the manuscript. Dave Sorem is the magazine's Managing Editor, and thanks to Dave for taking care of business on several occasions when I was just too stressed to deal with it.

My assistant Kerrie Swan proved again that she's priceless, with her help on this book. Kerrie researched many things for me, especially back in the days when we had advance copies of Word and incomplete documentation; several of her reports became the basis for topics (most notably the section on Microsoft Draw). On top of this, she took over many aspects of producing that magazine, and so kept a roof over my head and food on the table.

And thanks, too, to Joanne, for providing shelter from the storm, and for understanding and compassion bordering on sainthood.

Table of Contents

INTRODUCTION

Microsoft Word has a long and distinguished history, going back to 1985 with version 1.0 for DOS computers. Since then, Microsoft has produced a version of Word for the Macintosh, and in late 1989, Word for Windows 1.0. The first "WinWord" was a tremendous advance over its DOS ancestor, taking advantange of the Windows graphical user interface to provide very realistic document display, and a well organized and consistent user interface through menus and dialog boxes.

Word 2.0 was announced officially in November 1991. It's interesting to note that Microsoft often refers to the product simply as "Word," a sign that the DOS version may have a limited future.

The latest Word can properly be called a "feature-oriented" release. Although it expands on Word 1.0's basic design and corrects a few flaws, Microsoft seems to have put the bulk of its resources into adding features that induce you to spend more time inside Word (and not using products from other companies), and features directly targeted at competing with WordPerfect, the word processing program that's been in a neck-and-neck race with Word for many years. This will certainly benefit those of you moving to Word from Word-Perfect, and, in a roundabout way, will benefit everyone because WordPerfect Corporation's ideas and expertise have been added to Microsoft's product.

Is This Book for You?

If you were stunned (like the author) when you unpacked Word and found more than 1,200 pages of documentation, you'll really appreciate the months we've spent distilling that information down to its essentials. We've eliminated the redundancy, the long explanations of very basic concepts (we expect you to know how to operate Windows), and the tutorials and examples. We had to leave out information about features we believe aren't used often, and on occasion we'll refer you to Word's online help system or even to the manuals.

We intend for this book to serve you in the way that its title implies: as an "Instant Reference," the book you turn to when you have a specific question. It's organized alphabetically like an encyclopedia, into dozens of topics, from "Annotations" to "Viewing Documents." There are cross-references to other topics at the end of most topics, and the index lets you find the information you want quickly.

For a deeper understanding of Word, we highly recommend *Mastering Microsoft Word for Windows, Version 2.0* by Michael J. Young, just recently published by SYBEX. Our goal is to make these two books the only ones you'll need to successfully master and use Word.

Conventions

This book uses a few typographic and graphical devices to speed up your comprehension and to save space. We assume that you know what it means to "click a button," and how to select menu commands and work with the various dialog boxes and windows common to all Windows programs.

Keys are represented by small pictures of the top of the key. The Enter key looks like this: ⏎. When you must press several keys in combination, we'll connect them with a plus (+) sign; Shift + Ins means that you should hold down the Shift key while you press the Ins key.

Menu commands are distinguished by a special font and the use of an arrow to separate the name of a menu from the specific item on the menu. For example, we represent the Save command on the File menu as File→Save. Think of it as saying, "Pull down the File menu, then go to the Save command."

Because we assume that you're familiar with Windows, we don't bother to give you the keyboard equivalent for selecting a menu item; you should already know that you can hold down Alt while pressing the first letter of the menu name to display it.

Buttons are represented by the legend on the button inside a box. The familiar "OK" button looks like this: OK. Another assumption we've made is that you know how to use the OK and Cancel buttons in dialog boxes, and you don't need us to tell you about it every time we describe a dialog box.

ANNOTATIONS

Annotations are notes you insert into a document, much like foot-notes. Annotations have their own numbering system separate from footnotes, including the initials of whoever inserted the annotation (see the sample screen below). This makes annotation ideal for on-line review of documents—you can distribute one copy of the document file to several reviewers, perhaps on disk or over a network, and each reviewer can insert his or her comments directly into the document. When the review is complete, you can look at the comments in the document, in context, and incorporate suggestions. Annotations are printed at the end of the document, on a separate page.

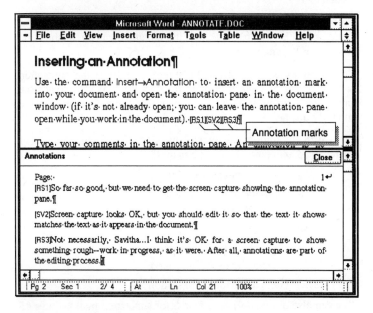

Inserting an Annotation

Use the command Insert→Annotation to insert an annotation mark into your document and open the annotation pane in the document window. If it's not already open, you can leave the annotation pane open while you work in the document.

Type your comments in the annotation pane. An annotation is no different from ordinary Word text, so you can format it any way you like—you can even include graphics.

Viewing Annotations

To display or hide annotation marks, use the Hidden Text display option in the View category of the Options dialog box (Tools→Options). Annotation marks are automatically (and permanently) formatted as hidden text, so hidden text must be visible for you to work with annotation marks. Visible annotation marks consist of a reviewer's initials and a number between square brackets, such as *[RS27]*. You can also click ¶ in the Ribbon to turn on display of hidden text.

To view a specific annotation, double-click its annotation mark. Word opens the annotation pane if it's not already open, to show the contents of the annotation.

To review annotations in a document, just leave the annotation pane open. As you scroll through the document, Word updates the annotation window to show the contents of the annotations on the currently displayed view of the document.

To search for annotation marks, use Edit→Goto and type one of the reserved annotation bookmark names:

a	Go to the next annotation
a-	Go to the previous annotation
an	Go to annotation n
a+n	Go forward n annotations
a-n	Go backward n annotations
pxan	Go to annotation n on page x
sxan	Go to annotation n in section x

You can also use Edit→Find to search for annotation marks. Enter ^5 (caret, five) in the Find What box of the Find dialog box. This finds all annotation marks. You can't search for a specific mark this way, even with hidden text visible.

Managing Annotations

One of the most important features of annotations is that you can lock a document for annotations before you distribute it for review. This means that reviewers must use annotations to insert their comments; they can't insert them directly into the document or change the document in any way. This assures you of control of the review process. Only the author of a document can unlock it. (Of course, as you probably guessed, impersonating the author is as simple as using the same name in the User Info category of Options.)

To lock a document for annotations, use File→Save As and click the File Sharing... button in the dialog box. A second dialog box comes up; check Lock File for Annotations. You can use the same name for the file if you want to, or give it a new name. (The Password box in the File Sharing dialog box sets a password for the document; anyone trying to open the document must have the password.)

You can **copy, cut, paste, or delete annotation marks**, and the annotation content goes with the mark. Word takes care of renumbering annotation marks automatically. If you paste multiple copies of an annotation, Word will renumber annotations accordingly.

Word takes the **initials** it uses in annotation marks from the User Info category in the Options dialog box (Tools→Options). Change these initials to change subsequent annotation marks; the previous initials remain in existing annotation marks. (It works this way to allow multiple reviewers to insert annotation marks with their initials.)

To incorporate something a reviewer has contributed in an annotation, select it in the annotation pane and copy or cut it, then paste it into the document. Don't select the final paragraph marker or the annotation mark in the annotation pane. Emptying the content of an annotation doesn't automatically delete the annotation mark; you must delete that yourself.

To print annotations with a document, use File→Print and click the Options button. In the Options dialog box, select Annotations in the Include with Document section, and click OK. Set any other printing options and print the document. **To print annotations alone,** use File →Print and select Annotations from the Print drop-down list box.

See also: Revision Marks, Footnotes

BOOKMARKS

Bookmarks are tagged locations in a document. They're one of the most widely used constructs in Word. They're used to move to specific locations in a document, as the source material for cross-references, as page range indicators in index entries, to select parts of one document to link to or insert in another, and even to provide input to calculations.

Every bookmark has a name up to 20 characters long. The name must begin with a letter, have no spaces inside, and consist of any combination of letters, numbers, and the underscore (_) character. Word remembers bookmarks exactly as you type them, with upper- and lowercase letters, but bookmark references aren't sensitive to the case of letters—BookMark, BOOKMARK, and bookmark are considered to be the same by Word.

A bookmark can specify a single location (with no text selected, the position of the text insertion cursor) or can span the length of selected text. Bookmarks at a single location are considered "empty," while bookmarks that span text can deliver what they cover to bookmark references; the reference shows the text covered by the bookmark. There will be more on this later.

To insert a bookmark, use Insert→Bookmark. The Bookmark dialog box displays a list of existing bookmark names and a box for typing a new bookmark name. If you select an existing bookmark, it's moved from its current location to the current location of the cursor or selected text.

To delete a bookmark, select an existing bookmark in the Bookmark dialog box and click Delete.

To go to a bookmark, use Edit→Goto. In the Go To dialog box (which looks astonishingly like the Bookmark dialog box), select a bookmark name and click OK. Alternatively, press F5 and type a bookmark name at the Go to: prompt in the status line. Word moves the cursor to the insertion point of an empty bookmark, or moves to and highlights the text spanned by the bookmark. If the bookmark spans more text than can be displayed on one screen Word displays the end of the highlighted text.

When you copy text containing a bookmark, the bookmark is removed from the original text and travels with the copied text; the bookmark moves to wherever the copied text is inserted. Bookmarks located in text that is cut or moved move with the text.

Bookmark References

You can insert the text covered by a bookmark elsewhere in a document with a bookmark reference field. You might do this to create cross references, or to insert the title of a figure or table into text referring to the table or figure.

To insert a bookmark reference, insert field characters by pressing [Ctrl]+[F9] and typing the bookmark name between the field braces. Bookmark references are the one kind of field that doesn't require a field type identifier, although you must preface the bookmark name with REF if the bookmark name happens to be the same as one of the field type identifiers. You can also insert a REF field with the Insert →Field command.

If the bookmark covers a number only, you can use the bookmark name in calculation fields. See the "=" field in the topic "Fields."

You can also insert a reference to the number of the page on which the bookmark appears with the PAGEREF field. Refer to the topic "Cross-References" for more information.

Bookmarks in Linked and Inserted Files

To insert part of a file covered by a bookmark, use the Insert→File command and select the file from the File Name list box. Type the bookmark name in the Range box in the Insert File dialog box to tell Word to insert just the text covered by that bookmark into the current document.

If you check Link to File when you insert the file, you create a link from the current document back to the text under the bookmark in the linked file. This link is inserted in the current (destination) document as an INCLUDE field with the bookmark name. If the linked text has changed in the source document, select the INCLUDE field and press [F9] to update the linked text. If you change the linked text displayed in the destination document, you can send the changes back to the source document by selecting the

INCLUDE field and pressing [Ctrl]+[Shift]+[F7]; only the area defined by the bookmark in the source document is changed.

Bookmarks as Variables

To a programmer, a *variable* is a place to store data. Word's quite useful analog to the variable is the SET field, which allows you to define the content of a bookmark without inserting it over existing text. The bookmark name can then be used just like any other. A good example might be a field like {SET ChapterName "Using Bookmarks"}; the bookmark reference {ChapterName} can be used in the chapter title and anywhere else in the document you want to insert the name of the chapter. SET fields are formatted permanently as hidden text.

See also: Fields, Navigating through Documents

BORDERS AND SHADING

Word gives you the ability to add borders and shading to many kinds of objects in your document:

Object	Exterior Border	Interior Lines	Interior Shading
Paragraphs	✔	✔(between)	✔
Tables	✔	✔	✔
Frames	✔		✔
Pictures	✔		

Caveat: Your printer must be able to print graphics for Word to be able to draw borders or shading.

Use the Format→Border command to control borders and shading. This command displays the Border Cell, Border Table, Border Paragraphs (shown below), or Border Picture dialog box, depending on whether the cursor is in one of those objects.

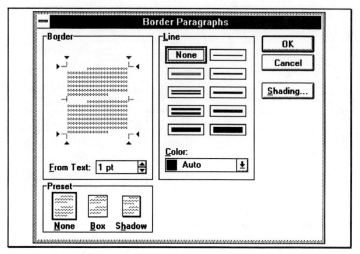

The From Text box controls how far outside the paragraph's text the border appears. The default is 1 point.

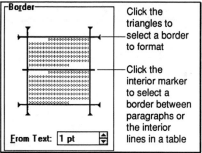

Click the triangles to select a border to format

Click the interior marker to select a border between paragraphs or the interior lines in a table

Word's paradigm for border formatting is illustrated by the sample shown in this dialog box. Each pair of triangles defines one edge of the border. Click on one of the triangles to select that edge to format; hold down ⟨Shift⟩ while you click to select more than one edge to format simultaneously.

Then apply a line style and width by clicking on one of the choices in the Line box. You can choose one of these line styles (the measurements in the figure are in points; a point is 1/72 of an inch):

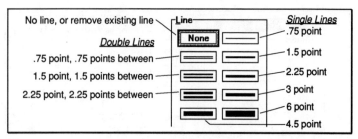

You can also set the line's color using the Color drop down list box. Even if your printer can't produce color, you'll find that light colors, such as gray or yellow, can produce lighter lines when printed in black and white, and this is often useful for adding subtle lines.

Paragraph and Frame Borders

When the cursor is in a paragraph or a frame, Format→Borders displays the Border Paragraphs dialog box. Its sample format has a set of handles in the center of the sample for controlling whether a line appears between paragraphs. This line is only printed or displayed if two or more consecutive paragraphs have this option set. If you select multiple paragraphs, Word formats the border around the paragraphs as a single unit:

These paragraphs...
...all have a shadow...
...boxed border.

These paragraphs have a thick border...
...and thin lines between...
...to make up a simple table.

At the bottom of the dialog box are samples of three commonly-used border styles: None, Box (.75-point rules around all four edges), and Shadow (.75-point rules on the left and top, thicker rules on the right and bottom). Click one of the samples to select a "canned" format.

Word formats paragraph borders so that they extend beyond the left and right indents of the paragraph, by the amount in the From Text box. Reducing From Text to zero will bring the inside of the border flush with the paragraph margins (and flush with the text), but wide borders may still extend outside the margins. A better solution is to have some amount of spacing in From Text (to leave some white space between the text and the border) and to adjust the paragraph's left and right indents to bring the border within the margin.

You can store a border and shading definition as part of a style, so that any paragraph with that style will have the border and shading.

Picture Borders

You can put a border *around* a picture by selecting a line style for each of the sides. You can't shade a picture's interior (the Shading... button is grayed-out) nor can you put lines inside it (without the help of Microsoft Draw, anyway; as far as Word is concerned, a picture is an indivisible object, and Word can't get "inside" it to shade it or put in interior lines).

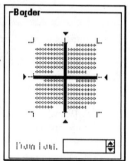

Table Borders

In addition to exterior borders, you can format interior lines in a table. If you currently have more than one cell in a table selected, the Border Cells dialog box (or Border Table, if you've selected the entire table) sample shows an interior line you can format. With multiple cells selected, the third preset format is Grid, which produces .75-point rules in the interior of a table and a 1.5-point line around the exterior.

When you have just one cell selected in a table, the border formatting options are identical to those for a paragraph border.

From Text is grayed-out because you control the distance between cell walls and text in a table with the Space Between Cols setting in the Column Width dialog box (displayed with the Table→Column Width command.

Shading

When you click the Shading... button in one of the Border dialog boxes, Word displays the Shading dialog box.

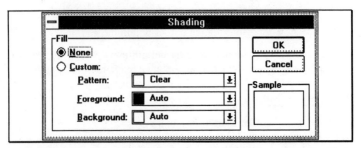

The default is to have no shading, so initially None is selected. Click Custom to select a pattern.

Select the basic pattern in the Pattern drop-down list box.

The Foreground list shows the available colors for the lines in the hatched patterns, and the dots in the percentage-shaded patterns. The Background list shows the available colors for the background of each pattern. As you select shading options, Word displays a sample of the shading in the lower right of the dialog box.

BREAKS

Broadly speaking, a "break" is a marker that delineates a change to the formatting of the page. Word lets you insert these breaks:

- **Page breaks** end the current page; any text following a page break appears at the beginning of the next page.

- **Column breaks** force the text following the break to begin at the top of the next column in a multicolumn page layout; in a single-column layout, a column break is equivalent to a page break.

- Various **section breaks** signal the beginning of a new section; the new section can have different margins and a different column layout. The types of section breaks are

  - **Next-page section breaks** that begin a new section and force that section to begin on a new page.

  - **Even and odd page section breaks** that begin a new section on a new page, and specify whether that page must be odd or even; if necessary, Word inserts a blank page to make it work.

· **Continuous section breaks** that start a new section without
forcing it to begin on a new page.

To insert a break, use the Insert→Break command to display the
Break dialog box, or use one of these keyboard shortcuts:

⟨Ctrl⟩+⟨Shift⟩+⟨↵⟩   To insert a column break in a multicolumn layout,
or a page break in a single-column layout

⟨Ctrl⟩+⟨↵⟩   To insert a page break

There are no predefined keyboard shortcuts for inserting section
breaks; you can write a simple macro to insert section breaks and associate it with a key combination if you frequently insert section breaks.

BULLETED LISTS

Bulleted lists are sequences of indented paragraphs introduced by a
symbol. Word provides an automatic facility for creating bulleted
paragraphs through the Tools→Bullets and Numbering command or
the 🗐 button on the Toolbar.

If you use the Toolbar, Word formats the current paragraph according to its default bullet paragraph parameters (the following paragraphs are formatted with the defaults):

- A .25-inch left indent

- A hanging indent (first line indented -.25" relative to the left indent)

- The standard bullet character from the Symbol font (•)

- A tab between the bullet and the start of the text

For more control, use the Tools→Bullets and Numbering command to
display the Bullets and Numbering dialog box. Select the Bullets
category if it is not already selected.

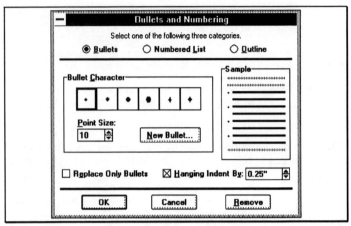

In this dialog box you can select a bullet character. If you click New Bullet..., Word displays the Symbol dialog box; select the character you want to use as a bullet. If you want the bullet to be a different size from the default 10 points, select a new size from the Point Size list.

If the Hanging Indent By box is checked (the default), Word formats the paragraph with the left indent shown in the box, formats the first line with the negative value in the box (a hanging indent), and separates the bullet and text with a tab. You can change the value in the box if you want a different hanging indent distance.

If Hanging Indent By is not checked, Word doesn't indent the paragraph and separates the bullet from the text with one space.

The Replace Only Bullets option controls whether Word adds (or updates) bullets to all paragraphs, or only to those that already have bullets. This is useful if you've selected several paragraphs, some already formatted with bullets and some not, and you want to change the bullet or the indentation; with Replace Only Bullets checked, Word only formats paragraphs already starting with bullets.

One limitation of Word's bulleted paragraphs is that they follow a fixed format with the bullet at the left margin. If you prefer a different style, such as indenting the bullet with a beginning tab, you'll have to format your bulleted paragraphs accordingly, manually or with a style.

See also: Paragraphs, Numbered Lists, Symbols

CHARACTER FORMATTING

Word can apply the standard character formatting options to text in your document:

- **bold**
- *italic*
- underlined in several styles: continuous underlining including white space; underlining words only; and double underlining
- strikethrough
- Small Caps
- all caps
- hidden text (which we obviously can't show on the printed page!)
- color (something else we can't show on this page); whether your document is printed in color depends on the printer.
- subscript and superscript text, by a distance you specify
- character spacing control, from very condensed to v e r y w i d e .
- fonts and point sizes, depending on what your printer offers; use the Windows Control Panel to select the printers Windows makes available, and Word's File→Print Setup command to select from the available printers.

The Character Formatting Tools

Character formatting selections take effect at the location in your document at which you apply them, as follows:

- If you have no text selected (the cursor is a vertical bar insertion point), any new text you type after selecting character formatting at that point will have the character formatting you selected. If you move the insertion point to another location, the character formatting at the new location determines the format of text you insert.
- If text is selected, the character formatting applies to the selected text.

The Ribbon comes standard with three buttons to apply common character formatting (you can add other buttons for the formatting you use most often), and list boxes to select the font and point size:

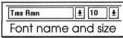

The left box lists the names of the fonts available on your system (a function of the selected printer and the screen fonts you've installed in Windows). The right box lets you select a point size.

These buttons apply bold (the B button), italic (*I*), or underlining (u) to selected text.

For complete control over character formatting, you'll want to use the Character dialog box; display it with the Format→Character command, or double-click in a blank area of the Ribbon.

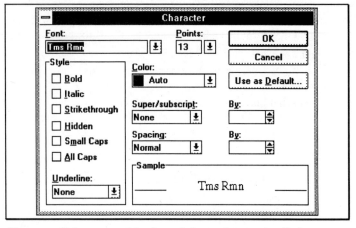

You can click any combination of the options under Style, except that Small Caps and All Caps are mutually exclusive. Click the arrow on the Underline box to see a list of underlining styles.

Drop down the Super/subscript list box to see a list of choices: None, Superscript, and Subscript. When you select Superscript or Subscript, Word enters 3pt into the By box as the default amount by which text is raised or lowered. You can enter another amount using the up or down arrows on the By box, or by typing the new value. Another way to select subscript or superscript is just to "dial in" an amount in the By box: starting from None, clicking the down arrow enters subscript amounts, and clicking the up arrow enters superscript amounts. The Super/subscript box will change to track your selection.

You set character spacing in a similar way. The Spacing box lists the choices as Normal, Expanded, and Condensed; and the adjacent By box controls the amount. The maximum compression (minimum spacing) is 1.75 points, while the maximum expansion is 14 points.

The Font list shows the fonts offered by the current printer, while the Points list shows the font sizes available. The Color list shows the 16 colors provided by Windows; Auto is the text color you set in the Windows Control Panel.

If you click the [Use as Default...] button, Word redefines the Normal paragraph style to use the character formatting you select with the Character dialog box. This change is automatically reflected back into the template associated with the current document—the change is not local to the document.

Hidden Text

The hidden text attribute lets you tag text so that you can select whether to display or print it; you might use hidden text to add notes to yourself, or to suppress the printing of boilerplate text in certain versions of a document and print it in others.

To control whether hidden text is displayed, use the Tools→Options command, select the View category, and check or uncheck the Hidden Text option in the Non-Printing Characters section of the dialog box. Or, click the [¶] button in the Ribbon. Word displays hidden text with a dotted underline.

To control whether hidden text is printed, select the Print category in the Options dialog box and check or uncheck the Hidden Text option in the Include with Document section of the dialog box. Word doesn't apply any special formatting to printed hidden text.

Whether hidden text is displayed or not affects your document's pagination. Be sure to have hidden text display turned off when you compile indexes and tables of contents, and when you update PAGEREF cross-reference fields.

Controlling Capitalization

The (Shift)+(F3) key combination lets you change the capitalization style of selected text. It's a "three-state toggle," meaning that each time you use this key combination it advances the capitalization style to the next style, depending on the style of the selected text:

word for windows instant reference	Starting with all lowercase letters,
WORD FOR WINDOWS INSTANT REFERENCE	the first time you press (Shift)+(F3) the text is formatted all caps;
Word For Windows Instant Reference	the second time it's formatted with initial caps;
word for windows instant reference	and the third time it's returned to all lowercase.

Copying and Repeating Character Formatting

To repeat character formatting that you just performed on a new text selection, use the Edit→Repeat Formatting command or press (F4) immediately after formatting one area of text and selecting another. The character formatting you applied to the first text selection is applied to the second selection.

To copy character formatting from one selection to another:

1. Highlight the text that you want to *receive* formatting.

2. Hold down the (Shift)+(Ctrl) keys and click the pointer inside text *supplying* the formatting you want to copy.

See also: Symbols, Styles

COLUMNS

Each section in a Word document can be formatted individually to arrange text in one or more columns. Since you can have several sections on one page you can mix column formats on a page, as this example illustrates. Text in a multicolumn layout "snakes" across the page: from top to bottom of the first column, continuing at the top of the next column, and on across the page for the number of columns in the format—these are called "newspaper-style" columns. You can have up to 100 columns in a section (the number that's actually practical depends on the width of the page, the font size, and so on). Columns can't be narrower than half an inch.

You can control these aspects of a multicolumn format:

- The number of columns
- The space between columns
- Whether Word prints a thin vertical line between columns

Each column has the same width, calculated as:

$$column\ width = \left(\frac{text\ width}{number\ of\ columns}\right) - space\ between\ columns$$

In Normal display mode, you see only a single column; Word displays text in a linear stream. In Page Layout, you can display and edit text in multiple columns, and in Print Preview you can display multicolumn formatting.

Formatting a Column Layout

You can specify up to five columns in the current section (or the entire document if it has only one section) with the Toolbar. Hold down the mouse button on the 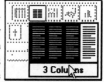 button; Word displays the pictorial control shown to the right. Drag the pointer to the right to highlight the number of columns you want in the section. If you drag the pointer off the control, the legend at the bottom changes to *Cancel* to allow you to release the mouse button without changing the number of columns.

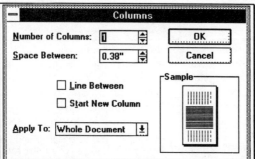

When you want precise control over column formatting, use the Columns dialog box; display it with the Format →Columns command.

Select the number of columns and specify the space between them. Check Line Between if you want Word to draw a thin rule between each column. Check Start New Column to have Word insert a column break at the insertion point.

The Apply To list box lets you choose the scope of column formatting:

- **This Section** applies the column formatting to the section containing the cursor.

- **Whole Document** makes the selected column formatting apply to the entire document, even if the document has multiple sections.

- **Selected Text** inserts a continuous section break before and after the selected text, converting the selection into a separate section.

- **This Point Forward** inserts a continuous section break at the beginning of the selected text; formatting applies from that point forward to the end of the document.

- **Selected Section** applies formatting to all selected sections when the selected text spans more than one section.

The Sample box shows a pictorial representation of how your selected formatting will look.

Column Breaks

On its own, Word applies the same rules for splitting paragraphs across columns as it applies to determining page breaks. Widow and orphan control, and Keep With Next and Keep Lines Together paragraph formatting all influence where Word breaks columns.

To insert a manual column break, use Insert→Break or press Ctrl + Shift + ↵ .

To insert a page break in a multicolumn format, use Insert→Break or press ⌈Ctrl⌋ + ⌊◢⌋.

Column Balancing

Word fills columns with text starting at the upper left of the page and snaking through the columns to the lower right. If the page doesn't have enough text to fill up the columns, one or more of them may be partially or completely empty.

The solution is to insert a continuous section break *after* the section mark ending the affected section. Since section breaks always span the width of a page, this has the effect of forcing Word to balance the columns in the previous section up against the top of the page; the leftover white space is collected at the bottom of the page in the "ghost" section created with the second section break.

See also: Sections

CROSS-REFERENCES

A *cross-reference* is text in one part of a document that refers to another part of a document. Word's approach to cross-references is based on bookmarks.

A typical cross-reference might look like this when printed:

> See "Cross-References" on page 28

It's produced using a bookmark field and a PAGEREF field:

> See "{CrossReferences}" on page {PAGEREF CrossReferences}

"CrossReferences" is the name of a bookmark identifying the text of the topic title we're in now. The first field inserts the text from the bookmark, and the second field (PAGEREF) inserts the page number on which the bookmark appears. In detail, the steps to create this cross-reference are

1. Select the entire text to be cross-referenced (the "source" of the cross-reference); in this example, select the text of the title, without the paragraph marker:

CROSS-REFERENCES

2. Use the Insert→Bookmark command, and enter the name **CrossReferences** in the Bookmark dialog box. Click OK.

3. Where you want the cross-reference to appear (the "destination"), type **See**, a space, and then a quotation mark. Insert an empty set of field marks by pressing Ctrl + F9.

4. Inside the field markers, type **CrossReferences**, then move the cursor to the right outside the right field marker.

5. Type the ending quotation mark, press the spacebar once, and then type **on page**.

6. Insert another pair of empty field markers (Ctrl + F9).

7. Type **PAGEREF CrossReferences** inside the new field markers.

8. Select the text containing both fields and update the fields by pressing F9.

   · If View→Field Codes is checked, you'll still see the fields themselves, rather than the text of the cross-reference.

   · If View→Field Codes is turned off (no checkmark), the fields will be replaced by the text of the cross-reference: the title under the bookmark CrossReferences, and the page on which the bookmark appears. The bookmarks are still there, as you'd see if you turned on View→Field Codes.

If the pagination of the document or the text under the bookmark changes, select the fields and update them again, to update the page number reference and the bookmark reference. Word also automatically updates fields when it prints a document.

Cross-Referencing Figure and Table Numbers

Sometimes in a cross-reference you want to show the sequence number of the figure or table you're referring to, in addition to (or instead of) referencing some text. The use of SEQ (sequence) fields in figure and table numbers allows you to insert new figures or tables and have Word update the numbering sequence to reflect the addition; you need a corresponding way to reference the updated sequence number in a cross-reference.

You do this with a special form of the SEQ field that names a numbering sequence and then displays the current value of the SEQ field in that sequence just before a bookmark. This form of the SEQ field looks like this:

{SEQ *SequenceName BookmarkName*}

As an example, let's assume you're setting up a figure with a caption, and later you want to refer to the figure number and figure title in a textual cross-reference. You've given your sequence of figure numbers the name "fig."

1. Set up the figure caption like this, with the bookmark Pie-Chart around the title of the figure:

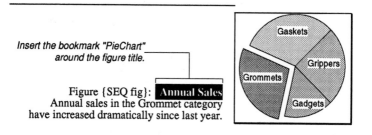

Insert the bookmark "PieChart" around the figure title.

Figure {SEQ fig}: Annual Sales
Annual sales in the Grommet category
have increased dramatically since last year.

2. At the location of the cross-reference, type:

...as shown in Figure {SEQ fig PieChart}, "{PieChart}," on page {PAGEREF PieChart}.

This produces the cross-reference

...as shown in Figure 1, "Annual Sales," on page 27.

Smart Cross-References

You can combine the cross-reference fields described above with other field types to create cross-references that adjust to changing pagination in your document. For example, if the source of a cross-reference appears on the same page as the cross-reference page, you wouldn't want to include the page number in the cross-reference; in other situations you'd want to give a page number, or say that the reference is on the next page. Here's a general cross-reference structure that handles this situation fairly elegantly:

{SEQ *SequenceName BookmarkName*}{IF {PAGE}={PAGEREF
BookmarkName} "" {IF {PAGE}={={PAGEREF *BookmarkName*}-
1} " on the next page" " on page {PAGEREF *BookmarkName*}}"}

Breaking this structure down into its component parts shows the
instructions it gives to Word:

{SEQ *SequenceName BookmarkName*}	Insert the current value of *SequenceName* nearest to *BookmarkName*.
	Notice that there's no space between these two fields. If the field doesn't produce a page reference, you'd want to be able to have a period immediately following the reference. If space is necessary, it's inserted by the field.
{IF	Start of a decision (IF) field.
{PAGE}={PAGEREF *BookmarkName*} ""	Is *BookmarkName* on the current page? If so, insert nothing (empty text between quotes).
{IF {PAGE}={={PAGEREF *BookmarkName*}-1} " on the next page"	On the other hand, maybe *BookmarkName* is on the next page. (Check to see whether the current page is one less than the page containing *BookmarkName*.) If so, insert the text to say so.
" on page {PAGEREF *BookmarkName*}}"	If it's neither on the current page nor on the next page, the default case is just to give the page number.
}	Finish with a closing field marker.

Be sure that you use ordinary vertical quote marks (") around text in
a field; don't use the typographer's fancy quotes (" and ").

See also: Bookmarks, Fields

CURSORS

As you move the pointer around the screen, you'll notice that it
changes shape in various parts of the screen, and changes during
certain operations. Here's what the various pointer shapes mean:

These pointers indicate that the cursor is in a text area.
The left "I-beam" cursor appears over text that's not
formatted italic; the slanted I-beam appears over italic
text, to make positioning the pointer easier. (Unfortunately, whether

it's available depends on your display.) This cursor also appears over dialog box text boxes.

This pointer shape signifies that the cursor is outside the document window: over menus; over the Ribbon, Toolbar, or Ruler; or inside a dialog box. It's also the sizing arrow when you have selected a picture.

This pointer appears when the cursor is near the left edge of the document window. Clicking here selects an entire line of text, or a row within a table.

Wait; Word is busy.

In Print Preview mode, this cursor appears over objects you can drag, such as margins or page breaks. In Page Layout view, this cursor appears when you insert a frame.

After you start context-sensitive help (⌈Shift⌉+⌈F1⌉), this pointer appears. Click it over the item (the command or part of the screen) about which you'd like help.

This pointer appears when the cursor is over the window-split control (the black bar just above the top vertical scroll button); hold down the mouse button and drag down to split the window.

This pointer can appear in two places: When you're in a table and move the pointer over a column boundary, this cursor appears to let you drag the column border left or right to change the column width. When the style area is displayed (as set in the View category of Tools→Options), you can drag the style area border left or right to change its width.

The select/drag pointer appears in page layout view before you've selected an object. It appears over frames and pictures, for example, indicating you can click to select the object, or you can hold down the mouse button and drag it into position. This pointer also appears in outline view, and lets you drag outline items to different positions.

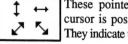
These pointers appear in page layout view when the cursor is positioned over a selected frame or a picture. They indicate that you can drag the selected item or border.

This pointer appears when the cursor is at the top border of a table. Clicking the mouse will select the entire column below the pointer.

 This pointer appears when you are dragging text or a graphic to a new location.

CUSTOMIZING WORD FOR WINDOWS

Word for Windows is extraordinarily customizable. In fact, at a fundamental level you can view the program not as a word processor at all, but a general purpose text-processing system that is configured *by default* as a word processor. You can change Word to suit yourself in many ways:

- **Menus.** You can add or remove items on all Word menus. You can't add or remove menus, however. Each item on a menu can be associated with a built-in command, or a macro from the global (NORMAL.DOT) template or a specific template.

- **Keys.** You can associate commands or macros with key combinations (and change existing key combinations).

- **Toolbar.** You can add or remove icons on the Toolbar, and associate icons with commands or macros. See the topic "Toolbar" for information about this.

- **Macros.** You can write small programs in WordBASIC, Word's "macro" language, to automate most tasks and change how Word behaves. The subject of WordBASIC programming is worthy of a book in its own right and, unfortunately, can't be covered in this one.

- **Options and Behavior.** You can control how Word behaves in areas such as saving files, printing, background repagination, typing, and on and on.

Since most Word customization is accomplished through the command Tools→Options, we'll organize this topic around that command's Options dialog box. The Options dialog box is really eleven dialog boxes in one. When you first use the command, it displays the options for the View category; when you select categories of options in the list of icons at the left of the dialog box, the dialog box will change appropriately. Some of the option categories are discussed elsewhere:

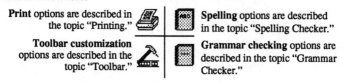

Print options are described in the topic "Printing."

Toolbar customization options are described in the topic "Toolbar."

Spelling options are described in the topic "Spelling Checker."

Grammar checking options are described in the topic "Grammar Checker."

View Options

The View category in the Options dialog box controls the appearance of the Word window, and controls how Word displays documents. Some of these options control Word's display for any document; others control only how specific document windows work.

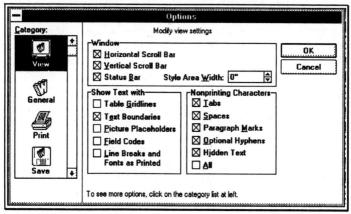

The Window Control Group

The **Status Bar** checkbox controls whether the status bar appears at the bottom of Word's main window.

The **Horizontal Scroll Bar** and **Vertical Scroll Bar** checkboxes control whether those scroll bars are displayed in document windows; the setting applies to the current document window, so you can set up document windows individually.

The **Style Area** box controls the width of the style area at the left of the current document window; you can set the style area width for each document window individually. The default setting of zero actually leaves just enough room for the cursor, so that you can use this area for selecting lines and paragraphs of text. When you increase the value in this box, you add additional room to allow Word to display the style name of each paragraph visible in the window.

The Show Text with Control Group—Controlling How a Document is Displayed

Each option in this group applies to the current document window, independently of the settings in other document windows.

Table Gridlines controls whether the boundaries of cells in tables are outlined. This means that, if a table doesn't have borders, Word will display faint lines showing you the rows and columns in the table. If a table has borders, those borders cover up the table gridlines.

Text Boundaries controls whether Word displays faint lines showing the boundaries of text in Page Layout view mode. These lines don't appear in Normal view mode. Text boundaries show the extent of text: the area within the margins within which you can type text. They're particularly useful if your page layout has frames.

Picture Placeholders controls whether Word displays pictures. If this option is checked, Word displays just empty frames showing the extent of each picture; with the option off, Word displays pictures.

Field Codes controls whether Word displays the codes making up fields (on), or whether it displays field results. The checkbox does the same thing as the command View→Field Codes.

Line Breaks and Fonts as Printed controls the extent to which Word is WYSIWYG (What You See Is What You Get). With this option off, Word determines line and page breaks based on displayed character widths; the printed page will have different breaks. With this option on, Word may allow lines to extend beyond the margins to show exactly how breaks will occur on the printed page.

If you have a display font manager in your system (such as Adobe Type Manager, or the Windows 3.1 TrueType system), the difference becomes essentially unnoticeable, and you should leave this option on.

The Nonprinting Characters Control Group

This option group controls whether Word displays symbols for non-printing characters to help you identify these characters on the display; or whether Word doesn't display them, showing either nothing at all at that location, or a space, as appropriate. The options control display of these symbols:

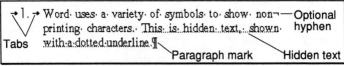

All turns all of these display options on or off together. With All off, Word displays only the non-printing characters selected by the other checkboxes . With All checked, Word displays all of the non-printing characters. This check box does the same thing as the ¶ button on the Ribbon.

General Options

Word's general options apply to all of Word, regardless of the template or document currently loaded.

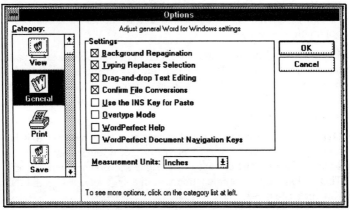

Background Repagination controls whether Word uses idle time (when it's not doing something else for you) to recompute and display page breaks. If it truly used only idle time, you could just leave this option turned on. But often, Word will start to repaginate automatically and won't let you do anything else until it's done. If you're working with a large document and find that Word spends too much time repaginating, turn this option off. You can tell Word to repaginate manually with Tools→Repaginate Now.

Typing Replaces Selection controls how Word handles text you type or paste from the Clipboard, while you have something selected in the document. With this option off, Word moves the insertion point to the beginning of the selection, cancels the selection, and inserts the new material in front of it; what was selected remains. With this option on, Word deletes what was highlighted and puts the new material in its place.

Drag-and-drop Text Editing controls whether you can highlight material and then drag it somewhere else (see the topic "Text: Inserting, Selecting, and Editing").

Confirm File Conversions controls whether Word asks you to confirm its judgement of the appropriate file converter to use, when you open a file in a non-Word format. When this option is on, Word displays a dialog box with the list of file conversions, with Word's best guess highlighted. You can accept Word's choice or make one of your own. With this option off, Word proceeds automatically according to its own judgement. Word is generally correct; however, since some conversions come in optional flavors (such as the variety of text-only conversions available) it's usually desirable to leave this option on.

Use the INS Key for Paste, if on, configures the [Ins] key to paste the contents of the Clipboard into the document at the insertion point. If this option is off, [Ins] toggles between insert and overtype mode. (Regardless of this setting, [Ctrl]+[V] and [Shift]+[Ins] perform the paste operation.)

Overtype Mode controls whether text you type replaces existing text, one character at a time (overtype on), or whether new text is inserted, pushing existing text to the right and down (overtype off). This option works in conjunction with the [Ins] key, if Use the INS Key for Paste is off.

WordPerfect Help controls whether Word provides help and other aids for WordPerfect users. Use the Help→WordPerfect Help command for more information.

WordPerfect Document Navigation Keys, if on, makes Word respond to the arrow, PgUp, PgDn, Home, End, and Esc keys (and shifted combinations of these keys) in the same way as WordPerfect would.

The **Measurement Units** list box lets you select the unit of measure that Word uses on the ruler, and the unit of measure Word assumes if you type just numbers in most dialog boxes. You can also specify a different unit of measure on an *ad hoc* basis when you type in a dialog box, by including an appropriate abbreviation: " (quote) or *in* for inches, *pt* or *pts* for points, *cm* for centimeters, and *pi* for picas.

Save Options

Word's save options apply to Word in general.

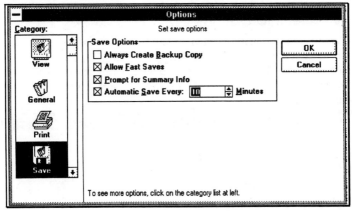

Always Create Backup Copy forces Word to save the previous version of a document file, with the extension changed to .BAK, when you save a document.

Allow Fast Saves allows Word to speed up the saving process, when possible, by saving only a record of changes to a document, rather than an exact image of the document after you've made changes. In other words, the saved document file contains the previous version of a document, plus a list of changes; from this information, Word reconstructs the latest version of the document. After a certain number of changes have accumulated, Word does a full save to create a fresh image of the current state of the document. When this option is off,

Word completely rewrites the document file each time you save it. The difference is most noticeable in the time it takes to save larger documents.

Always Create Backup Copy and **Allow Fast Saves** are mutually exclusive; checking one turns off the other.

Prompt for Summary Info, when on, causes Word to display the Summary Info dialog box the first time you save a document after creating it. Thereafter, Word doesn't display the dialog box, and you must use File→Summary Info to change this information.

Automatic Save Every:, when checked, causes Word to fast-save all open files (including templates) that have unsaved changes. The interval between automatic saves is set in the Minutes text box; ten minutes is the default.

User Info Options

Word's user information options record basic information about you, as the current user of a particular copy of Word. This information is separate from the information you supplied during installation (your name and organization), which is displayed initially each time you start Word.

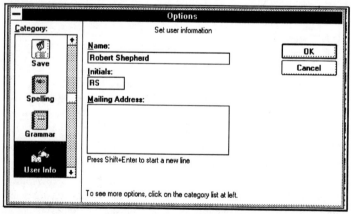

Name is the name that Word proposes by default in the Summary Info dialog box. The USERNAME field (see the topic "Fields") uses this name.

Initials contains the initials Word uses in annotation marks. The first time you enter a name, Word will propose the initials from that name; thereafter, changing the name has no effect on the initials (you must enter new initials manually). The USERINITIALS field uses this information.

Mailing Address contains your mailing address, as used by the Tools →Create Envelope command. The USERADDRESS field uses this information.

Menu Customization

The Menus category of the Options dialog box lets you add or delete menu items, either globally (by storing the definitions in NORMAL.DOT), or for the current document template. This means that the arrangement of Word's menus changes depending on which document window contains the cursor (the active window).

Each template inherits its menu setup from the global template NORMAL.DOT. When you customize menus in a template, Word records how the template's menus *differ* from the global menus. Deleting an item in a template menu suppresses the appearance of that item when the cursor is in a document window that uses that template. Adding an item to a template causes that item to appear only when the cursor is a document window using that template. If you add a menu item to the global menus, it will appear in the menus for all templates, until you specifically delete it from a template's menus. Finally, there's nothing to prevent you from assigning an identical menu item (that is, identical text for the item that appears in a menu) to one command or macro in the global menus, and to a different command or macro in different templates. Because of the potential for confusion, it's a good idea to add a description for each macro you add to a menu (in the Tools→Macro dialog box); that description appears in the status bar as you select menu items.

Caution: You'll notice that this dialog box doesn't have a Cancel button. That's because it's designed to allow you to make multiple changes to menus. As a consequence, as soon as you click Add, Delete, or Reset All, any changes you've made go into effect. There's no way, then, to undo a change, so if you change your mind you'll have to recreate a deleted menu item or delete a new menu item. If you mistakenly press Reset All, you'll really be in trouble, because then you'll have to customize the menus from scratch. Double check the selections you've made before you commit the changes.

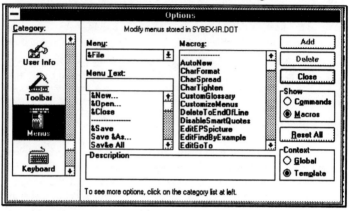

To add a menu item:

1. Select an option in the Context group to determine where the menu item appears:

   · **Global** causes the new menu item to appear on all menus, unless it's deleted in a particular template's menu setup; the menu assignment is stored in NORMAL.DOT.

   · **Template** causes the new menu assignment to be stored in the current template, and will appear when the cursor is in the document window of a document using that template.

2. In the Show option group, select

   · **Commands** if you want to associate the menu item with one of Word's built-in commands; the list box in the center of the dialog box will change to show a list of built-in commands.

   · **Macros** if you want to associate the menu item with a macro. The list box in the center of the dialog box will show a list of all available macros, from both NORMAL.DOT and the current template.

   The show option doesn't matter if you want to add a separator (a horizontal line dividing groups of items in a menu); both lists show a dashed line as their first item, signifying a separator.

3. Select a menu to customize from the Menu drop-down list box. When you do this, the Menu Text list box changes to show the items currently on the selected menu.

4. Select a command, macro, or the separator from the Macros/Commands list box. The Description box will show the description associated with the selected command or macro; this description will also appear in the status bar when you select the item from a menu, to provide a quick help message.

5. Word will propose the text of the menu item in the Menu Text box. Word's predefined commands and macros come with predefined menu text. In other cases, Word makes a guess (often wrong) based on the name of the selected command or macro. For example, if you select a macro named EditEPS-picture, Word will propose the text "&Edit E P Spicture", complete with inappropriate spaces between all capitalized letters. The ampersand (&) is a special character signifying that the next letter should be underlined in the menu item. This also specifies that character as the shortcut key you'd press in combination with ⌈Alt⌉ to select the item from the keyboard.

   Edit the Menu Text to make it correct. Use the ampersand to specify a shortcut key (if you want it; you don't have to have a shortcut key). Note that if you specify a shortcut key that's already used in the menu, Word resolves the conflict by only recognizing the shortcut key for the first item in the menu that uses it.

6. Click ⌈Add⌉ to complete the new menu item. Click ⌈Close⌉ if you change your mind; the new menu setup won't take effect until you click ⌈Add⌉.

To delete a menu item:

1. Select Global or Template in the Context option group to specify whose menu item you intend to delete.

2. Select a menu from the Menu drop-down list box.

3. Select the menu item to delete from the Menu Text list box.

4. Click ⌈Delete⌉ to remove the menu item.

To restore all menu assignments to the defaults, click ⌈Reset All⌉. *Think long and hard before doing this, because there's no way to* *undo it.* If you change your mind after it's too late, you'll have to recreate every menu assignment from scratch.

Tip If you have a complex custom menu setup, you might consider writing a WordBasic macro to customize the menus. This macro would then act as insurance in case you reset the menus by mistake, since all you'd have to do to recustomize the menus is to run the macro. The disadvantage of this, of course, is that you'd have to edit the macro each time you change your menu setup.

Customizing the Keyboard

You can associate various key combinations with commands or macros. For example, Word 2.0 changed the Undo key from ⟦Alt⟧+⟦←Back⟧ (an old Windows tradition) to ⟦Ctrl⟧+⟦Z⟧ to conform to the Apple Macintosh's use of "Command+Z" for undo. If you're used to the old Undo key, or you'd just like Word to behave like most other Windows applications, you can change the undo key assignment.

The Options dialog box looks like this when you select the Keyboard category.

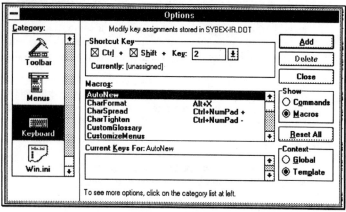

To assign a macro or command to a key combination:

1. Select an option in the Context group to determine when the key assignment functions:

   · **Global** causes the key combination to work no matter what template is used by your current document (unless you reassign or delete the key combination from the template); the key assignment is stored in NORMAL.DOT.

· **Template** assigns the key combination to the current template.

2. In the Show box, select Commands or Macros; the list box in the center of the dialog box changes to show one or the other.

3. Select a command or macro. As you click on a line in the list box, Word shows any current key assignments for the command or macro in the Current Keys For box at the bottom of the dialog box.

4. Define the key combination with the Shortcut Key controls.

· **Ctrl** determines whether the key combination includes the `Ctrl` key.

· **Shift** determines whether the key combination includes the `Shift` key.

· **Key** is a combination list box; you can type directly into the box, or drop down a list of keys. The list includes the letter and number keys, the function keys (except `F1`, which is reserved for help), INS, and DEL.

Word won't let you assign commands or macros to the letter or number keys alone (without `Ctrl` or `Shift`). Other keys can be used alone.

Word shows the macro or command, if any, currently assigned to the key combination you specify. Assigning the keys to a new command or macro removes the assignment from the old one.

5. Click `Add` to make the key assignment.

To delete a key assignment:

1. Select Global or Template in the Context group.

2. Select the assignment to delete:

· Specify the key combination; Word highlights the associated command or macro in the list, if it's part of the current list. Use the Show control group to select another list.

· Select the command or macro; Word shows its current key assignment.

3. Select the key combination to delete in the Current Keys For list; this is necessary because it's possible to have more than one key assignment for a command or macro.

4. Click [Delete].

To reset all key assignments to the default, select a Context (Template or Global), and click [Reset All]. *Use this procedure with caution—if you do this by mistake, you'll have to manually restore all key assignments.*

[Tip] You can write a macro to make your custom key assignments (and deletions). Having this macro available provides insurance against accidentally resetting all key assignments to defaults, since you can run the macro at any time to restore your key assignments.

[Tip] Word limits key assignments through the Options dialog box to combinations using the [Ctrl] and [Shift] keys. That's because [Alt] + combinations are generally reserved for menu and dialog box short-cut keys (such as pressing [Alt] + [F], [S] for File→Save). There's no technical reason you can't use [Alt] + combinations, however. You have almost unlimited freedom to assign keys with the WordBasic ToolsOptionsKeyboard command, so you can write a macro to make key assignments that the Options dialog box doesn't support.

Customizing WIN.INI Settings

WIN.INI is Windows' master configuration file. Windows uses it for system settings, and applications may store their own configuration information there as well. Word is one of those applications, although it has its own separate configuration file for detailed option settings. It uses WIN.INI for basic information about such things as where related files are stored, including its own configuration file— when Word starts, it has no idea where you stored its files, so it asks for that information from WIN.INI through Windows.

The WIN.INI category in the Options dialog box provides direct access to the parts of WIN.INI relevant to Word, saving you the trouble of opening WIN.INI and searching for the correct entries.

There are several sections in WIN.INI that contain Word configuration information. The main entry looks something like this (your configuration may differ in details):

```
[Microsoft Word 2.0]
DOC-path=C:\WINWORD
INI-path=C:\WINWORD
programdir=C:\WINWORD
Spelling 1033,0=C:\WINWORD\SPELL.DLL,C:\WINWORD\SP_AM.LEX
Hyphenate
1033,0=C:\WINWORD\HYPH.DLL,C:\WINWORD\HY_AM.LEX,C:\WINWORD\SP_AM.LEX
Grammar 1033,0=C:\WINWORD\GRAMMAR.DLL,C:\WINWORD\GR_AM.LEX
Thesaurus 1033,0=C:\WINWORD\THES.DLL,C:\WINWORD\TH_AM.LEX
ButtonFieldClicks=1
MACRODE=C:\WINWORD\macrode.exe
UpdateDictionaryNumber=2
AUTOSAVE-path=C:\WINWORD
```

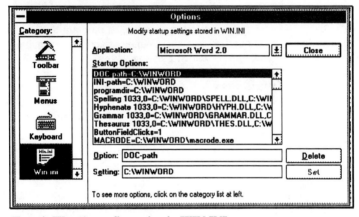

To edit Word's configuration in WIN.INI:

1. Select a configuration category from the Application list. The main category is *Microsoft Word 2.0*; others cover areas such as *Graphic Import Filters* and *Proofing Tools*. When you select a category, Word displays its entries in the center list box.

2. Select a line to edit from the center list box. Word breaks the line up into its two basic parts, and displays them in Option (the name of the option) box and the Setting box (the current setting of that option).

   If you want to add a line that doesn't yet exist, type its name in the Option box to start a new line.

3. Edit the information in the Setting box.

4. Click Set to put your edits into WIN.INI; click Close (before clicking Set) if you change your mind.

To delete a line from WIN.INI, select it as in steps 1 and 2 above, and click ⌊Delete⌋. *Be sure you know what you're doing—those settings wouldn't be there if Word didn't need them.* Do this only when necessary; for example, when you've deleted a conversion filter and need to tell Word about the change. See Appendix B in the Word manuals for information about specific WIN.INI settings.

DRAW (MICROSOFT DRAW)

Microsoft Draw is an "embedded application," a program that can't function on its own but works within a Windows application such as Word to create and edit embedded drawings. Word and Draw automatically manage the embedded graphic; when you double-click the graphic, Word starts Draw and loads the graphic into Draw, and when you exit Draw, it updates the graphic in the Word document. You don't have to use the Windows Clipboard to transfer anything; it happens automatically.

It's important to understand the distinction between "draw graphics" such as those Draw works with, and "bitmap" graphics that Windows Paintbrush can work with. Bitmaps are images composed of dots, or screen "pixels," that you work with on a dot-by-dot basis. Draw graphics, on the other hand, are collections of objects: lines, circles, rectangles, text, and so on. You manipulate objects in a drawing as units, for example changing the endpoint of a line, rather than editing the individual dots that make up the line. Microsoft Draw can include bitmaps within a drawing, and lets you scale them, but can't edit the individual pixels in the bitmap. For that you must use a bitmap editor such as Windows Paintbrush.

Technically, Draw works with "Windows metafiles," which is the standard Windows format for drawings. The format is also called WMF, and files containing metafiles usually end in ".WMF". This means that you can import .WMF files created with other applications into Draw, and you can copy Draw objects through the Clipboard into other drawing programs that work with Windows metafiles.

To create an embedded drawing and start Microsoft Draw, use the Insert→Object command, and select the Microsoft Drawing type.

To edit an existing embedded drawing, double-click on the embedded graphic. If the graphic is a bitmap, it's converted to a bitmap *within* a Draw object. (In other words, it's no longer a bitmap that can be edited by Windows Paintbrush; if you copy the resulting draw object to the Clipboard you won't be able to paste it into Paintbrush.)

The Microsoft Draw window looks like this:

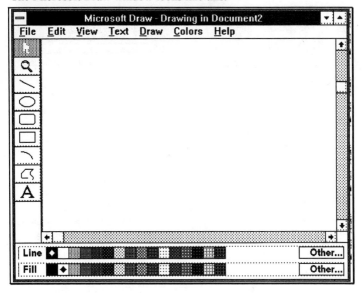

Drawing

You can begin drawing right away by clicking on one of the tool buttons at the left of the Draw window:

	Line	Hold down the mouse button where you want the line to begin, drag the pointer to the end of the line, and release the mouse button.
	Rectangle	Hold down the mouse button where one of the corners of the rectangle should be, drag to the opposite corner, and release the button.
	Rounded Rectangle	A rectangle with round corners; draw it in the same way you draw a rectangle.

Ellipse

An ellipse is defined by a rectangle; the height and width of the rectangle enclose the ellipse. A circle, a special case of an ellipse, would be enclosed in a square. To draw an ellipse, hold down the mouse button at one of the corners of the rectangle bounding the ellipse, drag the pointer to the opposite corner, and release the button. While you're dragging, Draw displays a rough outline of the ellipse to help you draw it.

Arc/Pie Wedge

An arc is a portion of an ellipse; initially the arc encompasses 90° (a "quadrant") of the ellipse, but you can change that later. To draw an arc, hold down the mouse button at one end of the arc and drag to the location of the other end. The direction you drag determines the quadrant of the arc, as shown to the left.

Freeform

The Freeform tool draws a sequence of connected straight lines. If you hold down the mouse button and drag, Draw produces a series of very small line segments, producing the illusion (at normal magnifications) of a continuous freehand line.

To create sequences of longer straight lines, click the mouse at each endpoint in the sequence. If you return to your starting point, you'll create a closed polygon.

Text

To draw text, click where you want the text to begin and type the text. Text is drawn according to the settings on the Text menu.

Manipulating Objects

Once an object is drawn, you can **select** it for editing. Draw gives you three ways to select an object or objects:

- **To select a single object,** click on it with the pointer tool .

- **To select all the objects in one area of a drawing,** first envision the objects you want to select as lying within an imaginary rectangle (put them in a mental box). Move the pointer to one corner of this box, press and hold down the mouse button, drag the pointer to the opposite corner of the box, and release the mouse button. This selects all objects that lie completely within the box; objects which extend outside the box in any way aren't selected.

- **To select several objects individually,** hold down the **⟦Shift⟧** key while you click on each object with the pointer tool ▣.

You can combine the methods for selecting multiple objects. For example, you could use the imaginary selection rectangle to pick most of the objects in one area of a drawing, and then the ⌗Shift⌗-click method to select other objects to add to the collection. As long as you hold down ⌗Shift⌗ key you won't cancel any previous selections. The first time you click the mouse after releasing ⌗Shift⌗, you cancel your previous selections.

Draw will display *handles* (small black squares) at each end of a selected line, or at each corner of the rectangle defining other objects. Once an object is selected you can:

- **Move** the object by holding down the mouse button inside the selection rectangle (but not on a handle) and dragging the object into a new position.

- **Resize** the object by dragging one of its handles; the object remains anchored at the handle opposite the one you're dragging, and its overall size changes relative to the anchor point.

  If you hold down ⌗Ctrl⌗ while sizing an object it is resized relative to the center rather than the opposite handle.

  If you hold down ⌗Shift⌗ while sizing an object, Draw constrains changes to its size: If you move the pointer vertically the object maintains its width; moving the pointer horizontally maintains its height; and when you move diagonally Draw maintains the proportions of an object (pure resizing without distortion).

  Bitmaps inside drawings have two special behaviors during sizing: If you've previously resized a bitmap, double-clicking one of its resizing handles restores it to its original proportions (aspect ratio). If you hold down ⌗Shift⌗ while double-clicking a handle, the bitmap is restored to its original size.

  You can't resize text; you must select a point size from the Text menu instead.

- **Copy** or **cut** the object to the Clipboard. You can then paste the object back into the drawing or into another application.

You can select more than one object at a time by pressing the mouse button away from the objects and dragging a selection box around the objects; or by individually selecting objects by clicking on them while holding down ⌗Shift⌗.

Line Styles

The lines making up all objects (except text, of course) are drawn in a particular style, selected with the Draw→Line Style command. This command pops up a submenu listing the available line styles. The figure below shows samples of the available styles.

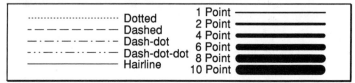

The menu selection Other lets you specify the width of a solid line in points.

Color

You control the color of objects by clicking on a color box at the bottom of the Draw window. Boxes to the right of the word *Line* select the color of lines and text; boxes beside *Fill* select the color of the interior of filled objects (see "Frames and Fills," next).

The colors listed in the boxes depend on the colors available on your display. If your display offers more colors than can fit at the bottom of the Draw window, scroll arrows appear at the left and right of the color boxes; click the arrows to scroll the list of colors.

You can add colors by editing the Draw *palette* using the Colors→Edit Palette command. The Edit Palette dialog box displays boxes for up to 100 colors. Click on a color box to select it, then click Change... to modify an existing color, Add to define a new color (in an empty box), or Delete to remove a

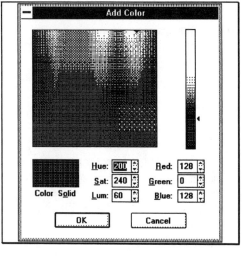

color. The Change... or Add buttons display the Add Color dialog box (shown here) that lets you select the color by clicking in a spectrum of colors, or by entering color values directly in terms of hue, saturation, and luminance; or as a mixture of red, blue, and green.

You may want to use the Colors→Save Palette to save a palette after you've customized it. You can then reuse the saved palette by selecting it with Colors→Get Palette.

Frames and Fills

Ellipses, rectangles and rounded rectangles, arcs, and polygons are made up of two elements: a *frame* defining the exterior of the object; and a *fill*, defining the appearance of its interior. When you first start Draw, these objects are drawn with a frame, but without a fill. The Draw→Framed and Draw→Filled menu settings control how new objects are drawn, and also control the frame and fill of existing objects.

The appearance of an object's frame depends on the line style and line color selected (and whether its frame is turned on, of course).

The appearance of filled objects depends on the selected fill color and on the pattern selected using Draw→Pattern. There are seven patterns:

solid

Drawing Aids

Holding down [Shift] while drawing an object constrains line drawing to the horizontal, vertical, or diagonal axes, and causes other objects to be drawn inside an imaginary square instead of a rectangle. (For example, rectangles are drawn as squares, ellipses as circles, and arcs as parts of circles.)

Similarly, holding down [Shift] while you drag an object constrains its movement to horizontal, vertical, or diagonal. Holding down [Shift] also constrains resizing: If you move the pointer up or down the object maintains its width; moving the pointer left or right maintains its height; and when you move approximately diagonally (from one corner toward the opposite corner) Draw maintains the proportions of an object (pure resizing without distortion).

Draw's **grid** constrains drawing (clicking points) and movement to an imaginary grid on the display. The grid has twelve intervals per inch horizontally and vertically. You control whether the grid is in effect with the Draw→Snap to Grid command.

The **guides** are moveable horizontal and vertical lines that you can use as straight-edges or to measure objects. Each guide line displays its distance from the left (vertical guide) or top (horizontal guide) edge of the drawing area when you drag the line with the mouse. If you hold down Ctrl while dragging a guide, it displays the distance you've moved it; this is useful for measuring distance in your drawing. You control whether the guide lines are displayed with the Draw →Show Guides command.

Grouping and Ungrouping Objects

It's often convenient to group several objects together so that you can manipulate them as a single entity. Select the objects you want to combine into a group, then select Draw→Group. You can combine groups inside other groups. Use the Draw→Ungroup command to break apart a selected group.

The Stacking Order

When objects in a drawing overlap, which one is visible depends on its order in the "stack," which you might look at as a stack of transparencies on which each object is drawn. By shuffling the stack of transparencies you can change which objects are visible and which are obscured by others.

In Draw, you shuffle the stack by selecting an object and using either Edit→Bring to Front or Edit→Send to Back.

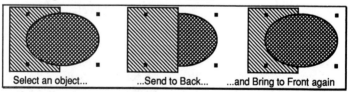

Select an object...   ...Send to Back...   ...and Bring to Front again

Text Formatting

The Text menu lets you control how text is formatted. If you have text selected, new formatting is applied to the selected text; otherwise, Text menu selections apply to the next text you draw. You can select:

- **Bold, italic,** or **underline** in any combination; selecting **plain** removes bold, italic, and underlining.

- **Left, right,** or **center** alignment (like the corresponding Word paragraph controls, except that you can draw only single lines of text with Draw). Text is enclosed in an imaginary rectangle that's slightly wider than the text; alignment determines whether the excess white space accumulates at the left (during right alignment), at the right (during left alignment), or is split in half and put at both the left and right (center alignment). This is mainly useful when you're aligning several lines of text, or aligning text relative to other objects (such as lines forming "callouts" in an illustration).

- The **font,** from the choices offered by the currently selected printer.

- The **font size,** depending on the capabilities of the currently selected printer.

To edit an existing line of text, select the pointer tool and double-click on the text. The cursor will change to a text-editing cursor, which you can move left and right on the line with the mouse or with the arrow keys.

Zooming the Display

You can control the magnification percentage with the View menu, from 25% to 800%. If you've selected an object, the magnified or reduced display is centered on the object; otherwise the new display is relative to the center of the old display.

The Zoom tool (🔍) also zooms the display by percentage. Each mouse click increases the magnification in the same steps as the View menu (25%, 50%, 75%, 100%, 200%, 400% and 800%), while each click with the ⬛Shift⬛ key depressed reduces magnification one step.

See also: Embedding and Linking, Frames, Graphics, Pictures

EMBEDDING AND LINKING

Word 2.0 lets you create "compound" documents that contain text as well as other objects that are created, and sometimes managed, by other Windows applications. The process goes beyond simply pasting or inserting objects from other applications into a document—using various techniques, Word can establish dynamic links capable of updating information from external sources as it changes, and build compound documents in collaboration with other Windows applications.

A very simple example is shown by the keycap symbols used through this book. Each symbol is actually a link to a file in a library of small keycap graphic files. This allowed us to change the graphics at one point, to lighten the captions in each symbol, then update the link fields to update the symbols throughout the entire book. The task would have been a nightmare if each symbol had been directly inserted into the document—there are hundreds of these symbols.

There are four concepts to understand about compound documents:

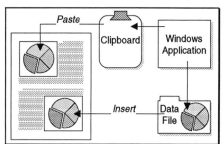

The **Clipboard** is the traditional way to get data from another Windows application into a Word document. Word also can insert data directly from an external file, as long as the file is in one of the formats Word can use directly or convert. In either case, the data is stored in the document.

The Clipboard has a fundamental limitation: It transfers data in a lowest common denominator form, using one of the "official" Windows data types, such as Windows Metafile (WMF), bitmap (BMP), or Rich Text Format (RTF). When you paste data from the Clipboard, Word and the other application negotiate the type of data the sender passes to Word, based on whatever format both programs understand. A similar thing happens to inserted files: Word must use one of its filters to convert the file's data to one of the standard Windows formats. In both cases, data may be lost or simplified in the conversion process.

Another limitation of both pasting and inserting is that the pasted or inserted data is a copy of the original; if the original data changes, the data in your document won't change.

Microsoft's first approach to the problem of keeping data current was Dynamic Data Exchange (DDE), in which Windows applications communicate directly, and exchange data upon request. DDE can be used

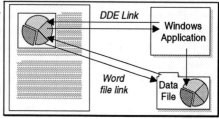

to establish *links* between data managed by different applications. Word implements links through a LINK field. In a "warm" link, Word checks with the originating application when you update the link field, to see if the data has changed. In a "hot" link, the other application can be instructed to "volunteer" data any time the source file changes (as long as both applications are running).

Word also uses the LINK field to link to external files. When you update the field, Word refreshes the field result by rereading the external file and updating the copy of its data stored in the document.

DDE and external file links still are subject to the limitations of the standard Windows data formats. If data can't be represented in one of those standard formats, the data is lost or must be simplified.

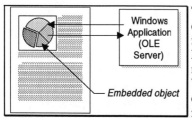

The state of the art (today) in creating compound documents is to use Object Linking and Embedding (OLE), a new technology that will be standard in Windows 3.1 and beyond (Windows 3.0 users get a limited form of OLE when Word 2.0 installs OLE applications like Microsoft Draw and Graph).

With OLE, Word maintains a document file itself, but sets aside parts of the file for other applications to manage. In effect, Word has this conversation with an OLE-aware application: "I need some data. I'll take it in the format you create and manage, and store it verbatim in my document file. When I need to display or print it, I'll call you to do it; when my user wants to edit the data, I'll call you to let you handle it." Any such OLE object in a document is said to be *embedded*, and the application that manages it is called an *OLE server*. OLE allows applications to specialize in areas such as graphics and database work, and to work together to create compound documents. Because an OLE application manages its own data, it isn't restricted to creating objects that can be stored in one of the Windows data formats.

Microsoft's Excel spreadsheet program was among the first applications to use OLE. Word is another. Both those programs were designed to run under Windows 3.0, and so had to install their own support for OLE. OLE will be officially integrated into Windows 3.1, and many of the traditional Windows accessories—Write and Cardfile, for example—will support OLE. You can expect most major Windows applications to be upgraded to support OLE in the very near future.

Using Linking and Embedding

Word automates the process of embedding objects in a document and creating links. It uses two fields, called EMBED and LINK, to represent the embedded or linked object. The codes in each field identify the object, and include formatting information.

In general, if it's possible to create a link or embed an object, Word will give you the opportunity to do so. Most Insert menu commands that insert objects (Picture and File, for example) include a Link to File checkbox in their dialog boxes; if you check that option, Word creates a link rather than inserting a copy of the file. When Word detects that the information on the Clipboard comes from an application that supports OLE (or DDE, in the case of older, non-OLE applications) Edit→Paste Special lists the types of links you can set up or the objects you can embed, and creates the fields necessary to do so. The Insert→Object command does nothing but embed objects. As you add OLE applications to your system, and they register themselves with Windows, Insert→Object will list the objects they produce.

When you embed an object, the object itself will be visible just like any other object in your drawing, contained in a rectangle just like a picture. You can double-click the object to edit it, and Word will start the associated application.

That's the quick overview. The following topics go into more detail about linking and embedding:

- "Draw" describes Microsoft Draw, the drawing program included with Word 2.0. Draw is used exclusively to create and edit embedded drawings (you can't even run it by itself; it has to have a host application like Word).

- "Fields"; see the entries for the DDE, EMBED, and LINK fields.

- "Pictures" has information about Windows metafiles and bitmaps, and about linking to an external graphics file.

ENVELOPES

If you have a printer capable of printing envelopes, Word gives you an easy way to address and print them. Use the Tools→Create Envelope command, or click the envelope button (⌨) in the Toolbar, to display the Create Envelope dialog box.

If you select the address in a document before you use this command, the dialog box will display it in the Addressed To box; otherwise, type the address in the box. Clicking Add to Document stores the address information in the document for future use. This can be very convenient if the document is a letter, for example.

The Return Address information is taken from the User Info category of the Tools→Options command. You can enter a different address here if you need to. Check Omit Return Address if your envelopes have a preprinted return address.

The Envelope Size drop-down list shows a wide variety of common envelope sizes used in both the U.S. and Europe. Pick the one corresponding to the envelope you're using.

When you've entered all the information to be printed on the envelope, click Print Envelope. If your printer has an envelope feeder installed (as indicated in the Print category of Tools→Options) it will be used automatically. Otherwise, Word will prompt you to insert an envelope into the printer's manual sheet feeder. (Some printers, such as dot-matrix printers, don't make any distinction between different paper sources, and so you may not be prompted.)

If you used the Add to Document button to add the address information to the document, you can also print an envelope with the File→ Print command. The envelope prints as a separate page, numbered zero. Word uses the envelope feeder on your printer, or prompts you to insert an envelope, as necessary. To print just the envelope with the Print command, tell Word to print only page zero.

You can repeat this procedure later, to update the address information if it's changed in your document.

EXCHANGING DOCUMENTS WITH OTHER PROGRAMS

Word has its own document file format (sometimes called "Word Normal"), and can also read and write files in formats used by other programs. Word comes with a comprehensive set of *filters* to convert documents and data between Word Normal and other formats, some or all of which you choose during installation. Once a filter is installed its format is listed in the dialog boxes associated with the File→Save As and File→Open commands. Not all conversion types are available for both saving and opening, as shown in the table below.

| Availability | | Common | | |
Open	Save	Extensions	Name	Comments
	**Document and Text Formats**
✔	✔	.DOC	Word for Windows 1.0 and 1.1	File format has changed with Word 2.0.
✔	✔	.DOC	Word for DOS 4.0, 5.0, 5.5	
✔	✔	.MCW	Word for the Macintosh 4.0, 5.0	
✔	✔	.DOC	WordPerfect 4.1, 4.2, 5.0, 5.1	
✔	✔	.RFT	RFT-DCA	DisplayWrite and IBM 5520
✔	✔	.WPS	Works for Windows, Works 2.0	Document files created with Microsoft Works
✔	✔	.DOC, .WS	WordStar 3.3, 3.45, 4.0, 5.0, 5.5	WordStar 2000 is not available for conversion.
✔	✔	.WRI	Windows Write	

(continued)

Availability		Common		
Open	Save	Extensions	**Name**	**Comments**
Document and Text Formats *(continued)*				
✔	✔	.TXT, .TX8, .ASC, .ANS	Text (various styles)	See "Text Formats" below for more information.
✔	✔	.RTF	Rich Text Format (RTF)	Microsoft's standard document interchange format
Data Formats				
✔		.WK1, .WK2	Lotus 1-2-3 2.x, 3.0	All conversions read data in only.
✔		.XLS	Excel BIFF 2.x, 3.0	Data is converted to a table if it
✔		.DBF	dBASE II, III, III+, IV	is less than 32 columns wide. Data larger than 32 columns is converted to paragraphs.
✔	✔	.MP	MultiPlan 3.0, 4.2	

Most file conversions are imperfect to some degree, because there may not be exact equivalents for something in two different file formats. See the file CONVINFO.DOC, included with Word 2.0, for specific limitations.

Opening a File in Another Format

Use the File→Open command to display the Open dialog box. Select the format you want to convert in the List Files of Type list box at the bottom of the dialog box (the formats listed will be those you chose to install). This çauses Word to change the file specification in this dialog box to show the common extension used for the selected file type (as shown in the table above). If the file you want to open uses a non-standard extension, or you already know its full name, you can type the file name directly into the File Name text box.

You don't have to identify the file type in the Open dialog box; you only have to get its name right. The List Files of Type feature is only a convenience. You actually tell Word what the file type is after you click OK in the Open dialog box, when Word displays the Convert File dialog box. In this dialog box, Word will show its best guess as to which file type you selected; you can take Word's recommendation (it's usually correct), or you can override Word and select another format.

Once the file has been converted, Word considers it to be in Word format *in memory*. It can be stored on disk in one of several ways:

- If you use the File→Save command, Word assumes you want to store the file on disk in Word Normal format, *under its original file name*. Word displays a message box asking you if that's really what you want to do. If that's correct, click $\boxed{\text{Yes}}$. If you click $\boxed{\text{No}}$, Word displays the Save As dialog box to let you change the name or format.

However, if you've opened a file in one of the text formats, and you *haven't made any changes that added formatting of any kind* (in other words, the file remains purely text), then Word will automatically save it in the original text format, under the same name.

- If you use the File→Save As command, you can choose whether to save the file in Word Normal format, and you can rename the file before saving it. If you don't change the name, Word will ask permission before overwriting the old format file.

If you're tempted to read in a file in a "foreign" format and save it in that same format—if you want Word to mimic another word processor—be prepared for Word to lose certain formatting information during this double conversion. That's because each conversion is not perfect, and you'll lose something each time you convert a file. Word is Word, and it can't do a perfect job pretending to be another program.

Saving a Word Document in Another Format

Use the File→Save As command to display the Save As dialog box. Select the format in which to save the file from the Save File As Type list box. If you're saving an existing document (one that already has a file name), Word will propose to use exactly the same name. You should change at least the file extension to one of the common extensions in the table above, to help you identify the file format later. When everything is set up, click $\boxed{\text{OK}}$.

Rich Text Format (RTF)

RTF is an exception to the general rule that file conversions are imperfect, simply because RTF is Microsoft's standard format for exchanging document information, and thus Microsoft can extend the format whenever necessary to track changes exactly in Word's .DOC format. Because of RTF's fidelity, it's the preferred format for exchanging documents with another program, if the other program supports it.

Where the .DOC format stores a document in *binary* form, in which even individual bits of data are significant, RTF uses only printable text to describe every aspect of a document. Thus .RTF files are generally much larger than .DOC files. They're also less likely to be damaged by small errors (such as disk errors) than .DOC files, and are therefore more robust. This fact leads to this tip:

| *Tip* | If you find yourself with a "killer document," one that crashes Word every time you open the file or when you switch to Page Layout view, the document file may be corrupted in a way that can be cured by converting it to RTF and then back to .DOC format. Open the file with Word set to Draft view (the simplest and safest display method), save it in RTF, then close the original file and open the RTF version. If this cures the problem, save the document in .DOC format, overwriting the original, damaged file.

Text Formats

A *text* file is a file containing only the text of a document, and none of the (normally) hidden coding that tells a program how to format the text. Word has several text options that provide two types of character code conversion and preserve (or simulate) some degree of formatting.

"Text" versus "DOS Text"

Windows uses what's called the ANSI character set for all text, while non-Windows (usually called "character-based") applications use a different character set called "PC" or "DOS." The two character sets are essentially identical in their first 128 codes (codes 0 to 127), but differ dramatically in the characters they assign to codes from 128 to 255. When you specify a "Text" conversion format, Word doesn't change any character codes; it assumes the ANSI character set. If you specify one of the "DOS Text" types, Word tries to find characters in one character set that are equivalent to characters in the other set, and substitutes the corresponding character code. If Word can't find an exact match it may just use the same numeric code, or it may not convert the character at all.

To put it in concrete terms, with either type of text conversion you won't be able to display or print many of the characters commonly produced by character-based applications; all the line drawing and shading characters and many of the special symbols will be unavailable.

If you've wondered why Word seems to "garble" text files, this character conversion is the reason. You're better off using a simple text editor like the Windows Notepad for editing small text files, particularly system files like WIN.INI or AUTOEXEC.BAT.

Word offers these options for converting between text files and Word documents:

Text only (.TXT) *DOS text only (.TX8)*	Word strips all formatting and saves only the text. It inserts carriage returns only where paragraph endings occurred in the file. All fields are converted to text strings with real curly braces in place of the field markers; all other non-text objects, such as pictures, are ignored. Each cell in a table is converted to a separate paragraph.
Text with line breaks (.TXT) *DOS text with line breaks (.TX8)*	Like Text only, except that Word inserts a carriage return where each line ended in the formatted version of the document.
Text with layout (.ANS) *DOS text with layout (.ASC)*	Word tries to simulate the formatting of the document by inserting spaces and tabs (for example, to simulate paragraph indents). The results can be particularly hideous for justified paragraphs.

The two tables below show how Word converts characters when importing (opening) DOS text files, and when exporting (saving) DOS text files. The reason there are separate tables for importing and exporting is that the conversions aren't symmetrical: Word doesn't "map" character codes the same way when it's exporting as it does when it's importing. The second table (the results of exporting) shows only characters changed during conversion.

Word Text File Import Character Conversions

DOS		→	ANSI	DOS		→	ANSI
Code	Char.	Code	Char.	Code	Char.	Code	Char.
128	Ç	Ç	199	135	ç	ç	231
129	ü	ü	252	136	ê	ê	234
130	é	é	233	137	ë	ë	235
131	â	â	226	138	è	è	232
132	ä	ä	228	139	ï	ï	239
133	à	à	224	140	î	î	238
134	å	å	229	141	ì	ì	236

(continued)

Word Text File Import Character Conversions *(continued)*							
DOS		**→**	**ANSI**	**DOS**		**→**	**ANSI**
Code	**Char.**	**Code**	**Char.**	**Code**	**Char.**	**Code**	**Char.**
142	Ä	Ä	196	175	»	»	187
143	Å	Å	197	176	▨	_	95
144	É	É	201	177	▨	_	95
145	æ	æ	230	178	▨	_	95
146	Æ	Æ	198	179	│	¦	166
147	ô	ô	244	180	┤	¦	166
148	ö	ö	246	181	╡	¦	166
149	ò	ò	242	182	╢	¦	166
150	û	û	251	183	╖	+	43
151	ù	ù	249	184	╕	+	43
152	ÿ	ÿ	255	185	╣	¦	166
153	Ö	Ö	214	186	║	¦	166
154	Ü	Ü	220	187	╗	+	43
155	¢	¢	162	188	╝	+	43
156	£	£	163	189	╜	+	43
157	¥	¥	165	190	╛	+	43
158	₧	p	112	191	┐	+	43
159	ƒ	f	102	192	└	+	43
160	á	á	225	193	┴	-	45
161	í	í	237	194	┬	-	45
162	ó	ó	243	195	├	+	43
163	ú	ú	250	196	─	-	45
164	ñ	ñ	241	197	┼	+	43
165	Ñ	Ñ	209	198	╞	¦	166
166	ª	ª	170	199	╟	¦	166
167	º	º	186	200	╚	+	43
168	¿	¿	191	201	╔	+	43
169	⌐	_	95	202	╩	-	45
170	¬	¬	172	203	╦	-	45
171	½	½	189	204	╠	¦	166
172	¼	¼	188	205	═	-	45
173	¡	¡	161	206	╬	+	43
174	«	«	171	207	╧	-	45

(continued)

Word Text File Import Character Conversions (continued)							
DOS	→	ANSI		DOS	→	ANSI	
Code	Char.	Code	Char.	Code	Char.	Code	Char.
208	⊔	-	45	232	Φ	_	95
209	⊤	-	45	233	θ	_	95
210	π	-	45	234	Ω	_	95
211	⊔	+	43	235	δ	_	95
212	⊦	+	43	236	∞	_	95
213	F	+	43	237	φ	_	95
214	π	+	43	238	∈	_	95
215	⫡	+	43	239	∩	_	95
216	÷	+	43	240	≡	_	95
217	⌐	+	43	241	±	±	177
218	⌐	+	43	242	≥	_	95
219	■	_	95	243	≤	_	95
220	■	_	95	244	⌠	_	95
221	▌	¦	166	245	⌡	_	95
222	▌	_	95	246	÷	_	95
223	▬	_	95	247	≈	_	95
224	α	_	95	248	°	°	176
225	β	ß	223	249	∙	·	183
226	Γ	_	95	250	·	·	183
227	π	¶	182	251	√	_	95
228	Σ	_	95	252	ⁿ	n	110
229	σ	_	95	253	²	2	178
230	μ	µ	181	254	■	¨	168
231	τ	_	95	255		_	95

Word Text Export Character Conversions							
ANSI	→	DOS		ANSI	→	DOS	
code	char	char	code	code	char	char	code
160		(space)	32	164	¤	✸	15
161	¡	i	173	165	¥	¥	157
162	¢	¢	155	166	¦	■	221
163	£	£	156	167	§	§	21

(continued)

Word Text Export Character Conversions (continued)

ANSI code	char	→ char	DOS code	ANSI code	char	→ char	DOS code
168	¨	"	34	220	Ü	Ü	154
169	©	c	99	221	Ý	Y	89
170	ª	ª	166	222	Þ	_	95
171	«	«	174	223	ß	ß	225
172	¬	¬	170	224	à	à	133
173	–	–	45	225	á	á	160
174	®	r	114	226	â	â	131
175	¯	_	95	228	ä	ä	132
176	°	o	248	229	å	å	134
177	±	±	241	230	æ	æ	145
178	²	z	253	231	ç	ç	135
179	³	3	51	232	è	è	138
180	´	,	39	233	é	é	130
181	µ	µ	230	234	ê	ê	136
182	¶	¶	20	235	ë	ë	137
183	·	·	250	236	ì	ì	141
184	¸	<not converted>		237	í	í	161
185	¹	1	49	238	î	î	140
186	º	º	167	239	ï	ï	139
187	»	»	175	241	ñ	ñ	164
188	¼	¼	172	242	ò	ò	149
189	½	½	171	243	ó	ó	162
190	¾	_	95	244	ô	ô	147
191	¿	¿	168	246	ö	ö	148
196	Ä	Ä	142	247	˜	1	108
197	Å	Å	143	249	ù	ù	151
198	Æ	Æ	146	250	ú	ú	163
199	Ç	Ç	128	251	û	û	150
201	É	É	144	252	ü	ü	129
209	Ñ	Ñ	165	253	ý	y	121
214	Ö	Ö	153	254	þ	_	95
215	ˆ	L	76	255	ÿ	ÿ	152

FIELDS

A *field* is a special region of a document that contains codes that Word interprets and acts upon. Some field types insert text or graphics into a document, and thus have a *result,* while others show no result at their location, but may affect other parts of a document.

You can choose to display either field results or the codes inside fields by using the View→Field Codes command. When that menu item is checked, field codes are displayed; when it is not checked, field results are displayed. With View→Field Codes off, fields that show no result are invisible.

Fields are enclosed between special markers that are displayed on your screen (when View→Field Codes is checked) as { and }. However, don't confuse these screen symbols with the characters produced when you type curly braces; they're special markers that only show up on the screen. All fields follow one of these three formats:

{*Bookmark*}   A field may contain the name of a bookmark (as long as the bookmark name isn't the same as one of the field type names). The field displays as its result the text identified by the bookmark.

{*FieldName*}
{*FieldName Instructions*}   All other field types start with a *FieldName,* a formal name such as "DATE" that identifies what the field does. Some field types require additional *Instructions* that change how the field works.

Inserting a Field

The easiest way to insert a field into a document is using the Insert→ Field command, which displays the Field dialog box.

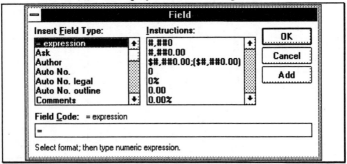

The Insert Field Type list shows only the fields you can insert your-self. Certain field types, as described later, can be inserted only by Word and aren't on this list. Click a field type to put it into the Field Code text box. At the same time, the contents of the Instructions list will change to show appropriate instructions for the field you selected. When you select an instruction the ⌈Add⌉ button will acti-vate; click ⌈Add⌉ to put the instruction into the Field Code box. For some fields you'll also have to type information, such as a bookmark name, into the Field Code box. When you click ⌈OK⌉, Word adds the field you "designed" to your document.

A second way to insert a field is to press ⌈Ctrl⌉+⌈F9⌉ to insert an empty set of field characters. You can then type the contents of the field. This is often the easiest way to create complex fields that have a lot of options and switches (see "Field Switches" below).

Finally, many commands automatically insert fields. For example, if you select the Link to File option using Insert→Picture, Word inserts an IMPORT field.

Manipulating Fields

With View Field Codes turned on, you can select text within a field and edit it. If you select one of the field markers, the entire field is automatically selected. With View Field Codes turned off, you can edit the field result (if any), but updating the field restores the field result to its previous state.

Very few field types automatically update their result when the conditions producing the result change. You must manually update a field by selecting it and pressing ⌈F9⌉; you can use Edit→Select All to select and update all the fields in a document. The File→Print Merge command also updates all fields in a document.

Field Switches

Switches are options that modify the action or result of a field; they're part of the *Instructions* in the description above of the general layout of a field. Some switches apply to specific fields; many switches apply to most field types, and are called "general" switches.

The general switches described below can be used with all field types except:

AUTONUM	GOTOBUTTON	TC
AUTONUMLGL	IMPORT	XE
AUTONUMOUT	MACROBUTTON	
EQ	RD	

You add a general switch (or more than one) inside a field, after the field type and instructions. Here's an example:

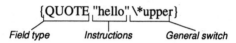

The field type QUOTE normally displays its instruction, in this case *"hello,"* exactly as it appears in the field code. The addition of the *upper switch changes "hello" to "HELLO."

Text-Formatting Switches

Text formatting switches control the capitalization (uppercase, lowercase, or mixed) of text, the format of numbers, and character formatting such as bold or italic. Word formats field results according to how the first character of the field is formatted, unless you modify that with a text formatting switch. A text formatting switch looks like this:

* *FormatName*

That is, each text formatting switch starts with a backslash and an asterisk, and then a word applying a specifying the formatting.

Case Conversion	The case conversion switches control how text in the field result is capitalized.
* upper	Converts text in the field result to uppercase.
* lower	Converts text in the field result to lowercase.
* firstcap	Formats text in the field result so that the first letter of the first word is capitalized.
* caps	Formats text in the field result so that the first letter of each word is capitalized.

Number-Formatting	These switches control how numbers in field results are displayed. Other text besides numbers in the field result is ignored; if there are no numbers in the result, then the switches are ignored.
* arabic	Numbers are displayed as arabic numerals.
* ordinal	Numbers are displayed as ordinal numbers: *1st, 2nd,* and so on.
* roman	Numbers are displayed as roman numerals.
* alphabetic	If the field result is a number, changes the result to display the letter at that position in the alphabet (1=A, 2=B, 26=D, and so on). Numbers from 1 through 26 display a single letter; from 27 through 52 a double letter; and so on in multiples of 26. If the first letter of the word "alphabetic" in the switch is capitalized Word uses uppercase letters; if the first letter is lower case then Word uses lowercase letters.
	*alphabetic produces a blank result if the number equals zero, and has no effect on non-numeric field results.
* cardtext	Spells out the number. For example, {QUOTE "225" *cardtext} displays *Two Hundred Twenty-Five.*
* ordtext	Spells out the number as an ordinal. For example, {QUOTE "225" * ordtext} displays *Two Hundred Twenty-Fifth.*
* hex	Converts the number in the field result to hexadecimal form. For example, {QUOTE "15" * hex} displays *F.*
* dollartext	Spells out the number in the field result in currency format, with the fractional part formatted as a fraction. For example, {QUOTE "225.99" * dollartext} displays *Two Hundred Twenty-Five and 99/100.*

Character-Formatting	These switches control the character formatting of the field result. *Without* one of these switches most fields use the character formatting, if any, of the source of the result.
* charformat	The formatting of the first character in the field after the opening field mark is applied to the entire field result. In many cases this is the default. However, some field types, notably bookmark reference fields, take their formatting from the source of the reference (the text identified by the bookmark) and ignore the formatting of the field. The *charformat switch overrides this behavior and forces the field result to match the formatting of the field.
* mergeformat	Uses the formatting of the previous result on the new result when a field is updated. This is useful if you've manually formatted a field result and want the formatting to become permanent. Without the *mergeformat switch, that formatting would disappear the next time the field was updated.

(continued)

> Character-Formatting *(continued)*
>
> For example, if you format the result of a TIME field without *mergeformat so that the minute digits are bold (11:**27**:42) and then update the field, the minutes digits would revert to normal text (no bold). With the *mergeformat switch in the field, the minute digits would remain bold no matter how many times the field is updated.

Numeric Picture Switches

The various numeric picture switches provide more detailed formatting of numbers, by providing a string of characters that represents a "picture" of the format. Each such picture begins with the backslash and asterisk characters (*).

If the field result does not include a number, these switches are ignored; if the field result includes text in addition to a number, the text is not used. You can include commas, periods, numbers other than zero, and currency and other symbols as literal parts of the picture; they appear in the result exactly as they appear in the picture. Some characters have a special meaning, as described below.

A common numeric picture formats a number as currency, and might look like \# $###,##0.00; this says that the field result, if it's a number, will:

- Start with a dollar sign (this is a "literal" because it appears in the result literally as it appears in the picture).

- Use a comma between the third and fourth digits of numbers with more than 3 digits to the left of the decimal.

- Always have at least one digit to the left of the decimal.

- Have exactly two digits to the right of the decimal.

These characters have a special meaning in numeric pictures:

0 (zero)	Each zero is a digit placeholder. On the left side of a decimal point it specifies that the number will be at least as many digits long as there are zeros. If the number has fewer digits, zeros are added to pad the result; if the number has more digits, all digits are displayed. For example, {QUOTE "27" \#0000} displays *0027*.
	On the right side of a decimal point, zeros specify the exact precision of the displayed text—extra digits are rounded off, and the result is padded with zeros if there are fewer significant digits.

#	The pound sign is a conditional placeholder to the left of a decimal point—if the number at that position is not zero, it is displayed; otherwise nothing is displayed. The pound sign is typically used in combination with zero.
X	Digits to the left of X, when it appears to the left of the decimal point, will be discarded. When X appears to the right of the decimal point, digits beyond X are rounded off. For example, formatting 277.7875 with the picture \# X#.#X results in 77.79.
Decimal Separator	The character used as a decimal point must match the decimal character specified in WIN.INI (a comma or a period, depending on your location).
Thousands Separator	The thousands separator (the character separating groups of three digits to the left of the decimal point) must match the thousands separator specified in WIN.INI (a comma or a period).
-	The negative sign (actually a hyphen) is displayed if the result is negative, a space if the result is positive.
+	The positive character signifies that a sign must be displayed: - (a hyphen) if negative, + if positive. Without this switch only negative numbers would have a sign.
PositivePicture; *NegativePicture*	You can specify alternative pictures depending on whether a result is positive or negative; the two pictures are separated by a semicolon (with no additional space). For example, the picture \# $#0.00;($#0.00) formats a positive value like .75 as $0.75 and a negative value like -27.935 as ($27.94).
PositivePicture; *NegativePicture; ZeroPicture*	This variation on the use of the semicolon lets you specify an additional picture if the result is zero. (For example, in some cases you might want the word "zero" to appear if the number is zero.)
'text'	Any text between single quotes is displayed literally. For example, the picture \# #0.00' Dollars' applied to the number 99.44 produces the result *99.44 Dollars*. Notice the space in front of "Dollars" in the picture; normally, spaces in a picture don't appear in the result, but in this case the space is inside the single quotes.
`sequence-name`	Enclose a sequence name between grave accent (`) characters to display the current value of the sequence. Be careful not to confuse the grave accent with the ordinary single quote—type a grave accent by activating NumLock on the keyboard, and holding down Alt while typing **096**.

Date and Time Pictures

The date and time picture strings format field results that can be interpreted as a date or time. A date or time picture begins with a backslash and the "at" symbol (\@).

If Word can't recognize the result as a date or time these switches are ignored. Some kinds of fields can produce a result that represents a date or time in the future (which really means that the date or time result has yet to be determined). The PRINTDATE field, for example, will have an indeterminate result until the first time the document is printed. In these cases, Word displays all zeros where the specified format called for numbers, and Xs where the format called for letters.

Date Pictures   In date pictures, the letter M must always be capitalized, to distinguish month formatting in date pictures from minute formatting in time pictures. You can include literal characters such as hyphens or spaces; for example, on the 24th of January, 1995 the date picture "D-MMM-YY displays *24-Jan-95*, while the date picture MMMM D, YYYY displays *January 24, 1995*. (The letters D and Y may be upper- or lowercase, as long as they are all the same case.)

M	Displays the month as a number, without a leading zero for single-digit months.
MM	Displays the month as a number; single-digit months have a leading zero.
MMM	Displays the month spelled out as a three-character abbreviation (Oct for October, for example).
MMMM	Displays the month spelled out fully.
D	Displays the day of the month without leading zeros for single-digit months.
DD	Displays the day of the month; single-digit months have a leading zero.
DDD	Displays the day of the week as a three-letter abbreviation (Mon for Monday, for example).
DDDD	Displays the day of the week fully spelled out.
YY	Displays the year as a two-digit number (the year within a century), with leading zeros for single-digit years. The year 2001 would be displayed as 01, for example.
YYYY	The year is displayed with all its digits. The year 2001 would display as *2001*, and the year 969 would display as *969*, for example.

Time Pictures   The letter m in time pictures must always be lowercase to distinguish minute digits from month digits. The letter H produces 24-hour time formats, while h produces 12-hour time. You can include literal characters such as colons to separate parts of a time.

h	Displays the hour as one or two digits, in 12-hour format.
H	Displays the hour as one or two digits, in 24-hour format.

(continued)

Time Pictures *(continued)*	
hh	Displays the hour as two digits (single-digit hours have a leading zero), in 12-hour format.
HH	Displays the hour as two digits (single-digit hours have a leading zero), in 24-hour format.
m	Displays minutes in one or two digits.
mm	Displays minutes in two digits, with leading zeros added to single-digit minutes.

The following switches control the display of AM and PM in 12-hour time formats. The actual text used depends on the setting in the Windows Control Panel, and may not be literally "AM" or "PM." When you use these switches, you must enclose the entire picture in quotes (for example, "HH:mm AM/PM").

AM/PM	Displays the appropriate legend (by default, AM for morning hours, PM for afternoon hours) in uppercase.
am/pm	Displays the appropriate legend in lowercase.

Literal Text and Sequence Names in Date or Time Pictures	
'text'	Any text between single quotes is displayed literally.
`` `sequence- name` ``	Enclose a sequence name between grave accent (`) characters to display the current value of the sequence. Be careful not to confuse the grave accent with the ordinary single quote—type a grave accent by activating NumLock on the keyboard, and holding down Alt while typing **096**.

Locking a Field

When you want to protect a field from being updated, add the lock-result switch: a backslash and an exclamation point (\!).

The lock-result switch is easiest to understand when contrasted with unlinking a field. Unlinking converts a field's result to text, making the result permanent and not subject to updating. However, this is a one-way operation, since to update the (former) result you'd have to recreate the field. The lock-field switch, on the other hand, leaves the field in place, but makes its result *semipermanent*—it can't be updated until you edit the field codes to remove the lock-result switch.

Field Cross-Reference

Word's fields can be categorized as shown below. Detailed information about each field follows, in the next section.

Bookmarks and Cross-References	ASK (prompt for bookmark text), Bookmark, PAGE (the current page number), PAGEREF (the page number of a bookmark), FTNREF (footnote reference), REF (reference a bookmark), SET (set bookmark text), STYLEREF (get the text from a paragraph in a specified style)
Information	AUTHOR, COMMENTS, CREATEDATE, DATE (the current date), EDITTIME (elapsed time a file has been open), FILENAME, INFO, KEYWORDS, LASTSAVED-BY, NUMCHARS, NUMPAGES, NUMWORDS, PAGE (the current page number), PRINTDATE, REVNUM (revision number), SAVEDATE, SUBJECT, TEMPLATE, TIME, TITLE, USERADDRESS, USERINITIALS, USERNAME
User Interaction	ASK (prompt for bookmark text), FILLIN (prompt for text to insert), GOTOBUTTON (move the cursor), MACRO-BUTTON (run a macro)
Numbering and Outlines	AUTONUM (automatic numbering), AUTONUMLGL, AUTONUMOUT, PAGE, SEQ (sequence numbers)
Print Merge	DATA, MERGEFIELD, MERGEREC, NEXT, NEXTIF, RD (referenced document), SKIPIF
Linking	DDE, DDEAUTO, EMBED, IMPORT, INCLUDE, LINK,
Mathematical	Expression (=), EQ
Miscellaneous	FTNREF (footnote reference), GLOSSARY (insert a glossary entry), GOTOBUTTON, MACROBUTTON, IF (control the field results based on a condition), PRINT (send printer codes to the printer)
Tables and Lists	INDEX, XE (index entry), TC (table of contents entry), TOC (table of contents)
Text and Characters	DATE, TIME, QUOTE (insert text), SYMBOL (insert a character), STYLEREF, GLOSSARY

Field Syntax

The format and usage of each Word field is described on the next several pages.

Note: Many fields, such as ASK and QUOTE, take text as part of their instructions. If the text consists of more than one word (if it has any spaces), then you must enclose the text in double quotes ("). Rather than remembering a rule like "single word, no quotes; multiple words, add quotes," you might want to get into the habit of putting *all* text in quotes; it makes no difference to Word.

Ask	{ASK *BookmarkName Prompt*} {ASK *BookmarkName Prompt switches*}

Displays a message (*Prompt*) asking for text, and assigns the text to the bookmark *BookmarkName*. ASK functions when fields are updated (manually or at printing time), and during print merge before each document is printed. An ASK field doesn't display any result; only the bookmark field for the named bookmark shows the entered text.

Prompt must be enclosed in quotes if it consists of more than one word.

Switches

\o   During print merge, prompts only before printing the first document.

\d   Specifies the default response; the text following \d is used as the response if the user clicks OK or presses ⌐ without typing a response.

ASK fields cannot be used in footnotes, headers, footers, annotations, or macros.

Author	{AUTHOR} {AUTHOR "*NewName*"}

Inserts the contents of the Author section in the Summary Info dialog box. If *NewName* is included, the Author section of Summary Info is changed to *NewName*.

Auto Numbering	{AUTONUM}

Inserts an automatic numbering field in arabic number format into the document.

The automatic numbering fields follow the outline hierarchy (see the topic "Outlines" for more information). All paragraphs formatted with the *heading 1* style are numbered in sequence; the first *heading 2* paragraph after a *heading 1* starts at 1; and so on. Each paragraph must have its own AUTONUM field. The left example below shows a series of heading paragraphs as they'd appear with View→Field Codes turned on, while the right example shows the field results (View→Field Codes turned off).

{AUTONUM} *heading 1*	*1. heading 1*
{AUTONUM} *heading 2*	*1. heading 2*
{AUTONUM} *heading 2*	*2. heading 2*
{AUTONUM} *heading*	*1. heading 3*
3	*2. heading 3*
{AUTONUM} *heading*	*3. heading 2*
3	*2. heading 1*
{AUTONUM} *heading 2*	*1. heading 2*
{AUTONUM}. *heading 1*	
{AUTONUM} *heading 2*	

Automatic numbering fields produce a result when they're inserted, and are updated after printing or after display in Print Preview. Pressing ⌐ doesn't update the field.

Auto Numbering Legal	{AUTONUMLGL}

AUTONUMLGL works like AUTONUM, except that it uses the legal numbering format, as shown to the right.	1 heading 1
	  1.1 heading 2
	  1.2 heading 2
	      1.2.1 heading 3
	      1.2.2 heading 3
	  1.3 heading 2
	2 heading 1
	  2.1 heading 2

Autonumber Outline	{AUTONUMOUT}

AUTONUMOUT inserts an automatic numbering field with outline number format, when used in a heading. In body text it uses arabic numerals, and so has the same result as AUTONUM. See the example to the right.	I heading 1
	  A heading 2
	  B heading 2
	    1 heading 3
	    2 heading 3
	  C heading 2
	II heading 1
	  A heading 2

Bookmark	{*BookmarkName*}

Inserts the text defined by the bookmark *BookmarkName*:

- If *BookmarkName* was inserted into the document with Insert→Bookmark and spans text (text was selected when the bookmark was inserted), *BookmarkName* defines that text, and the BOOKMARK field reproduces that text at its own location.

- If *BookmarkName* doesn't define text (for example, if it was inserted into the document while the cursor was an insertion point, with no text selected) then the BOOKMARK field produces no result.

- If *BookmarkName* was defined with a {SET *BookmarkName)* field, then the BOOKMARK field produces the text defined by the SET field.

If *BookmarkName* happens to be the same as the name of a field code, use a {REF *BookmarkName*} field instead.

You cannot insert this field from the Insert Field Type dialog box; you must insert field characters using [Ctrl]+[F9] and then type BOOKMARK *BookmarkName*.

Comments	{COMMENTS} {COMMENTS "*NewComments*"}

Inserts the contents of the Comments section in the Summary Info dialog box. If text for *NewComments* is included, Comments in Summary Info is changed to *NewComments*.

Creation Date	{CREATEDATE} {CREATEDATE "*DatePicture*"}

Inserts the date the document was created, taken from the Summary Info dialog box. The format of the date is determined by Windows' default date format; you can specify a different format using the *DatePicture* (see "Date and Time Pictures" at the beginning of this topic).

Data	{DATA *datafile*} {DATA *datafile headerfile*}

Names the source file containing the data to be inserted during print merge. If you don't specify a file name extension, Word assumes .DOC. This field does not display a result (it's permanently formatted as hidden text), and must appear at the very beginning of a document.

The *headerfile*, if included, names a header file in addition to a data file. A header file defines the relationship between field names in a data file and the corresponding bookmark references in the master document.

The DATA field cannot be used in footnotes, annotations, headers or footers, or in data files. It cannot be part of (nested within) any other field.

If the header or data file names do not specify a path, Word assumes that they're in the current directory. If you include a path, each backslash in the path must be doubled (for example, D:\\SYBEX\\WINWORD).

Date	{DATE} {DATE "*DatePicture*"}

Inserts the date, formatted according to your default date format in Windows.

The *DatePicture*, if included, inserts the date with custom formatting (see "Date and Time Pictures" at the beginning of this topic).

The date displayed is the date on which the field was last updated when you pressed [F9] or printed the document.

DDE **(Dynamic Data** **Exchange)**	{DDE *AppName Filename*} {DDE *AppName Filename PlaceReference*}

Establishes a DDE link with the application *AppName*; the application supplies the contents of *Filename*, which is a file in that application's format.

PlaceReference further specifies the part of *Filename* that is the subject of the link. For example, the field

{DDE Excel budget.xls R1C1:R12C99}

establishes a DDE link with Microsoft Excel, opens the file BUDGET.XLS, and links to the cells outlined by R1C1 to R12C99.

(continued)

DDE *(continued)*

The DDE field result remains unchanged until you update the field with ⟦F9⟧ or print the document. (In contrast, the DDEAUTO field will update the result whenever the source information changes.) If the DDE link is broken, the last available results remain displayed.

LINK is preferred for new applications (and DDE is no longer listed in the Insert Field dialog box); DDE is a subset of the types of links that LINK can establish.

DDEAUTO (Automatic DDE)	{DDEAUTO *AppName Filename*} {DDEAUTO *AppName Filename PlaceReference*}

DDEAUTO functions like the DDE field, except that the results it displays are updated automatically whenever the source information (the information in *Filename* controlled by the application *AppName*) changes. The other application must support DDE "hot links" for the DDEAUTO field to work.

LINK is preferred over DDEAUTO for new applications.

Edit Time	{EDITTIME}

Inserts the total number of minutes that the document has been open for editing. This information is taken from the Summary Info dialog box.

Embed	{EMBED *ClassName*} {EMBED *ClassName switches*}

The EMBED field is created when you insert an object using Insert→Object or Edit→Paste Special, and creates a link to the object. You cannot insert an EMBED field from the Field dialog box or by typing it explicitly between field characters, because the EMBED field is really more of a marker for a substantial amount of information that Word maintains buried inside your document. You can, however, modify the switches of an existing EMBED field.

ClassName identifies the application that manages the embedded object; common class names include:

MSDraw	*Microsoft Draw*
MSGraph	*Microsoft Graph*
WordArt	*WordArt*
WordDocument	*A Word document*

Expression	{= Expression}

EXPRESSION fields perform a calculation and display the result. *Expression* is an equation using any combination of the math functions listed below, and may include bookmarks to reference numbers in another part of the document.

The equation can be any combination of the following mathematical operations or functions.

Arithmetic Operators			
Operator	*Description*	*Operator*	*Description*
+	Addition	-	Subtraction
*	Multiplication	/	Division
%	Percentage (unary operator, as in 2%; divides argument by 100)	^	Powers and roots (roots are expressed as decimal fractions)
Relational Operators			
Operator	*Description*	*Operator*	*Description*
=	Equal to	<>	Not equal
>	Greater than	<	Less than
>=	Greater than or equal	<=	Less than or equal to
Table References			
Operator	*Description*	*Operator*	*Description*
[R*n*C*n*]	The contents of row *n*, column *n* in the current table	[R*n*C*n*:R*n*C*n*]	Operates on a range of cells in the current table
[R*n*]	The contents of row *n* in the current table	*Bookmark* [R*n*C*n*]	Contents of the specified cell in the table containing *Bookmark*
[C*n*]	The contents of column *n* in the current table	*Bookmark* [R*n*C*n*:R*n*C*n*]	A range of cells in the table containing *Bookmark*
Functions			
Function	*Returns...*		
TRUE	Equivalent to a non-zero number; useful as a placeholder when testing IF functions (see below) to simulate a true result from an expression.		
FALSE	Equivalent to a zero result from an expression; like TRUE, useful as a placeholder when testing IF functions.		
AVERAGE()	The average of the items; may include table cell references.		
COUNT()	The number of items between parentheses; items may include table cell references; items must be separated by commas.		
MAX()	The largest of the items in parentheses; items may include table cell references; items must be separated by commas.		
MIN()	The smallest of the items in parentheses; items may include table cell references; items must be separated by commas.		
SUM()	The sum of the items in parentheses; items may include table cell references; items must be separated by commas.		
PRODUCT()	The result of multiplying all the items in parentheses; items may include table cell references; items must be separated by commas.		

(continued)

Functions *(continued)*	
Function	*Returns...*
ABS()	The absolute value of the expression in parentheses (always a positive number, regardless of the sign of the argument).
INT(*x*)	The integer part of *x*; for positive numbers, any fractional part (to the right of the decimal point) is discarded; for negative numbers, rounds to the next highest (more negative) integer (for example, INT(-8.4) returns 9).
SIGN(*x*)	1 if *x* is positive, zero if *x* is zero, and -1 if *x* is negative.
DEFINED(*x*)	1 if the expression *x* evaluates without error; zero if the result has an error (such as division by zero).
MOD(*x,y*)	*x* modulo *y*; that is, the remainder after *x* is divided by *y*.
ROUND(*x,y*)	*x* rounded to *y* decimal places; if *y* is positive, signifies digits to the right of the decimal point; if *y* is negative, signifies digits to the left of the decimal point.
AND(*x,y*)	1 if both *x* and *y* are true; otherwise zero.
OR(*x,y*)	1 if either *x* or *y* is true; returns zero if neither are true.
NOT(*x*)	The reverse value of *x*; that is, returns false if *x* is true.
IF(*x,y,z*)	Returns *y* if expression *x* is true, otherwise returns *z*.

File Name	{FILENAME}

Inserts the file name of the document. The drive and path are not included.

Fill-In	{FILLIN *switches*} {FILLIN "*Prompt*" *switches*}

FILLIN prompts you for text each time the field is updated (with ⊞ or by printing); the text is then inserted at the field location. Each time FILLIN works it collects new text. *Prompt* is an optional message to display.

Switches

\d *text*   *text* is the default if the user enters nothing; enclose *text* in quotes if it's more than one word.

\o   Prompts only for the first document during print merge. If a SKIPIF field causes Word to skip the first document then the FILLIN field will never function.

Footnote Reference	{FTNREF *Bookmark*}

Inserts the reference number of the footnote specified by *Bookmark*.

| **Formulas** | {EQ *Instructions*} |

The EQ field was the only way to create mathematical formulas prior to Word for Windows 2.0. While 2.0's equation editor is easier to use for complex formulas, the EQ field still has some uses, such as putting boxes around text, and for creating simple formulas.

If you open a pre-2.0 document and double-click on an EQ field Word reads the formula into the Equation Editor and translates it into Equation Editor format. You can also paste an EQ field into the Equation Editor.

One use for an EQ field (even with the Equation Editor available) is to put a box around text within a paragraph; this can often work better than using a Draw graphic or the Equation Editor. That's how the symbols representing Windows buttons were done in this book. For example, this OK button was created with the EQ field {EQ \x(OK)}. Refer to the Word Help topic Field Types and Instructions if you'd like more information about the EQ field.

| **Glossary Reference** | {GLOSSARY *GlossaryName*} |

Inserts the contents of the glossary entry named with *GlossaryName*. Each time the field is updated, it retrieves the contents of *GlossaryName,* so that if the glossary entry represented by *GlossaryName* changes the field will reflect the new content.

| **Goto Button** | {GOTOBUTTON *GoToInstruction Display*} |

GOTOBUTTON fields are Word's method of implementing simple "hypertext" links. (The Windows help system contains many examples of hypertext links, in the form of highlighted text that you click to move to another part of the help information.) GOTOBUTTON fields, together with MACROBUTTON fields, let you create rather sophisticated online documents.

A GOTOBUTTON field displays *Display* as its result (with View→Field Codes turned off).

When you activate this field, Word moves the cursor as directed by *GoToInstruction.* You "activate" a GOTOBUTTON in one of three ways:

· Double-click the result text

· Press Alt + Shift + F9 with the result text selected

· Run the DoFieldClick macro with the result text selected

Display can be text or a graphic, as long as the result fits on a single line. Text cannot contain spaces, even if you enclose it in quotes (in fact, if you enclose the text in quotes Word displays nothing at all). If you're using a graphic, just insert the graphic in the appropriate part of the field. For example,

    {GOTOBUTTON SomewhereElse Click Me! }

(continued)

GOTOBUTTON *(continued)*

produces what looks remarkably like a standard Windows button embedded in the middle of a document (when the document is displayed, of course; the printed result is somewhat less lifelike). This example was created using Word's dialog editor to make the pushbutton with the legend "Click Me!"; then a screen capture to get the image, which was simply pasted into the field in the Word document. When this "button" is clicked, Word moves the cursor to the bookmark *SomewhereElse*.

GoToInstruction can be a bookmark name or instructions you'd type with the Edit→Go To command (a page number, a relative number of pages to move, or a section number plus a page number).

If	{IF *Expression IfTrueText IfFalseText*}

IF displays *IfTrueText* if *Expression* evaluates true, *IfFalseText* if it is false.

Expression itself should be made up of two items (text, numbers, bookmark references, or arithmetic expressions) separated by a relational operator that tests the items (see the table "Relational Operators" under the discussion of the Expression [=] field in this topic for a list of valid operators).

If you are comparing text strings with IF, the second text expression can contain the wildcard character * (asterisk) to signify "match any characters" or ? (question mark) to signify "match any single character at this location."

Don't confuse the IF *field* with the IF() *function* used with the Expression (=) field. The IF() function in an = field is used in mathematical or logical comparisons. The purpose of the IF field, on the other hand, is to choose between two different results to display based on some condition. For example, you might use an IF field like {IF {=MOD({PAGE},2)}=0 Even Odd} to display the word "Even" on even-numbered pages (when MOD({PAGE},2)}=0 is true) and "Odd" on odd-numbered pages.

Import	{IMPORT *Filename*}

IMPORT inserts the contents of a graphic file (*Filename*). The file must be one of the graphic file types Word recognizes and for which a graphic import filter is installed. If you're not sure which formats are valid, check the WIN.INI options through Tools→Options.

If *Filename* contains a DOS path, each backslash in the path must be doubled (for example, D:\\SYBEX\\BITMAPS\\FILEOPEN.BMP).

If you double-click on an IMPORT field, Word turns it into a Microsoft Draw object (the IMPORT field is changed to an EMBED field).

Include	{INCLUDE *Filename switches*} {INCLUDE *Filename BookmarkName switches*}

INCLUDE inserts the contents of a text file identified by *Filename* into the document. (We'll use the terms "external file" and "current document" to distinguish between the file being inserted and the document containing the INCLUDE field.)

(continued)

INCLUDE *(continued)*

If the external file is a Word document, you can use *BookmarkName* to tell Word to insert only the text identified by the bookmark (in the other document) into the current document. Without *BookmarkName,* Word inserts the entire file.

INCLUDE maintains a link back to the external file. Each time you update the INCLUDE field Word reinserts the external file; as a result, your current document is updated if the external file is changed.

The link formed by INCLUDE can work both ways—that is, you can make changes to the included text in the current document, then send the changes back to the external file by pressing `Ctrl` + `Shift` + `F7` . (This assumes that the external document is in Word file format.)

Use the \c (convert) switch when the source file is in another format. Word will examine the extension in the filename, and the external file itself, to determine which document conversion filter to use. A special form of this switch, \c *text,* tells Word to insert the external file as plain text, regardless of its actual format.

Caveats: Microsoft recommends using INCLUDE when you're working with a "long" document, one longer than approximately 20 or 30 pages. Documents that are longer than that tend to become hard to work with, as pagination, saving, scrolling (and so on) times become excessive. The idea is to create a "master" document that references two or more "component" documents through INCLUDE fields.

What the Microsoft documentation glosses over is that INCLUDE fields don't improve things much at all, for a simple reason: INCLUDE fields *incorporate* the other file in the current document, so that it behaves as if it's just as long as if you'd used Insert→File or pasted the contents of the external file into your document (the size of the master document isn't just equal to the sum of the sizes of the component files—it's slightly *larger* due to the overhead of the INCLUDE fields). Further, you may run into problems using cross-references and other bookmark references between component documents. The INCLUDE field doesn't live up to its promise, as was discovered producing this book.

You can solve the problem with the size of the master file in a roundabout way by using print merge instead of INCLUDE fields (using bookmarks in the component files as if the entire file were one field in the merge), but then you lose the ability to preview the results and control things like pagination.

In fairness, INCLUDE fields do have their strengths: the ability to update the current document if the external file changes; the ability to make changes in the current document and reflect the changes back to the external file; and INCLUDE files can be very useful if you have a library of boilerplate text that's used by a number of documents.

Index	{INDEX} {INDEX *Switches*}

INDEX inserts an index into the document. Each time the field is updated, when you press `F9` with the field selected or print the document, Word collects XE (index entry) fields and compiles an index. The compiled index becomes the result of the INDEX field. See "Index Entry" below for information about the XE field.

(continued)

INDEX *(continued)*

The index is formatted using the standard Word paragraph styles "index 1" through "index 7." By default Word compiles an index from entries only in the current document. You can use the RD (referenced document) field to tell Word to collect entries from specified external document files.

Switches

There are a number of switches that you can use with the INDEX field. However, most of the time it's easier to use the Insert→Index command, whose dialog box lets you set the commonly-used INDEX options: whether the index style is "run-in" or entries as separate paragraphs, and how to mark the transition when the letter-group (the letter of the alphabet currently being indexed) changes. For more precise control, and additional options, you can add these switches:

\b *bookmark*	Collects index entries only from the pages marked by *bookmark*.
\e *"page number separator"*	Specifies the characters separating the index item and its page numbers. There can be no more than three separator characters. A tab character is used by default.
\g *page range separator*	Specifies the character used as a page range separator (for example, \g: specifies a colon as the separator, so that 5:99 in the index signifies a range from page 5 to 99). A hyphen is used by default.
\h *"letter-group separator"*	Specifies the format of the paragraph separating groups of letters in the index. For example, \h" " specifies a blank paragraph, \h"A" specifies heading letters, while \h"--A--" includes hyphens before and after the letters. \h"" (two quotes with nothing between them) specifies that letter groups should not be separated; this is the default.
\l *"page number separator"*	Specifies the character or characters separating page numbers, when an index entry appears on multiple pages. If the pages are contiguous, Word uses the page range format set by the \g switch. The default separator is a comma followed by a space.
\p *StartLetter-EndLetter*	Specifies the range of a partial index; the index is compiled only for entries beginning with the letters from *StartLetter* to *EndLetter*.
\r	Specifies a "run-in" index, in which a topic and its subtopics are combined into a single paragraph. A colon separates the topic and the subtopics, and a semicolon separates multiple subtopics.
\d *"character"*	Specifies a separator other than a hyphen to separate sequence numbers from page numbers.

(continued)

Index *(continued)*		
	\s *sequence*	Uses sequence fields to form the page number; that is, Word finds the value of the sequence field *sequence* on the page where it collects the index entry, and makes a page number consisting of the value of *sequence*, a hyphen, and the page number. This is most useful for collecting index entry page numbers when your document uses chapter numbering (for example, "8-3").

Index Entry	{XE "*Text*"} {XE "*Text*" *Switches*}

The XE field inserts an index entry into a document. Index entries are automatically formatted as hidden text.

When Word compiles an index, it collects the text from XE fields and notes the page number on which the entry appeared. See the previous topic "Index" for more information about indexes.

Text is the text of the index entry, and can be no more than 64 characters long, including spaces, tabs, paragraph and newline characters, and other special characters. It must be enclosed in quotes.

To create a multi-level index entry, separate each level of the entry with a semicolon (:). For example, the XE field

{XE "level 1:level 2:level 3:level 4"}

produces this index entry:

level 1
    level 2
        level 3
            level 4

Switches

\r *bookmark*	Tells Word to use the beginning and end of *bookmark* for the page range of the entry. If the bookmark spans only a single page, Word creates a single-page entry.
\t "*text*"	Uses *text* after the index entry instead of a page number. A common use for this switch is to insert a "see another entry" index entry.
\b	Makes page numbers bold.
\i	Makes page numbers italic.

Info	{INFO *InfoType*} {INFO *InfoType* "*NewValue*"}

INFO is the general case of the fields that take or update document information from the Summary Info dialog box; in other words, you could use a field with *InfoType* alone, without the word "INFO," for the same result. These are the equivalent fields:

(continued)

INFO *(continued)*			
AUTHOR	FILENAME	NUMPAGES	SAVEDATE
COMMENTS	KEYWORDS	NUMWORDS	SUBJECT
CREATEDATE	LASTSAVEDBY	PRINTDATE	TEMPLATE
EDITTIME	NUMCHARS	REVNUM	TITLE

Keywords	{KEYWORDS} {KEYWORDS "*newkeywords*"}

KEYWORDS inserts the contents of the Keywords section of the Summary Info dialog box. If you include *newkeywords,* it replaces the contents of the Keywords section of Summary Info.

Last Saved By	{LASTSAVEDBY}

LASTSAVEDBY inserts the name of the person who last saved the document; this information is taken from the Summary Info dialog box.

Link	{LINK *ClassName FileName* } {LINK *ClassName FileName format*} {LINK *ClassName FileName PlaceReference*} {LINK *ClassName FileName PlaceReference format*}

LINK establishes a link with a file created by a program other than Word, using "object-linking and embedding" (OLE). The content of that file is displayed in your Word document, while the external file itself is managed by the other application. When you double-click on a LINK field, Word invokes the other application to let you edit or create the linked object.

The linked application must support OLE; if it doesn't, Word uses DDE (dynamic data exchange) instead, and inserts a DDE or DDEAUTO field.

You cannot enter a LINK field yourself; Word must do it using the Edit→Paste Special command, or one of the other commands that contains a "Link" check box.

A link can be updated manually or automatically. After you've inserted the LINK field, select it and use the Edit→Links command to select manual or automatic updating.

ClassName	Identifies the application that manages this type of object; Windows uses this information to determine what application to start in response to Word's request for an OLE link. A typical classname might be "excelsheet" to identify a spreadsheet created with Microsoft Excel. Word determines the classname when it pastes the link.
FileName	The name of the file being linked.
PlaceReference	The portion of the specified file to be linked. For example, if you're linking to a spreadsheet that supports OLE, you can use the RnCn:RnCn notation to indicate a region of the spreadsheet to link.

(continued)

LINK (continued)	
format	One of the following formatting switches:
	\a To update the link automatically
	\t To insert the linked object as text
	\r To insert the linked object as RTF text
	\p To insert the linked object as a picture
	\b To insert the linked object as a bitmap

Macro Button	{MACROBUTTON *MacroName DisplayText*}

A MACROBUTTON field embeds a "button" in your document that runs a specified macro when you double-click the text of the button. MACROBUTTON fields, along with GOTOBUTTON fields, let you create sophisticated on-line documents.

The *DisplayText* should *not* be enclosed in quotes. You can format the text for emphasis, or put the field by itself in a paragraph and then add a border to the paragraph. You can even use a graphic for the display text (see the discussion of the GOTOBUTTON field for an example). However, the result must appear on a single line; it can't wrap to another line.

Merge Field	{MERGEFIELD *FieldName*}

MERGEFIELD is used during print merge to insert the contents of the named field from the data file. *FieldName* is displayed while you're editing the document, but the value of the field is printed.

Merge Record	{MERGEREC}

MERGEREC inserts the record number of the record currently being printed during print merge. Most of the time this number is incremented with each copy printed.

Next Record	{NEXT}

NEXT displays no result of its own; it selects the next record in the data file during print merge. NEXT allows you to insert information from multiple records into a single copy of a print-merged document. It cannot be used in footnotes, annotations, headers or footers, or in data files; nor can it be used inside another field. There is no equivalent field that selects a previous record.

Next IF	{NEXTIF *Expression Operator Expression*}

This is a conditional version of NEXT; it selects the next record in the data file during print merge only if *Expression Operator Expression* is true. See the table "Relational Operators" in the discussion of the Expression (=) field for a list of comparison operators you can use. NEXTIF cannot be used in footnotes, annotations, headers, or footers, or in data files; nor can it be used inside another field.

Number of Characters	{NUMCHARS}

NUMCHARS inserts the number of characters in the document the last time it was printed, or the last time the statistics in the Summary Info dialog box were updated.

Number of Pages	{NUMPAGES}

NUMPAGES inserts the number of pages in the document the last time it was printed, or the last time the statistics in the Summary Info dialog box were updated.

Number of Words	{NUMWORDS}

NUMWORDS inserts the number of words in the document the last time it was printed or the last time the statistics in the Summary Info dialog box were updated.

Page	{PAGE} {PAGE *NumericPictureSwitch*}

The PAGE field inserts the number of the page on which it's located. The page number is displayed using the number format specified in the Header/Footer dialog box, unless you specify another format with *NumericPictureSwitch*.

Page Reference	{PAGEREF *Bookmark*} {PAGEREF *Bookmark NumericPictureSwitch*}

PAGEREF inserts the page number on which *Bookmark* appears. All of the cross-references in this book use PAGEREF fields.

For example,

"see the PAGEREF field on page {PAGEREF Field_PAGEREF}"

produces

"see the PAGEREF field on page 80"

when the field is updated.

The page number format is taken from the Header/Footer dialog box, unless you specify another format with *NumericPictureSwitch*.

Print Codes	{PRINT "*PrinterInstructions*"} {PRINT \p *Size* "*PostScriptCode*"}

The PRINT field sends literal text to your printer; that is, it bypasses the Windows printer driver and sends *PrinterInstructions* directly to the printer. It's useful for creating special effects directly with printer codes; there are sample macros included with Word that show how the PRINT field can be used.

(continued)

PRINT (continued)

Each type of printer uses different codes (for example, PostScript versus Hewlett-Packard's Printer Control Language), so you have to know the kind of printer the document will be printed on, and you have to know the appropriate print codes for that printer. You'll get results ranging from merely amusing to downright disastrous if you send the wrong codes to a printer.

PostScript

PRINT has special extensions for use with PostScript printers. These extension are introduced with the \p switch. The following information assumes that you're familiar with PostScript programming. For more information about PostScript, see *Understanding PostScript, Third Edition,* published by SYBEX.

PRINT PostScript commands use the same coordinate system as PostScript: origin (0,0) in the lower left corner, positive dimensions up and to the right, and units in points. The origin and clipping rectangle for the PRINT field code is defined by the *Size* part of the field; *Size* can be one of these words:

page	The current page; origin is the lower-left corner of the page, and the clipping rectangle encompasses the entire page; this is the default.
para	The current paragraph; the clipping rectangle is the size of the extents of the paragraph (the space it occupies on the page). The paragraph must be at least one inch tall.
pic	The clipping rectangle is defined as equal to the next picture following the PRINT field. The picture must be after the PRINT field but before the end of the current paragraph.
row	The clipping rectangle is equal to the current table row.
cell	The clipping rectangle is equal to the current table cell.
dict	Specifies that the PostScript code defines a dictionary entry, rather than produces a printed result. The defined PostScript routine can then be used later in another PRINT field, but only on the same page. (The dictionary is reset after each showpage.) This is a powerful command, because it's not subject to clipping nor is its origin set by Word; use it carefully.

Word defines several variables in the header file downloaded with each print job, and your code can use some of these (all units are in points):

wp$y	The height of the current clipping rectangle.
wp$x	The width of the current clipping rectangle.
wp$page	The current page number, in the form of a number.
wp$fpage	The current page number as a formatted string.
wp$date	The current date as a formatted string.
wp$time	The current time as a formatted string.
wp$box	The path containing the drawing rectangle.
wp$top	The top margin in the page clipping rectangle; the space-before (as set in the paragraph's formatting) in the para clipping rectangle. Not valid for other clipping rectangles.
wp$bottom	The bottom margin in the page clipping rectangle; the space-after (as set in the paragraph's formatting) in the para clipping rectangle. Not valid for other clipping rectangles.

(continued)

PRINT *(continued)*	
wp$left	The left margin in the page clipping rectangle; the left indent in the para clipping rectangle. Not valid for other clipping rectangles.
wp$right	The right margin in the page clipping rectangle; the right indent in the para clipping rectangle. Not valid for other clipping rectangles.
wp$first	The first line indent of the paragraph defining the para clipping rectangle. Not valid for other clipping rectangles.
wp$style	The name of the style of the paragraph defining the para clipping rectangle. Not valid for other clipping rectangles.
wp$col	The number of columns on the current page, in the section in which the PRINT field appears; valid in the page clipping rectangle only.
wp$colx	The width of the columns on the current page, in the section in which the PRINT field appears; valid in the page clipping rectangle only.
wp$colxb	The space between columns on the current page, in the section in which the PRINT field appears; valid in the page clipping rectangle only.

PostScript Code Considerations

The *PostScriptCode* part of the PostScript PRINT field must be enclosed in quotes. Avoid operators that alter the PostScript environment, because that would alter how the rest of the page prints (Word wouldn't know that the PostScript environment has changed, and so might make incorrect assumptions about the state of the PostScript environment). In particular, avoid these operators:

banddevice	framedevice	initmatrix	nulldevice	
copypage	grestoreall	initgraphics	renderbands	showpage

Print Date	{PRINTDATE} {PRINTDATE *Date-TimePictureSwitch*}

PRINTDATE inserts the date the document was last printed, taken from the Summary Info dialog box.

Quote	{QUOTE "*LiteralText*"} {QUOTE *CharacterCode*}

QUOTE inserts text into your document. That's not very useful for text you'd simply type anyway, but the QUOTE field is more useful when you want to insert nonprinting characters, or characters not easily available on your keyboard. In that role, QUOTE works like SYMBOL field, without SYMBOL's ability to specify a font or font size, but with the additional ability to specify multiple character codes, and the ability to mix character codes with literal text.

(continued)

QUOTE *(continued)*

You specify character codes in a QUOTE field by their numeric value. Character codes must appear outside any quotes (numbers inside quotes would be printed as numbers, and not converted to a character code). The numeric value is based on the ANSI character set; see the ANSI character set table at the back of this book.

Numbers are interpreted as decimal. If you prefix the number with 0x Word interprets it as hexadecimal (base 16), allowing the use of the letters A through F in addition to the digits 0 (zero) through 9.

Here's an example of a QUOTE field, showing a mixture of literal text and character codes:

{QUOTE "SYBEX" 174 " is a registered trademark"}

produces

SYBEX® is a registered trademark

Reference	{REF *Bookmark*}

REF inserts the text encompassed by *Bookmark*. You can dispense with the word REF as long as *Bookmark* is not the same as a field name. See the discussion on the BOOKMARK field earlier, and the topic "Bookmarks."

Referenced Document	{RD Filename}

RD identifies a document file to be included in the compilation of an index or a table of contents. RD doesn't include the file itself (that's the job of the INCLUDE field). RD only causes Word to open the named document and scan it for index or table of contents entries.

Reference Internal Link	{REF intern_link*n*}

This variation of REF establishes a link with the contents of another part of the same document. What's special about it is that this link is established by Word when you copy a part of a document to the Clipboard, select the Edit→Paste Special command, and click the [Paste Link] button. The location of the linked text is maintained internally in the document by Word and isn't shown in the REF field thus created; this is why you can't manually create this field by inserting field characters and typing, or select it from the Fields dialog box.

Revision Number	{REVNUM}

REVNUM inserts the document's revision number. This is the number of times the document has been saved, taken from the Summary Info dialog box.

Save Date	{SAVEDATE} {SAVEDATE *DatePicture*}

SAVEDATE inserts the date the document was last saved, taken from the
Summary Info dialog box. See "Date and Time Pictures" at the beginning of
this topic for information about *DatePicture*.

Sequence	{SEQ *Identifier switches*} {SEQ *Identifier Bookmark switches*}

SEQ inserts the next available number from a sequence of numbers. A document can have multiple, independent numbering sequences, each distinguished
by its *Identifier*. You can, for example, have separate number sequences for
tables and figures.

The number produced by a SEQ field is one more than the number produced by
a preceding SEQ field in the same *Identifier* sequence. The first SEQ field in a
document starts at zero, unless you modify the starting number with the reset
(\r) switch (explained below). You can use the \r switch in a sequence more than
once, resetting the sequence each time.

If you include *Bookmark*, the SEQ field becomes a reference to the value of the
SEQ field closest to (and before) *Bookmark*; the field doesn't increment the
current sequence but, rather, shows the value of the referenced field. You can
use this to create a cross reference to a number in a sequence. For example, if
the field {SEQ Tables} is marked with the bookmark TrajectoryTable, then you
could write "see Table {SEQ Tables TrajectoryTable}" to cross-reference that
table number.

If a SEQ field is part of the text defined by a bookmark, a reference elsewhere
to that bookmark (such as a BOOKMARK field) will reproduce the SEQ field,
rather than just the number it produces. In other words, the BOOKMARK field
will have its own, unique, SEQ field, with its own number—*not* the number at
the source of the reference. Odd, but true.

The number produced by a SEQ field when it is inserted is one more than the
previous number in the same sequence. If the field is inserted between two existing SEQ fields (with the same *SequenceIdentifier*), it will produce a number
one more than the previous field, but the following, existing SEQ field won't be
updated, and will show the same number as the new field. The same thing happens if you delete a SEQ field. Sequence numbers are updated only when the
field is updated with the [F9] key or when the document is printed.

Switches

\c   Inserts the most recent, earlier sequence number; doesn't create a new one.

\r*n*   Resets the sequence number to *n*.

\n   Inserts the next sequence number (the default action).

\h   Hides the field result. (Like hidden text, it won't print; this is useful for
creating a cross-reference, for example.)

Set	{SET *Bookmark* "*Data*"}

SET defines the text of a bookmark. Instead of having a bookmark span text that prints, the SET field prints nothing at its location, but sets what will be printed by bookmark fields that reference *Bookmark*. One use might be to set a name that appears several places in a form letter. Another common use is to define a chapter title in one place, with a SET field, so that bookmark fields in several places can refer to it; if you want to change the chapter title, you need only change the SET field to change the title throughout the document.

You can't use SET in footnotes, annotation, or headers and footers.

Skip If	{SKIPIF *Expression Operator Expression*}

SKIPIF cancels the current copy during print merge and skips to the next record, if the expression is true. SKIPIF won't work in conjunction with NEXT. Refer to the IF field discussed earlier. For information about expressions and operators see the discussion of the Expression (=) field earlier.

Style Reference	{STYLEREF "*StyleIdentifier*"} {STYLEREF "*StyleIdentifier*" *Switch*}

STYLEREF inserts the text of the most recent paragraph formatted with *StyleIdentifier*. The headers in this book have a STYLEREF field that picks up the text of the most recently-used heading 1 paragraphs to help you find topics.

The default search direction is backward, toward the beginning of the document; Word uses the text of the most recent previous *StyleIdentifier* paragraph. In a header or footer the \l switch searches for the last paragraph of style *StyleIdentifier* on the current page. By using two STYLEREF fields in a header, one without the \l switch and the other with it, you can create telephone-book style headers that list the first and last items on a page.

If STYLEREF is in a footnote, the search begins from the point of the footnote reference mark.

Subject	{SUBJECT} {SUBJECT "*NewSubject*"}

SUBJECT inserts the contents of the Subject section in the Summary Info dialog box. You can change the Subject section in Summary Info by including *NewSubject*, enclosed in quotes.

Symbol	{SYMBOL *Character*} {SYMBOL \f *FontName Character*} {SYMBOL \s *FontSize Character*} {SYMBOL \f *FontName* \s *FontSize Character*}

SYMBOL inserts a single character specified by its numerical code; you can optionally specify the character's font and size.

Character is a number identifying the character. Refer to the character set tables at the back of this book to locate the numerical code for a particular character. If you don't specify a font SYMBOL inserts a character in the current font and size. Precede hexadecimal numbers with 0x (zero, x).

Table of Contents Entry	{TC "*Text*"} {TC "*Text*" \l *Level*} {TC "*Text*" \f *TableIdentifier*} {TC "*Text*" \l *Level* \f *TableIdentifier*}

TC is used to insert a table of contents entry. When Word compiles a table of contents (see the TOC [Table of Contents] field discussed later), it collects *Text* from each entry and the number of the page on which it occurs. TC fields are automatically formatted as hidden text.

You can create multiple tables (such as tables of figures or tables) using unique *TableIdentifier* characters (such as F for figures, T for tables, and so on). Word will compile each such table separately, collecting TC entries with the same *TableIdentifier*.

Word can also generate a table of contents from the "heading *n*" paragraph styles, but TC fields are the only way to generate other kinds of tables.

Switches

\f *character*   Specifies the *TableIdentifier*; table identifiers must be single characters.

\l *n*   Specifies the level of the entry; that is, the entry in the compiled table is formatted with the "toc *n*" style. The number must be from 1 to 9, inclusive.

For more information on tables of contents, see the topic "Tables of Contents and Other Lists." See also the information about the TOC (Table of Contents) field later in this topic.

Template	{TEMPLATE}

TEMPLATE inserts the name of the document template.

For reasons known only to Microsoft, TEMPLATE inserts nothing (an empty string) when the template is NORMAL.DOT. You can work around this feature by enclosing TEMPLATE in an IF field, like this:

{IF {TEMPLATE}="" "NORMAL.DOT" {TEMPLATE}}

Time	{TIME} {TIME *TimeFormatPicture*}

TIME inserts the time that the field was last updated. The time is formatted according to the Windows default setting, unless you include *TimeFormatPicture* (see "Time Pictures" at the beginning of this topic).

Title	{TITLE} {TITLE "*NewTitle*"}

TITLE inserts the contents of the Title section of the Summary Info dialog box. If you include *NewTitle*, the Title section of Summary Info is changed to *NewTitle*.

Table of Contents	{TOC} {TOC *Switches*} {TOC \b *Bookmark*} {TOC \f *Table*} {TOC *Switches* \b *Bookmark* \f *Table*}

TOC inserts a table of contents (or other list) compiled by Word.

A plain TOC field—one with no switches—compiles an outline-style table of contents; the entries are collected from the "heading *n*" paragraphs and formatted in the corresponding "toc *n*" paragraph style (for example, the text of each heading 2 paragraph is collected and formatted, in the table, with the toc 2 style).

Switches

\b *bookmark*	Compiles a partial table only from entries covered by *bookmark*.
\f	Compiles a table from TC fields that don't have a table identifier or use the default "c" identifier.
\f *table*	Compiles a table from TC fields that specify table identifier *table*.
\o *first level-last level*	Compiles a table of contents from "heading *n*" paragraphs, including only those headings whose level is within the range *first level-last level*. (For example, if you specify \o2-3, Word collects entries only from heading 2 and heading 3 paragraphs.) To specify a single level, use the same number for *first level* and *last level*.
\s *chapter*	Preface the page numbers in the table with the sequence number identified by *chapter*. This is commonly used when a document is organized by chapter page numbers (for example, "2-12" is page 12 in chapter 2). See the "SEQ" field for more information.

(continued)

TOC *(continued)*

\d *separator*	Use *separator* to separate the page numbers in a chapter-style table (see the previous entry for the \s switch). *Separator* can be from one to three characters long. The default separator is a hyphen.

See the TC field for information about inserting table of contents entries. See also the topic "Tables of Contents and Other Lists."

User Address	{USERADDRESS}

USERADDRESS inserts the contents of the Mailing Address section of the User Info category of the Options dialog box.

User Initials	{USERINITIALS}

USERINITIALS inserts the user's initials, taken from the User Info category of the Options dialog box.

User Name	{USERNAME}

USERNAME inserts the name of the user, taken from the User Info category of the Options dialog box.

FINDING AND REPLACING

Word's search and replace facilities have been greatly expanded and reorganized in Word for Windows 2.0, from changing the command name from "Search" to "Find," to completely redesigned dialog boxes with new secondary dialogs, to extensive changes to any macros you wrote for the earlier version that use the old EditSearch and EditReplace commands. If you're upgrading from an earlier version, you'll have a lot of adjusting to do. The new design actually works better, but it's much more complex than before.

What makes the subject so gnarly is that you can search for text and formatting in any combination, and replace the found text or formatting with yet another combination of text and formatting—there are a *lot* of permutations. Let's start with searching, then build on that with replacing.

Finding *Anything*

You can use Edit→Find to search for any combination of text, character formatting, paragraph formatting, or paragraph style name. Here's a table listing all the permutations.

Text	Formatting			Finds...
	Char	Para	Style	
✔				Specified text; modified by Match Case and Match Whole Word Only options.
	✔			Any text with the specified character formatting.
		✔		Entire paragraphs formatted as specified.
			✔	Entire paragraphs formatted with the specified style.
✔	✔			Text matching the specification *and* having the specified character formatting.
✔		✔		Text matching the specification *and* located in paragraphs formatted as specified.
✔			✔	Text matching the specification *and* located in paragraphs formatted with the specified style name.
✔	✔	✔		Text matching the specification *and* with the specified character formatting *and* located in paragraphs formatted as specified.
✔	✔		✔	Text matching the specification *and* having the specified character formatting *and* located in paragraphs formatted with the specified style name.
✔		✔	✔	Text matching the specification *and* located within paragraphs formatted with the specified style name *and* having additional paragraph formatting as specified.
✔	✔	✔	✔	Text matching the specification *and* having the specified character formatting *and* located in paragraphs formatted with the specified style name *and* having additional paragraph formatting as specified.
	✔	✔		Any text with the specified character formatting *and* located in paragraphs formatted as specified.
	✔		✔	Any text with the specified character formatting *and* located in paragraphs formatted with the specified style.
	✔	✔	✔	Any text with the specified character formatting *and* located in paragraphs formatted with the specified style name *and* having additional paragraph formatting as specified.
		✔	✔	Entire paragraphs formatted with the specified style name *and* having the specified paragraph formatting (useful for finding paragraphs whose style specifications have been overridden with manual formatting).

All these search options are controlled by one simple Find dialog box, which you display with the Edit→Find command.

Finding Text—the Basics

Type the text you want to find into the Find What box. You can paste text from the Clipboard into the Find What box; however, Word may have trouble with non-printing characters contained in what you paste. Refer to the section "Finding and Replacing Special Characters" later in this topic for codes to use to specify non-printing and other special characters.

To find text capitalized exactly as you type it, check Match Case.

To find text that occurs only in the form of a whole word, check Match Whole Word Only; this makes sure that if you're searching for the word "the," for example, you'll find only that word and not also "there," "thesaurus," "wither," and every other word that has those three letters within it.

To search forward from the insertion point, select Down in the Direction box. If the cursor isn't at the very beginning of the document when you start searching, when Word reaches the end of the document it will ask you if you'd like it to start over at the beginning of the document. Similarly, **to search backward,** select Up as the search direction.

The Word for Windows 2.0 Find system is optimized for repetitive searches; unlike with earlier versions, the Find dialog box stays on the screen after a search (whether or not the search is successful). You can keep clicking Find Next to continue searching. When you're done searching, click Cancel.

Another quirk of the Find system is that all your search specifications are retained after you put away the dialog box, so that the next time you use Edit→Find you'll see your earlier search specifications. Pay special attention to the Format line below Find What (explained next)—it's easy to overlook previous formatting specifications and end up baffled when Word can't find text you know perfectly well exists.

Finding Formatting

Three buttons at the bottom of the Find dialog box add formatting specifications to the search criteria (if there's nothing in the Find What box, Word searches only for the specified formatting). As you add format specifications, Word adds a description below the Find What box. In the example to the right,
Word will search for
text that is form-

Fi_n_d What:	
Format:	Style: Syntax, Font: StoneInformal, Bold, Flush Right

atted bold *and* in the StoneInformal font *and is located* inside paragraphs formatted with the Syntax style *and* aligned flush right. Formatting search specifications are additive; anything found must satisfy *all* the search criteria.

To remove *all* existing formatting specifications, click ⬚Clear⬚. If you want to remove only some format specifications but leave others, you must remove the unwanted specification individually by resetting its options to "don't care" as explained next.

To specify the character formatting to find, click the ⬚Character...⬚ button. Word will display the Find Character dialog box, which has an uncanny resemblance to the Format Character dialog box. Notice that all the options in this dialog box are grayed-out initially; each grayed-out option is something that's *ignored* in the character format find specification. If an option is checked it means that Word will search for text formatted with that option on. (For example, if the Bold option is checked Word will find only bold text.) If an option is unchecked (empty) Word searches for text with that option off. (For example, if Bold is not checked, Word excludes bold text from the search.) If you want to find text regardless of whether it's formatted with a particular option, click the option's checkbox until it turns gray. Select just the format options you want to find, then click ⬚OK⬚.

To specify paragraph formatting to find, click the ⬚Paragraph...⬚ button. Not surprisingly, the Find Paragraph dialog box also bears a striking resemblance to its formatting counterpart. It also will have grayed-out options; select just the paragraph formatting you want to find and click OK.

To find paragraphs formatted with a particular style, click the Styles... button; Word displays a small dialog box with a list of style names to choose from. The first item in the list is *(No Style)*; select it to clear the style name from the formatting specification. Click OK after you've selected a style name.

Replacing *Anything* with *Anything*

To replace something with the Edit→Replace command, you must first find it; luckily the Replace dialog box incorporates all the features of the Find dialog box to make finding and replacing a one-step operation. (However, there's no selection for search direction; all searches proceed forward from the insertion point.)

There is still only one set of buttons for specifying formatting options. In the Replace dialog box they specify search formatting if the cursor is in the Find What box, and replacement formatting if the cursor is in the Replace With box.

Like the Find dialog box, the Replace dialog box is optimized for repetitive find and replace operations. The Find Next button initiates the search phase. If the search is successful the Replace button is active; click it to replace whatever's found with whatever you've specified as its replacement, and find the next occurrence of the object of the search. Click Replace All if you're confident that all your find and replace criteria are correct and you want Word to perform the find and replace operation on the entire document. (You can always use Edit→Undo Replace or Ctrl+Z to reverse the replacement operation.) When you're all done click Cancel to put away the Replace box.

Another table like the one under "Finding *Anything*" earlier would help make sense of all the ways you can find and replace things, but the four possible find types plus the four possible replace types would result in a table with 256 entries. Here's a general principle instead: *All of the replace options that you specify are applied to whatever's found as a result of the find specification.* This can lead to some amazing (as well as unintended) find and replace operations, so it's a good idea to test your specifications by using only Find Next and Replace until you're sure they're safe, before taking the plunge with Replace All.

After all that buildup the instructions are quite simple:

1. Set up the find specification as described under "Finding *Anything*": Type text (if any) to find in Find What, and (with the cursor still in Find What) click the formatting buttons to set up any format specifications.

2. Move the cursor to the Replace With box, and enter text (if any) to replace what's found; click the formatting buttons to set up formatting to be applied to what's found. As you add replacement formatting, Word adds a description below the Replace With box.

3. Use Find Next, Replace, and Replace All to perform the search and replace.

Finding and Replacing Special Characters

There are many objects or characters in a Word document that you can't type into a Windows dialog box. For these objects you must use special codes to tell Word what to find or replace.

The table below lists these special codes. Note that not all of them are available for both searching and replacing. The symbol ^ in many codes is the caret character, produced on most keyboards with [Shift] +[6]. Letters must be lowercase.

Code	Find	Replace	Description
?	✓		Finds any single character in the same position as the ? in the search text. For example, *c?t* finds both "cat" and "cot." ? used in a replace specification inserts a literal question mark.
^t	✓	✓	Find a tab character, or replace with a tab character.

(continued)

Code	Find	Replace	Description
^?	✓		Find a question mark. (The caret is required to distinguish searching for a real question mark from its use as a placeholder for "find any character.") Not necessary in a replace, since the question mark character is treated as a printable character.
^^	✓	✓	Find or replace the caret. Necessary because the caret otherwise introduces a special character.
^p	✓	✓	Find a paragraph marker; or replace with a paragraph marker. When replacing, the new paragraph marker takes on the style and formatting of the paragraph in which it's inserted, unless you've specified replacement paragraph formatting or a style name.
^n	✓	✓	Find a line break; or replace with a line break. This is the break produced with [Shift] + [↵].
^d	✓	✓	Find a page or section break; or replace with a page break.
^s	✓	✓	Find a nonbreaking space; or replace a nonbreaking space.
^w	✓		Find white space: any combination of spaces or tabs; and empty paragraphs (isolated paragraph markers).
^0nnn	✓	✓	Find any character code; or replace with that character. nnn is the three-digit code.
^1	✓		Find a graphic. (This is the numeral "1," not a lowercase "L".)
^2	✓		Find a footnote reference mark.
^5	✓		Find an annotation mark.
^14	✓	✓	Find a column break; or replace with a column break. (14 is the ANSI character code used in the document to identify a column break.) This is the break inserted with [Ctrl] + [Shift] + [↵].
^19	✓		Find a field code, of any type; View→Field Codes must be turned on. If used in a replace specification, merely inserts ANSI code 19.
^_	✓	✓	Find an optional hyphen; or replace with an optional hyphen (these are displayed with the ¬ symbol). Normally, Word ignores the presence of optional hyphens in found text, on the theory that you don't care (and you usually don't). When you include an optional hyphen in a search specification, however, any found text *must* have an optional hyphen at the specified location.

(continued)

Code	Find	Replace	Description
^~	✔	✔	Find a nonbreaking hyphen; or replace a nonbreaking hyphen.
^c		✔	Pastes the Clipboard as the replacement item. Especially useful to insert graphics or with blocks of text too large for a dialog box (255 characters).
^m		✔	Uses the contents of the Find What box in the replacement text. Usually part of a larger replacement line (otherwise, it doesn't change anything), when you want to add something to existing text. For example, instead of typing *Baggins* in the Find What box and *Bilbo Baggins* in the Replace With box, type *Bilbo ^m* in Replace With.

Find and Replace with Macros

This section is particularly important if you've upgraded to Word for Windows 2.0 from an earlier version and have macros that use search and replace commands; and it's useful for anyone writing new macros that use find and replace commands.

First, all the earlier macro commands in the EditSearch family (EditSearch, EditSearchChar, EditSearchPara, and EditSearchFound()) have been renamed to begin with EditFind, as a result of changing the name of the command from "search" to "find."

Second, the .Style parameter in EditSearchPara (now EditFindPara) and EditReplacePara has been removed. Instead there are new commands called EditFindStyle and EditReplaceStyle to set up formatting options prior to performing the operation. When Word tries to convert your old macros to the 2.0 format, it may guess wrong about your intentions in using this parameter, and your macros may now fail to operate correctly. You'll have to examine each such macro and possibly rewrite it.

Two new commands, EditFindClearFormatting and EditReplaceClearFormatting eliminate the need for the awkward workarounds that used to be necessary to remove format specifications from the old Search and Replace dialog boxes. Unfortunately, Word can't tell that that's what you were doing, and will probably make mistakes converting your old macros. Again, review the converted macros.

Here are some general suggestions for any macro that uses find or replace commands:

- Because format specifications persist after you've used a find or replace command, always use EditFindClearFormatting and EditReplaceClearFormatting *before* setting up a new find or replace specification. Don't assume that the .Format=0 parameter will always cause Word to ignore an old format specification.

- Although most of the parameters to the find and replace commands are technically optional, the way that parameters hang around to surprise you means that you should specify *every* parameter for each command exactly as you want it to work. This protects you from such annoyances as having your search proceed in the wrong direction because a previous command changed the .Direction parameter, or having a simple text search fail because a format specification is still in effect.

Keep in mind that your macro will inherit whatever specifications a user entered previously in the Find or Replace dialog boxes, as well as any specifications set up by a macro that ran previously. Always remember that your macros are part of the larger Word environment.

FOOTNOTES

Footnotes are supplemental comments that you add to a document, and that Word prints at the bottom of the page. Printed footnotes are visually separated from the body of the document by a *footnote separator,* usually a thin horizontal line. A *footnote mark* in the body of your document keys to the footnote.* Word has a predefined paragraph style called *footnote text* that it uses by default to format footnotes. In normal and outline views, you work with footnote text in a separate part of the document window called the *footnote pane.* In Page Layout view you work with them directly.

---

* When you have just one footnote on a page, you usually use the asterisk (*) in text to signify a footnote; if you have multiple footnotes on a page you generally use numbers. Oh, yes...this is a footnote.

Inserting Footnotes

Word's default footnote style uses numbered footnotes, located at the bottom of the page. To insert a default footnote:

1. Position the insertion point in the document text where you want the footnote mark to be inserted. If you have a block of text selected, Word inserts the footnote mark at the beginning of the selection.

2. Use the Insert→Footnote command to display the Footnote dialog box.

3. Click OK to insert the footnote in the default style; footnote options will be covered below.

    If you're in normal view, and the footnote pane is not already open, Word splits the current document window to add the footnote pane at the bottom.

    In page layout view, Word moves the insertion point into the footnote text.

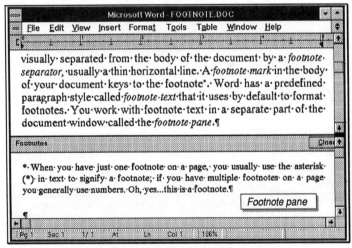

4. Type the text of the footnote in the footnote pane.

5. When you're done, you can click Close to put away the footnote pane; or you can leave the footnote pane displayed if you intend to insert other footnotes.

Viewing and Editing Footnotes

To view the footnote associated with a footnote mark, double-click the footnote mark. In normal and outline views, Word opens the footnote pane; in page layout view, Word positions the insertion point in the associated footnote. Alternatively, select the mark and use the View→Footnotes command to display the footnote pane.

To view a footnote in page layout view, you can scroll to the bottom of the page and work with the footnote text. You can also select the footnote mark and use View→Footnotes to have Word move the insertion point into the footnote.

Another way to display the footnote pane in normal view is to hold down [Shift] while you drag the split box down from its location at the top of the vertical scroll bar.

Once the footnote is visible, you edit it like any other Word text. You can add or delete text, reformat the text or the paragraph, and so on. Footnotes can consist of multiple paragraphs. Word uses the *footnote text* style by default, but you can apply other styles.

To copy or delete a footnote, select its footnote mark in the document and copy or delete the *mark*. Deleting the *text* of a footnote doesn't delete the footnote; it just leaves an empty footnote associated with the footnote mark.

As you add or delete numbered footnotes, Word automatically renumbers them.

Finding Footnotes

You can use the Edit→Go To command (or its shortcut [F5]) to find and move to footnotes. Use one of the following codes in the Go To box:

Type...	To move to...
fn	Footnote number n (works only with numbered footnotes)
f	The next footnote
f-	The previous footnote
f+n	The nth footnote after the current footnote
f-n	The nth footnote before the current footnote

You can also search for footnotes with the Edit→Find command. Word encodes footnote marks with the ANSI code 2; in the Find dialog box, enter ^2 (caret, two) to search for this code.

Customizing and Formatting Footnotes

The default footnote style is set up like this:

- Numbered footnote marks
- Footnote numbering starts at 1, and continues throughout a document.
- A short single line is used as the footnote separator; a long single line (margin-to-margin) denotes the continuation of a long footnote.

Footnote formatting options are controlled through the Footnote dialog box, and an associated Footnote Options dialog box.

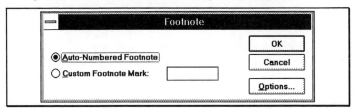

To use a custom footnote mark (not numbered), select the Custom Footnote Mark option in the Footnote dialog box, and enter up to 10 characters in the text box.

All other footnote options are controlled by the Footnote Options dialog box. Display it by clicking Options... in the Footnote dialog box. You can set options and then close this dialog box without actually inserting a footnote.

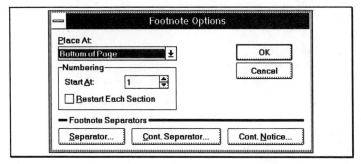

Footnote Positioning

To control the position of footnotes, select an option from the Place At drop-down list:

Bottom of Page	Word prints the footnotes associated with each page at the bottom of the page. Footnotes are based on the bottom margin, and grow upward, displacing text on the page (default).
Beneath Text	Like Bottom of Page, except that Word begins footnotes immediately after the end of text. Has an effect only if text doesn't fill up the current page; otherwise, Word puts footnotes at the bottom margin.
End of Section	Word collects all footnotes in a section and prints them at the end of the section.
End of Document	Word collects all footnotes in a section and prints them at the end of the document.

In a multicolumn layout, Word positions footnotes from each column below that column (in other words, footnotes are arranged in the same multicolumn format).

Footnote Numbering

By default, footnotes start at 1. You can specify a different starting number by entering the number in the Start At box.

By default, footnote numbering continues sequentially throughout a document. If you'd like footnote numbering to start over (at the number in the Start At box), check Restart Each Section. Although this option uses the word "Section," its action is modified by the level selected in the Place At drop-down list:

Bottom of Page, Beneath Text, and *End of Section*	Footnote numbering is restarted at the beginning of each section.
End of Document	Footnote numbering is restarted at the beginning of the document (equivalent to leaving Restart Each Section unchecked).

When you're using more than one file to create a document, and you want their footnote numbering to be sequential across the entire document, you'll have to manually set the starting footnote number in each document. However, if you're using INCLUDE fields to create a long document, Word will maintain footnote numbering across all the files.

Footnote Separators

Word recognizes three ways of setting off footnotes from text, all of which may appear in your document:

- The *footnote separator* separates the start of footnotes from the body of text on the page. By default, it's a short, thin line.

- The *continuation notice* is printed at the end of the footnotes on a page if Word has to continue the footnotes on the next page. By default, it's blank.

- The *continuation separator* is printed above footnotes continued from the previous page. By default, it's a long, thin line.

You can customize each type of separator from the Footnote Options dialog box by clicking the Separator..., Cont. Separator..., or Cont. Notice... buttons. When you do so, Word changes (or displays) special versions of the footnote panes that let you enter your own separator.

The Footnote Reference Field

When you want to refer to the number of a footnote (for example, "see note 3"), use Word's FTNREF footnote reference field. The FTNREF field includes the name of a bookmark that identifies the footnote marker you want to refer to. To use the FTNREF field:

1. Select the footnote marker you want to refer to.

2. Use Insert→Bookmark to insert a bookmark around the footnote marker.

3. Position the insertion point where you want the reference to appear, and press Ctrl+F9 to insert empty field characters.

4. Type **FTNREF**, a space, and the name you gave the footnote marker.

When you update a FTNREF field Word updates the number it produces. You can include FTNREF fields in footnotes, to refer to other footnotes.

See also: Annotations; Cross-References; Fields

FRAMES

Frames are a new feature of Word 2.0 that simplifies positioning objects on the page. Visually—in page layout view—a frame is a rectangle containing text or graphics. You can resize a frame with the mouse, and move it to a fixed position on the page or specify that the frame should be positioned relative to the page, margins, or associated text. Frames can have borders, and you can store frame specifications as part of a paragraph style. (The frame data is stored in the paragraph mark with all the other attributes of a paragraph.)

A Word document without frames is a single "stream" of text and graphics that begins at the upper-left corner of the first page, and flows down through the document to its end. Objects placed in a frame are removed from this flow and become an independent (or semi-independent) part of the document. Historically, word processors have been "stream-oriented," while desktop publishing programs have been frame-oriented; Word's frames transform it into a powerful hybrid with the best features of both.

Word 1.0/1.1 users: Word's old positioning features (the old Format →Position command) have been incorporated into Word 2.0's new concept of frames. Frames provide a visual representation of positioning, and frames have a few new positioning options.

Creating and Removing Frames

Word creates new frames with a single-line border initially. You can change that later with the Format→Border command. There are three ways to insert a frame into a document:

- **To insert an empty frame,** make sure that the cursor is an insertion point (no objects selected), and use the Insert→Frame command. If you're not currently in page layout view, Word asks you if you'd like to switch to it; because you draw an empty frame on the page, you must be in page layout view to see where the frame will be positioned.

  The cursor changes to a small cross (+). Move the cursor to where you want one corner of the frame to be, hold down the mouse button, and drag. Word displays an outline of the frame between the first corner and the current cursor position.

Release the mouse button when the frame is approximately the size you want. Don't worry about getting the frame sized and positioned correctly at this stage; it's easier to take care of that later when you move and resize the frame.

- **To frame existing text or graphics,** select the material you want included in the frame, and use Insert→Frame.

  If you've selected an entire paragraph (including the paragraph marker) Word creates the frame at the location of the paragraph, and sizes it around the existing material (the frame width and height are set to Auto so that the frame size changes if margins change). The frame positioning settings allow it to "float" as the surrounding material moves, anchored to its position relative to the surrounding material. In other words, the default frame characteristics are such that the frame doesn't modify the position or size of the enclosed material.

  If you've selected less than an entire paragraph, Word extracts the material, positions the frame before the paragraph that contained the selected material, and inserts the extracted material inside the frame as a new paragraph (with the same style as the original paragraph). The frame is formatted as above.

  If your selection spans more than one paragraph, Word combines these two techniques, and selects in their entirety all paragraphs touched by the selection; the selected material is moved to a frame containing two or more paragraphs, all enclosed by a single frame.

- **To use frame formatting stored with a paragraph style,** simply apply that style to a paragraph. Word automatically adds the frame to the material.

Once you've created a frame, you can treat it like a "sub-document," a semi-independent small document embedded inside its larger "parent" document. Frames exhibit the following behavior:

- You can insert new material, or edit or delete existing material.

- Pressing ⏎ when the cursor is inside a frame creates a new paragraph *inside the frame*.

- When you delete the last paragraph marker inside a frame you also delete the frame.

- If you apply a paragraph style to material inside a frame, any frame formatting in the style overrides the current frame formatting. If the style has no frame formatting, then the frame is removed.

  In a frame containing multiple paragraphs, applying a style with different frame formatting to one of the paragraphs may break the frame into two or more new frames. For example, in a frame that has three paragraphs, applying a new style with a different frame format to the middle paragraph creates three frames: first, a frame with the original formatting; a second frame with the new formatting; and a third frame with the original formatting. If you're in page layout view, you may see the middle paragraph's frame move to a completely different location, depending on its frame formatting.

- If you format several *consecutive* paragraphs with styles that contain identical frame formatting (even if the style names are different), Word collects the paragraphs into a single frame.

  This behavior can be very useful when you want a family of paragraph styles to be contained in a single frame. Set up the basic formatting in a parent style, and then create variations ("children") based on the parent. Since each child inherits its frame formatting from the parent style, all consecutive members of the same paragraph family will automatically be contained in a single frame (as long as the changes to the child paragraphs don't affect the frame; paragraph indents are one paragraph setting that will affect frames).

To remove a frame from around material, make sure the cursor is inside the paragraph whose frame you want to remove. Select the Format→Frame command and click the ⬚Remove Frame⬚ button in the Frame dialog box. Word removes the frame formatting, but doesn't change anything else.

If you select a frame in page layout view and press ⬚Del⬚, you remove the frame *and its contents*. Word treats the frame as a unit when you cut or copy it to the Clipboard, and will paste the frame and its contents.

Frame Formatting Basics

You control the size, position, and border of frames, independent of the frame contents. Frame formatting is stored in paragraph markers, along with other paragraph formatting, and frame formatting can be defined as part of a paragraph style.

When Word is in normal view it flags paragraphs with frame formatting with a solid square symbol in the style area at the left of the screen; there is no other visual indication of a frame in normal view, although if you've applied border formatting to the frame, *that* will be visible.

In page layout view, the appearance of frames depends on several factors:

- If a frame has a border, you'll see the border.

- If a frame has no border, but the Text Boundaries option in the View category of Tools→Options is turned on, Word shows the outline of the frame the same way it shows other text boundaries.

- If a frame has no border and Text Boundaries display is turned off, the frame itself is invisible; its contents display normally.

To work with a frame, you must first select it:

- **To select a frame in normal view,** position the cursor in a paragraph that you know is in the frame (your only clue is the solid square next to the paragraph in the style area). You can use Format→Frame to enter frame specifications, but you can't use the mouse to visually move or resize a frame.

- **To select a frame in page layout view,** move the cursor over the frame until the cursor changes to the frame tool (✥). You now have several options:

  · You can hold down the mouse button and drag the frame to a new position.

  · You can click once to select the frame. Word adds selection handles to the frame (eight solid squares at each corner and in the middle of each side). With the frame selected, you can use Format→Frame or Format→Border on it, or you can drag it to a new position. Also, as described under "Sizing Frames" below, you can use the selection handles to resize the frame.

· While the cursor is over the frame, it becomes an I-beam cursor (the text insertion point cursor). If you click a second time over the frame, Word assumes you want to edit the material in the frame, and puts the insertion point at a location approximately where you clicked. You can then proceed with ordinary editing tasks. To select the frame again, first move the insertion point outside the frame and then select it again as described above. Selecting Format→ Frame while the insertion point is inside a frame selects the frame, and cancels any selection inside the frame.

Once you've selected a frame you can:

- **Format the frame's borders** with the Format→Border command. Note that if you've selected material inside a frame, border formatting applies to the current paragraph rather than the frame. See the topic "Borders and Shading" for more information.

- **Use the mouse to move or resize the frame**; this visual formatting gives you a degree of precision consistent with your display's resolution, and is useful for tasks that don't require a high degree of precision.

- **Use the** Format→Frame **command** for precise control of frame formatting.

The Format→Frame command displays the Frame dialog box:

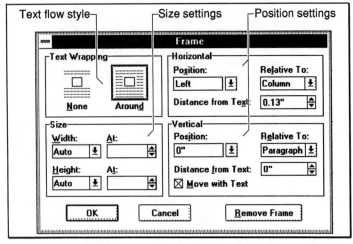

Sizing Frames

You can use the mouse to size a frame while you're in page layout view. Just select the frame, then drag one of the eight handles to resize the frame. Dragging to size a frame is useful for visually aligning a frame in relation to other objects on the page, and when you need no more precision than your display offers (approximately 1/72 of an inch on a typical VGA display).

For more control, use the size controls in the Frame dialog box:

- In the Width drop-down list, select Auto to let the frame adjust itself to the current page margins. Select Exactly if you want to specify a fixed width, and enter the width in the At text box.

- In the Height drop-down list, select Auto to the let the frame adjust its height to accommodate the tallest object it contains (much the way Auto line spacing works in paragraph formatting). Select At Least and enter a value in the At box to establish the minimum height of the frame. Select Exactly and supply a value to specify the exact height of the frame.

New frames start with their height and width both set to Auto. Using the mouse to resize a frame changes the settings to Exactly, and the At boxes show the size of the frame after dragging.

Flowing Text Around Frames

The Text Wrapping group on the Frame dialog box controls whether text flows around the frame. The Around setting enables text wrapping; it means that Word puts text to the left or right (or both) of a frame if there is sufficient room (if the frame doesn't extend the full width of the margins). The Text Wrapping group sample above shows a frame with the Around text-wrapping style. Selecting None means that Word leaves empty space to the left or right of a frame if the frame doesn't extend the full width of the margins. The default is Around for new frames.

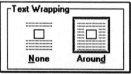

When text wrapping is enabled, the Distance from Text setting in the Horizontal control group in the Frame dialog box controls the distance between the frame and adjacent text.

Positioning Frames

Word offers an almost baffling array of frame positioning options. It helps to categorize frames according to how they're positioned:

- **Fixed frames** have an *absolute* position relative to the page, margins, or column boundaries. They remain at the same location on the current page regardless of how the material around them changes. This relationship holds for the current page; if enough material is added or deleted ahead of the frame, it will move to the same position on another page.

- **Floating frames** move vertically on the page as material on the page changes (frames can't float horizontally). The position of a floating frame is specified relative to an *anchor point*, which is the beginning of the next paragraph after the frame. As the anchor paragraph moves, the floating frame moves in a fixed relationship. (Some desktop publishing programs use the term "anchored frame" to describe this kind of frame; we use the term "floating" because "fixed" and "anchored" are too easy to confuse.)

Horizontal Positioning

A frame's horizontal positioning is controlled by the Horizontal control group in the Frame dialog box.

The Relative To drop-down list establishes the frame's horizontal reference; the Position box controls horizontal position relative to that reference point. The Relative To list has these options:

Page   Means that the setting in the Position box is relative to the left edge of the paper, and is independent of margin or column settings.

Margin   Means that the Position box setting is relative to the current left margin. As the margins change, the frame will maintain the same relative position.

Column   Means that the setting in the Position box is relative to the left edge of the column in which the frame resides. In a single-column layout, this is the same as the left margin.

The Position box sets the horizontal position relative to the reference established by the Relative To box. You have these choices:

Left   Means that the frame will be positioned at the left edge of the page or column, or at the left margin.

Right   Means that the frame will be positioned at the right edge of the page or column, or the right margin.

Center   Positions the frame in the horizontal center of the page or column, or centered between the margins.

Inside   Changes the horizontal position of the frame depending on whether it appears on an odd or even page (to the left on an odd page, to the right on an even page). This is analogous to the way that the gutter in page margins establishes an "inside" for each page for binding.

Outside   Is the opposite of Inside; the frame appears to the right on an odd page, to the left on an even page.

(number)   You can specify an absolute distance from the reference point to the frame.

You can add additional horizontal space between the frame and surrounding text (if you've enabled text wrapping) with the Distance from Text box.

Vertical Positioning

The Vertical control group in the Frame dialog box controls a frame's vertical position. The function of these controls changes slightly depending on whether you're formatting a fixed or floating frame.

To format a fixed frame, select either Page or Margin in the Relative To drop-down list to establish the reference point. In the Position drop-down list select Top, Bottom, or Center to position the frame relative to the reference point. You can also enter an absolute distance in the Position box.

To format a floating frame, select Paragraph in the Relative To drop-down list; this establishes the reference point as the beginning of the paragraph following the frame. Then enter an absolute distance in the Position box (if you select Top, Bottom, or Center, Word changes the Relative To box to Margin; those settings are incompatible with a floating frame). Position values specify the distance from the top of the frame to the top of the anchor paragraph. Positive values indicate the distance the frame lies below the anchor paragraph, negative values the distance above.

The Move with Text checkbox actually serves no purpose, since it's automatically checked when you select Paragraph in the Relative To list, and unchecked when you select Page or Margin. It's more of a visual reminder of which type of frame you're creating.

The Distance from Text box controls the amount of additional vertical space (beyond the space before and space after adjacent paragraphs) between the frame and the paragraphs before and after it.

In the initial release of Word 2.0*, Word seems to become confused if you have consecutive floating frames. That's probably because a floating frame uses the next paragraph as an anchor point, and if that paragraph is itself a floating frame, Word isn't quite sure what to use as a reference. If this happens, you'll see such strange things as a block of white space materializing in the middle of a preceding paragraph, splitting the paragraph vertically. A partial solution is to put extra paragraph markers ahead of the first floating frame to distance it from the preceding text. You might also play with the vertical Distance from Text setting to find a compromise point where the white space disappears.

> **See also:** Borders and Shading, Draw (Microsoft Draw), Embedding and Linking, Graphics, Pictures

GLOSSARIES

A *glossary* is a part of a Word template used to store *glossary entries*. Glossary entries can be anything that appears in a Word document—text, pictures, charts, WordArt, embedded objects, and so on—and so the ability to store these objects in a central location lets you build libraries of commonly-used parts of documents. You

---

* That slightly awkward phrasing is necessary because Microsoft is notorious for revising its software without changing the version number.

might, for example, store your company logo and address in a glossary, so that you can use them in many documents.

Glossary entries stored in the global template, NORMAL.DOT, are available when you're working in any document. Entries stored in another template are available only while you're working in a document based on that template. Don't put entries in NORMAL.DOT's glossary unless you'll really need them in all documents; it's all too easy to let NORMAL.DOT grow to an unmanageable size.

Each glossary entry is identified by a *glossary name* that you assign to it when you store the entry in a glossary. Glossary names can be up to 31 characters long and contain spaces. You use the glossary name when you want to insert the entry in a document. You can also redefine a glossary entry by storing new material under an existing glossary name; the new material replaces the old.

You can store up to 150 entries in a template glossary.

Word has a special glossary entry called the "Spike" that you can use to collect material from several sources. Unlike other glossary entries, storing new material in the Spike doesn't delete old material. The Spike is covered in more detail later in this topic.

Creating or Deleting a Glossary Entry

Where glossary entries are stored is controlled by options in the Template dialog box, displayed with the File→Template command. These options are:

- Global (Available to All Documents)—Entries are stored in NORMAL.DOT.

- With Document Template—Entries are stored in the template on which the current document is based.

- Prompt for Each New—Word displays a dialog box after you define a glossary entry, asking you where to store the entry.

To **define** a glossary entry:

1. Select the material in a document to become the entry. If you want the entry to be stored in a specific template, the document must be based on that template.

2. Select the command Edit→Glossary to display the Glossary dialog box.

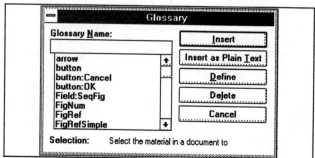

The bottom of the dialog box shows part of your selection (if it's displayable as text).

3. Enter the glossary entry's name in the Glossary Name box. Glossary entries can be up to 31 characters long, including spaces. Consider using colons (:), underscores (_), or mixed capitalization like the examples above, to make glossary names more readable.

   If the name you enter already exists in the glossary, Word brings it to the top of the list. You will then have the additional option of redefining the existing entry, if you have material selected in the document.

4. Click Define to create (or redefine, as noted above) the glossary entry.

   If you used the File→Template command to configure Word to ask you where to store new glossary entries, Word will now display a dialog box asking you whether it should store the entry in the global template or the current template. Pick the appropriate destination and click OK.

To **delete** a glossary entry:

1. Select the command Edit→Glossary to display the Glossary dialog box.

2. Select the name of the entry to delete from the list in the dialog box.

3. Click Delete to delete the entry.

Word keeps the dialog box displayed to allow you to delete multiple entries, or to do other glossary tasks.

4. Click $\boxed{\text{Close}}$ to put away the dialog box.

Note: It's possible to assign the same name to glossary entries stored in different templates, including NORMAL.DOT. When you have a document open that's based on another template besides NORMAL.DOT, and both that template and NORMAL.DOT have entries with the same name, the first entry you will delete will be the one in the document template. After it's removed, the name will still be in the list, this time representing the entry in NORMAL.DOT. Deleting the entry a second time deletes it from NORMAL.DOT. If you want to delete a duplicate-name entry from NORMAL.DOT without deleting the corresponding entry in a document template, make sure you're either in a document based on NORMAL.DOT or some other template.

To rename a glossary entry, first insert the contents of the entry under its current name into a document, and select the just-inserted material. Then delete the old glossary name, and define a new glossary entry with the new name.

Inserting a Glossary Entry

There are three ways to insert a glossary entry: from the Glossary dialog box, or by typing the name of the entry and "expanding" it into the entry it represents. The third method, using fields, is described later.

To insert a glossary entry using the Glossary dialog box, use the Edit→Glossary command to display the dialog box. Select the name of the entry from the list, then click $\boxed{\text{Insert}}$. Word normally preserves character formatting in glossary entries; if you'd like to insert just text, with formatting stripped away, click $\boxed{\text{Insert As Plain Text}}$.

To insert a glossary entry by typing its name, type the name, then press $\boxed{\text{F3}}$. Word interprets the text before the cursor, back to the first preceding space or punctuation, as a glossary name and tries to find it in the glossaries (first the document template; then, if it doesn't find it there, in NORMAL.DOT's glossary).

Referencing a Glossary Entry with a Field

You can also use Word's GLOSSARY field to reference the contents of a glossary entry. This doesn't actually insert the entry, but rather references the entry each time you update the field. An important consequence is that you can change a glossary entry, update the GLOSSARY fields that reference it, and have the change made automatically.

You could, for example, define a glossary entry named simply CompanyLogo, and reference it with a GLOSSARY field, like this:

{GLOSSARY CompanyLogo}

If your company logo changes, you can update all documents that use it by simply redefining CompanyLogo, and updating references to it.

See the topic "Fields" for information about inserting fields and about the GLOSSARY field.

The Spike

The Spike is a special glossary entry, stored in NORMAL.DOT (that is, globally), that you can use to accumulate material from several different parts of a document. Unlike ordinary glossary entries, new material placed into the Spike doesn't replace existing material. This makes the Spike useful for collecting material from several parts of a document in one place (for example, deleting material on a topic that you've decided not to write about at the current time, but want to save in a separate file for later use).

Each time you put material in the Spike, Word deletes it from the document. This is analogous to a cut operation to the Clipboard (though Spike does not affect the Clipboard).

To cut material to the Spike, select the material in the document and press ⌈Ctrl⌉+⌈F3⌉. Word deletes the material from the document and adds it to the material already in the Spike.

To insert the Spike without emptying it, type "Spike" and press ⌈F3⌉. In this case, you treat the Spike just like any other glossary entry, since inserting the Spike this way leaves the material in the Spike intact.

To insert and empty the Spike, press ⌈Ctrl⌉+⌈Shift⌉+⌈F3⌉. Word inserts the contents of the Spike and clears it out.

Printing a Glossary Catalog

The Glossary dialog box displays a fragment of the beginning of the contents of each glossary entry you select from the list. Word can only display a text sample here, and can't display graphics at all. If you'd like a complete listing of the contents of every entry in a glossary, you can print a glossary catalog.

Select the File→Print command. In the Print dialog box, select Glossary from the Print drop down list. Click OK to start printing. Word prints the name of each glossary entry and the contents (including any formatting) of that entry.

THE GRAMMAR CHECKER

Word 2.0 comes with a utility to check the grammar in a document, and to evaluate your writing style according to various readability indexes. It offers specific corrections, as well as general advice about common grammatical errors.

The grammar checker is the highest level of proofing tool offered by Word, because it tries to take meaning into account. That is, while the spelling checker won't know that you should have used "there" when you used "their," the grammar checker will catch the error. And, if the grammar checker doesn't recognize a word, it will run the spelling checker to give you a chance to correct the word. Last, but not least, the grammar checker sometimes works like a "reverse thesaurus"; while you might use the thesaurus to find a fancier word, the grammar checker will sometimes tell you to use a simpler one.

Using the Grammar Checker

You can use the grammar checker on all of a document, or just part of it. To check part of a document (preferably, whole sentences), select the part you want to check. Then, start the grammar checker with the Tools→Grammar command. If it finds nothing wrong with selected text, the grammar checker will ask you if you'd like to proof the entire document. If the grammar checker finds something objectionable, it will display the Grammar dialog box.

```
┌─────────────────────────────────────────────────────────┐
│ ▭              Grammar: English (US)                      │
│ ┌──────────────────────────────────────┐  ┌───────────┐ │
│ Sentence:                                  │  Ignore   │ │
│ │Never in the field of human conflict was so much owed by so many ▲│ └───────────┘ │
│ │to so few.                              │  ┌───────────┐ │
│ │                                      ▼│  │  Change   │ │
│ └──────────────────────────────────────┘  └───────────┘ │
│ Suggestions:                               ┌───────────┐ │
│ ┌──────────────────────────────────────┐  │Next Sentence│
│ │This sentence does not seem to contain a main clause. ▲│ └───────────┘ │
│ │                                      │  ┌───────────┐ │
│ │                                      │  │Ignore Rule│ │
│ │                                      │  └───────────┘ │
│ │                                      │  ┌───────────┐ │
│ │                                      │  │  Cancel   │ │
│ │                                      │  └───────────┘ │
│ │                                      │  ┌───────────┐ │
│ │                                      │  │  Explain..│ │
│ │                                    ▼│  └───────────┘ │
│ └──────────────────────────────────────┘  ┌───────────┐ │
│                                            │ Options...│ │
│                                            └───────────┘ │
└─────────────────────────────────────────────────────────┘
```

Word displays the suspect sentence in the Sentence box. If it identifies particular words associated with the error—a verb and noun in
disagreement, for example—it will highlight them.

The grammar checker provides an explanation of what's wrong in
the Suggestions box. If you agree with its evaluation, click Change
to let the grammar checker rewrite the sentence. If the grammar
checker can't figure out how to rewrite the sentence, the Change
button will be grayed-out. If you'd like a more detailed explanation,
click Explain...; the grammar checker will open another window with
a paragraph or two from its library of advice.

Click Next Sentence to leave the current sentence unchanged (even
if it may have further errors), and advance to the next sentence. Click
Ignore to skip the current error in a sentence, and advance to another
error in the same sentence.

Click Ignore Rule to have the grammar checker suppress checking
further material against the rule it's currently using. That is, if the
grammar checker is complaining that you've violated a particular
rule of grammar, and you want to continue doing so anyway, click
this button. Remember, the grammar checker is only a computer program, and you're allowed to overrule its judgment.

The Options... button is explained in the next section. Click Cancel
to end grammar checking.

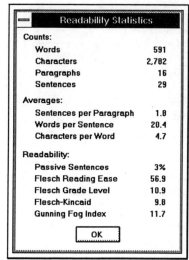

If you've configured the grammar checker to display readability statistics, it displays a dialog box similar to this one after the grammar check.

The Counts group shows the number of words, characters, paragraphs, and sentences in the document checked. The second group massages those statistics to give you ratios of sentences to paragraphs, words per sentence, and characters per word.

The last group of statistics applies several commonly used measures of readability. They're too complex to explain here; the Word manual has a table explaining these scales in the chapter "Proofing a Document," and you might want to refer to *The Chicago Manual of Style,* or Strunk and White's *The Elements of Style* for advice about readability. In general, the higher the numbers, the less readable is the material (except for the Flesch Reading Ease scale, which awards higher scores for better readability). In this example, the grammar checker found the topic you're reading fairly difficult to follow; the Flesch Grade Level rating indicates that you need almost an eleventh grade education to make sense of it.

Grammar Checker Options

If you click the Options... button in the Grammar dialog box, or select the Grammar category in the Tools→Options command, Word displays the Options dialog box for grammar checker options.

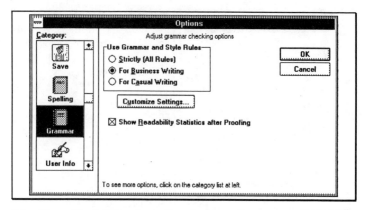

The Show Readability Statistics after Proofing checkbox controls whether Word displays the Readability Statistics dialog box, described earlier, after completing its grammar check.

The Use Grammar and Style Rules control group lets you select how strictly the grammar checker applies its rules, and the style of writing it assumes you're using (business or casual). Customize Settings... lets you control individual rules in the Customize Grammar Settings dialog box.

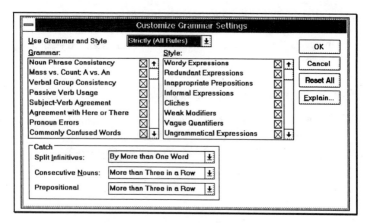

Select a category of rules to modify from the Use Grammar and Style drop-down list; these categories correspond to the Use Grammar and Style Rules control group in the grammar checker Options dialog box.

The Grammar list shows the rules of grammar that Word will apply. The Style list shows the writing style guidelines that the grammar checker will use. Check or uncheck the rules you want Word to use.

The Catch options control how severely Word checks phrases. For example, the default More than Three in a Row setting for Consecutive Nouns causes the grammar checker to question any sentence that has more than three nouns in a row.

Click OK to return to the grammar checker Options dialog box. From there, click OK or Cancel to return to the grammar checker (if that's where you started from), or to your document.

See also: The Spelling Checker; The Thesaurus

GRAPHICS

Word for Windows 2.0 provides a rich set of features for including graphics in your documents, and tools for manipulating graphics. Refer to these topics for specific information:

- "Borders and Shading" for techniques to create borders around graphics.
- "Draw (Microsoft Draw)" to learn about using Microsoft Draw to create embedded drawings.
- "Fields" for information about the fields that import graphics into a document.
- "Frames" for information about inserting, formatting, and positioning frames containing graphics.
- "Embedding and Linking" for information about embedding graphic objects and linking graphic files into a document.
- "Pictures" for information about the Insert→Picture command.

HEADERS AND FOOTERS

A *header* is material that prints near the top of each page of a document. The header on each page of this book shows the current topic title and the page number. A *footer* is material that prints near the bottom of each page of a document.

Word lets you create different headers and footers for each section of a multi-section document, or link headers and footers in one section to those of the previous section. New sections inherit the headers and footers of the previous section. You can control whether headers and footers are the same or different on odd and even pages, and whether a different set of headers and footers is used on the first page of a section.

In normal view, you must open a separate pane in the current document window to edit the contents of headers and footers. In page layout view, you can directly edit headers and footers.

Almost anything that you can put in a document can appear in headers and footers—text, pictures, graphs, WordArt, and most field types. Although headers and footers are nominally printed in the top and bottom margins, you can create headers and footers larger than the margins and Word will increase the margins to accommodate them. (Word gives headers and footers preference over other material in a document when it lays out each page for printing.)

The characteristics of headers and footers are controlled by settings in the Header/Footer dialog box, which you display with the View→ Header/Footer command. (Word 1.0/1.1 users: This command was located on the Edit menu.)

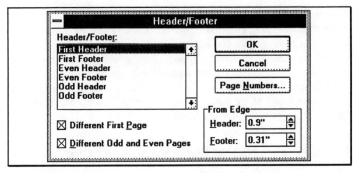

The Header/Footer list box lets you select the header or footer to edit. If you're in Normal view, Word lists the various permutations of headers and footers in the current section (first-page, even-page, and odd-page headers and footers, depending on the options checked at the lower left of the dialog box). Clicking OK opens the Header/Footer pane. In page layout view the list box shows only Header and Footer; selecting one of these causes Word to position the insertion point in the header or footer on the current page.

Header/Footer Types

You often want different headers and footers to appear on odd or even pages of a document (like the headers in this book, which always have the page number on the outside). Further, you might want to have different headers/footers (or none) on the first page of a section, where, for example, title page material might clash with the headers or footers.

The Different First Page and Different Odd and Even Pages checkboxes in the Header/Footer dialog box control the types of headers and footers available in the current section, as shown in the Header/Footer list box. The various combinations of those checkboxes produce the following types of headers and footers:

Different Odd and Even Pages checkbox		
	Different First Page checkbox	
		Header, Footer
✕		Even Header, Even Footer, Odd Header, Odd Footer
	✕	First Header, First Footer, Header, Footer
✕	✕	First Header, First Footer, Even Header, Even Footer, Odd Header, Odd Footer

Notice that Word doesn't give you all possible combinations of header/footer types: You don't have odd/even variations of first-page headers or footers. As a consequence, you can't have first page headers/footers that are different depending on whether they appear on odd or even pages. This can be a problem if, for example, you don't want headers on a first page, but want to keep a standard odd/even alternating footer at the bottom. See "Fields in Headers and Footers" below for a workaround using fields.

Header and Footer Paragraph Formatting

Word has two predefined paragraph styles for use in headers and footers; they're named, logically enough, *header* and *footer*. Header/footer paragraphs are assigned to these styles by default, but you can freely use other paragraph styles in headers and footers. However, it's best to customize *header* and *footer* appropriately, to save yourself the trouble of having to manually apply another style each time you create a header or footer.

You're free to format headers and footers any way you like, including manual paragraph and character formatting, tabs, and frames for positioning.

Positioning Headers and Footers

The From Edge control group in the Header/Footer dialog box lets you control the position of headers and footers.

The Header box specifies the distance from the top edge of the page to the *top* of the header (you can look at this as a "local" margin for the header). If your header consists of multiple lines of text or tall graphics, Word extends the header down from the top header margin. If this causes the header to protrude inside the top text margin, Word adjusts the text margin down to make room for the header.

The Footer box specifies the distance from the bottom edge of the page to the base of the footer. This is a "local" bottom margin, and Word extends the footer up toward text, and will adjust the bottom text margin to accommodate tall footers.

You can have different header and footer margins in different sections.

Linking Headers/Footers Across Sections

Word lets you set up headers and footers individually for each section, but often you simply want all headers and footers to be the same throughout a document, or throughout some series of sections.

When you start a new section by inserting a section break, it inherits the headers and footers and their style, positioning, and page numbering characteristics from the previous section. This forms a chain of linked headers and footers. When you change headers/footers in one section of a document, you break this chain. Subsequent sections linked to the changed section inherit the new headers and footers.

You can restore the link between a section and the previous section by clicking the Link to Previous button in the header/footer pane. Word asks you to confirm that it should delete the contents of the current header or footer and link it to the previous corresponding header or footer. Note that you must do this for each header and footer in a section individually. Note also that this only affects the contents of a header or footer; it doesn't change the odd/even or first-page settings or page numbering style of the current section to match the previous section. (This is quite useful behavior, since you often want to add special first-page headers or footers to a section, or keep a specific starting page number, without affecting the contents of headers or footers.)

Page Numbering

Because page numbering is usually associated with headers and footers, Microsoft has located Word's page numbering controls in a dialog box that's linked to the Header/Footer dialog box. You click Page Numbers... in the Header/Footer dialog box to display the Page Number Format dialog box.

You'll most often use the Page Numbering control group to either allow page numbers to continue automatically from section to section, or set a specific starting page number.

To number pages automatically, select Continue from Previous Section. This causes the current section to inherit its page number from the previous section—the same page number if the section begins on the same page as the previous section, or the next page number if the section begins on a new page. With automatic numbering, the first section in a document begins on page one.

To specify the starting page number of a section, select Start At and enter the page number in the text box to its right.

The Number Format drop-down list selects the format of page numbers (produced by PAGE fields) in the current section's headers and footers:

1 2 3...   Arabic numerals

a b c...   Lowercase letters of the alphabet

A B C...   Uppercase letters of the alphabet

i ii iii...   Lowercase Roman numerals

I II III...   Uppercase Roman numerals

Fields in Headers and Footers

Most of Word's fields can be inserted into headers and footers. Fields are the only way to insert such things as the page number, date, or time into a header/footer.

You can't use ASK, DATA, NEXT, or NEXTIF fields in a header or footer.

When you're in normal view and open the Header/Footer pane, a bar at the top of the pane has three buttons to insert the three most commonly used field types:

This button inserts a TIME field, which produces the time whenever it is updated. (Fields are updated when you print a document, so this field results in the placement of the time of printing in a header or footer.) The format of the time is controlled by your Windows time format setting, by default; you can edit the field to produce other time formats.

This button inserts a DATE field, which produces the date the field is updated. The format of the date is controlled by your Windows default date format; you can edit the field to produce other date formats.

This button inserts a PAGE field. Its result is the number of the page on which it's printed. The page number format is, by default, the format set in the Page Number Format dialog box (linked to the Header/Footer box by the Page Numbers... button in the Header/Footer dialog box). You can edit the field to customize the page number format.

Earlier, we mentioned a quirk in Word's approach to headers and footers that doesn't allow you to specify odd or even variants of first page headers and footers. This can be a problem, for example, if you must maintain an odd/even alternation in the placement of page numbers on a first page footer. A workaround is to use a series of fields that display different results on odd or even pages. Here's an example that produces the name of a magazine and a page number on even pages, and the issue date and a page number on odd pages:

{IF {=MOD({PAGE},2)}=0 "{PAGE}<tab>Net/One Technical Journal" "December 1991<tab>{PAGE}"}

It works like this:

IF {=MOD({PAGE},2)}=0

The MOD (modulo arithmetic) operator divides the current page number by 2, and returns the remainder: zero on even pages, one on odd pages. This is the test condition for the IF statement, which returns one of the following footer layouts depending on the result.

"{PAGE}<tab>Net/One Technical Journal"

If the current page number is even, these instructions print the page number on the left, a tab (represented above by <tab>), and the name of the magazine. This document's *footer* paragraph style has a right-justified tab at the right margin, so the magazine name appears at the right edge of the page.

"December 1991<tab>{PAGE}"

If the current page number is odd, these instructions print the issue date on the left and the page number on the right.

Other fields are available for use in headers and footers. See the topic "Fields" for information about field types and the procedures for inserting and using them.

HYPHENATION

Hyphens are the small dash characters (-) that you use to split words at the end of a sentence, to reduce the amount of white space added to justified lines, or the raggedness of the margins in left, right, or centered paragraphs. (You also use hyphens to create compound-words, but we're not concerned here with that use of hyphens.)

Word recognizes three kinds of hyphens: hard (sometimes called "normal"), optional, and non-breaking. You can also have Word automatically hyphenate a document.

Hard Hyphens

When you press the 🔲 key, Word inserts a "hard" hyphen; it's a character in your document like any other. If the word that it's part of happens to fall at the beginning of a line (except the first line in a paragraph), Word will break the word at the hyphen, moving the first part of the word (including the hyphen) up to the previous line, and leaving the remainder of the word on the next line. Word only does this, of course, if there's room on the preceding line for the part of the word before the hyphen.

If you add or delete text before the word with the hard hyphen, the word may move to a position where it no longer needs to be split. Since hard hyphens are always printed, this has the undesirable effect of putting a hyphen in a word in the middle of the line. It's better to use Word's *optional hyphen.*

Optional Hyphens

Insert an optional hyphen by pressing 🔲+🔲. An optional hyphen in a word tells Word:

- If you have to split this word, split it here, and print a hyphen.

- If you don't have to split this Word, don't print a hyphen.

Display of optional hyphens is controlled by the Optional Hyphens check box in the View category of the Tools→Options command. When optional hyphen display is turned on, Word shows each optional hyphen with the ¬ character (on the screen only; optional hyphens print with the ordinary hyphen character).

Non-Breaking Hyphens

Sometimes you want to use a hyphen that Word is not allowed to break at the end of a line (a classic example is the minus sign; Word might leave an ordinary hyphen at the end of a line and move the number to the next line). Word treats a non-breaking hyphen like a character, and won't break the word where it appears. Press Ctrl +Shift+☐ to insert a non-breaking hyphen. Non-breaking hyphens are displayed as em-dashes (—), but print as ordinary hyphens.

Automatic Hyphenation

You can have Word scan a document and use its own judgement to insert optional hyphens where necessary to tighten up text. Word examines the first word on each line (except the first line of a paragraph), looking for doubled characters or syllables that it can separate with an optional hyphen, to move part of the word up to the previous line. Word is often correct, but it's not perfect, and so you should tell Word to ask you for confirmation before it inserts each optional hyphen.

To start automatic hyphenation, use the Tools→Hyphenation command. If you have text selected, Word will hyphenate only the selected text. If the cursor is an insertion point (no text selected), Word hyphenates from the insertion point toward the end of the document. At the end of the document, Word gives you the option of continuing at the beginning of the document.

Tools→Hyphenation displays the Hyphenation dialog box. This dialog box remains on the screen as you hyphenate, until the entire selection or document has been hyphenated, or until you click Cancel.

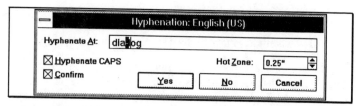

When you begin hyphenation, if there's nothing selected, the first button is OK. This gives you the chance to set up hyphenation options:

- *Hyphenate CAPS* controls whether Word tries to hyphenate words that consist entirely of capital letters. If this option is turned off, Word ignores words in all-capitals.

- *Confirm*, when checked, has Word stop at each candidate for hyphenation and wait for you to confirm. Your options at this point are explained below.

- The *Hot Zone* is the minimum length for hyphenated word fragments at the end of a line; it controls how "aggressively" Word hyphenates. A smaller setting allows Word to hyphenate more often, leaving smaller word fragments at the ends of lines. You specify a distance rather than a number of characters, because you often use proportional fonts that may have a variable number of characters in any given distance.

When you've selected hyphenation options, click OK to have Word start looking for likely candidates for hyphenation. If Confirm is turned off, Word proceeds to hyphenate automatically. If Confirm is checked (recommended, and the default), Word stops at each word it wants to hyphenate.

Each time Word finds a word that it thinks it can hyphenate, it displays it in the Hyphenate At text box. If the word already has optional hyphens, and Word thinks it can improve on the hyphenation, Word displays those words with their hyphens; if Word finds existing hyphenation acceptable it won't suggest hyphenating the word.

Word highlights its recommendation for locating the hyphen. If Word's recommendation is correct, click Yes. If you want to change the location of the optional hyphen, use the mouse or the ⬅ and ➡ keys to move the insertion point to the new location in the text box before clicking Yes. You'll notice a tall vertical bar in the Hyphenate At text box. This is the limit for hyphenation; if you place an optional hyphen past this point, Word still inserts it, but it has no effect because the part of the word to its left is too long for Word to leave at the end of the line.

To skip hyphenating a word, click No . Click Cancel to end hyphenation before the entire document or selection has been hyphenated.

The title of the sample Hyphenation dialog boxes shown here reads "Hyphenation: English (US)." Word hyphenates different languages according to different rules, determined by the default language you specified during installation. You can also specify a language for each paragraph with Format→Language, so that Word will use the appropriate rules in the paragraph (the language specification also controls how the spelling checker works).

Finding and Replacing Hyphens

You can include the ordinary hyphen in the text used in a find or replace operation.

To specify an optional hyphen in a search or replace, type ^- (caret, hyphen). To specify a non-breaking hyphen, type ^~ (caret, tilde).

See also: Text: Inserting, Selecting, and Editing

INDEXES

You create an index for a Word document in two phases: insert *index entries*, using XE fields; then have Word collect all the index entries and compile them to create the index.

Inserting Index Entries

Each index entry is an XE field, which you can insert with the assistance of the Insert→Index Entry command, or directly by typing the field.

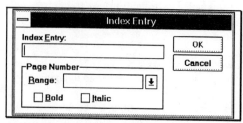

Insert→Index Entry displays the Index Entry dialog box. Its OK button is initially grayed-out, until you enter text in the Index Entry box.

To insert an index entry:

1. Position the index entry:

   · If the cursor is an insertion point (no text selected), Word puts the XE field at that location, and you must type the text of the entry in the Index Entry dialog box. Generally, position the XE field immediately before the item the entry references (if you put it after the item, there's a danger that Word may separate the index entry from its reference at a page break, causing the page number to be wrong).

   · If you have text selected, Word assumes that you want to use that text as the index entry. Later, after you close the Index Entry dialog box, Word inserts the XE field at the end of the selection.

2. Use Insert→Index Entry to display the Index Entry dialog box.

3. If you had text selected, that text will be in the Index Entry text box. Type new text, or edit the existing text.

   Colons have a special meaning in index entries: they separate the parts of a multilevel entry (explained below). If a colon must appear as part of the text of the entry, precede it with a backslash (\); for example, **Star Trek\: The Next Generation**. If a backslash is part of the text, double it (\\).

4. If you want the index entry to identify a range of pages, select a bookmark identifying the material from the Range drop-down list. (You must have previously inserted the bookmark.)

   You may want to use page ranges for any material longer than a paragraph, even if the material is initially on one page. If Word has to break the material across a page break, the index entry will correctly reflect the range; while, if the material all fits on one page, Word will show just a single page number. The drawback, of course, is that you must insert bookmarks for every page range.

5. If you want the page numbers in the entry to be bold or italic, check the appropriate Bold or Italic options.

6. Click OK. Word inserts an XE field into your document.

XE fields are automatically and permanently formatted as hidden text. If hidden text display is turned off when you create an index entry, it will seem to disappear into your document.

You can edit existing XE fields with hidden text display turned on. Edit the text between quotes, inside the field, to change the entry.

Multiple-Level Index Entries

Using single-level index entries results in an index that is organized alphabetically. You can add a *hierarchical* organization to your index by inserting multilevel index entries, in which certain *primary* entries have *subentries* listed below them.

Separate levels in the index entry text with colons (:). As noted earlier, colons that are part of the text must be prefixed with a backslash (\). Here's an example, showing the difference:

Star Trek: The Next Generation	Star Trek\: The Next Generation
produces a two-level index entry:	*produces a single index entry:*
Star Trek	**Star Trek: The Next Generation, 12**
The Next Generation, 12	

Of course, the left example may be exactly what you intend, if you're writing about all the different incarnations of *Star Trek*.

You can have as many as seven levels in an index. Try to avoid using more than three or four, since too many levels can be confusing and hard to read.

Index Entry (XE) Fields

The Index Entry dialog box lets you set up most features of XE fields, but it leaves out support for using text instead of page numbers in the entry; for that, you must insert the field and work directly with the field contents.

Here's the complete layout of the XE field:

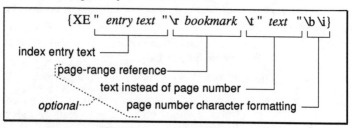

Each part of the field has the following purpose:

- *Index entry text* must be enclosed in quotes ("); be careful to use the standard straight quote, and not the fancy typographer's quotes (" and "). Colons in the text must be preceded by backslashes (\).

The index entry text is required, and the remaining parts of the field are optional. You may use \b or \i (or both) with any switches; \r and \t are mutually exclusive.

- *Page range references* begin with the "switch" \r, followed by the name of the bookmark defining the page range. The bookmark name should not be in quotes.

- The *Text instead of page number* switch, \t, introduces text that Word will use instead of a page number when it compiles this entry into the index; the text must be within quotes in the field. This is most commonly used for "See" cross-reference index entries; for example:

  {XE "Trek, Star" \t "see Star Trek" \i}

  produces the entry

  Trek, Star *see Star Trek*

  (Note the use of the \i switch to make the cross-referenced text italic.)

- *Page number character formatting* is controlled by the \b (bold) and \i (italic) switches.

Compiling an Index

Indexes are produced by INDEX fields. Word provides a lot of options for formatting and organizing indexes. Some of them are available when you create an INDEX field with the Insert→Index command; to get the full range of index features you'll have to work directly with the field.

When Word compiles an index, it formats the entries with a set of standard paragraph styles: *index 1* through *index 7,* and *index heading.* The numbered styles correspond to the level of the entry in a multilevel index, while *index heading* is used to format the paragraph that separates groups of letters in the index. You can define these styles to suit yourself, typically with increasing levels of indenting for lower levels, and possibly other visual cues such as reduced font size.

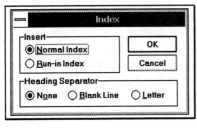

Insert→Index displays the Index dialog box. This dialog box lets you select the way multilevel index entries are formatted, and what Word does when the initial letter of the index entries changes (in other words, how Word formats alphabetical groups of entries).

The Insert control group gives you two options:

- **Normal Index** formats each entry at the same level in a multilevel entry on a separate line, like this:

Enterprise
    Crew
            Crusher (Beverly), 28
            Crusher (Wesley), 29
            Picard, 27
            Riker, 27
            Worf, 31

- **Run-in Index** collects each entry at the same level in a multi-level entry into a single paragraph; entries are separated with semicolons, like this:

  Enterprise: Crew; Crusher (Beverly), 28; Crusher (Wesley), 29; Picard, 27; Riker, 27; Worf, 31

The Heading Separator control group selects the way that Word breaks up alphabetical groups (entries with the same first letter) in the index:

- **None** means that Word doesn't do anything to denote the change from one initial letter to another.

- **Blank Line** has Word put a paragraph marker between alphabetical groups.

- **Letter** means that Word inserts a paragraph containing the letter of the new alphabetical group, formatted with the paragraph style *index heading*.

The INDEX Field

The heading separator and the run-in index style exhausts the repertoire of the Insert→Index command, but Word lets you control several other aspects of creating an index with options in the INDEX field.

INDEX fields have this general layout:

{INDEX *Switches*}

Switches are the options you can add to INDEX to customize the index it produces. An INDEX field can combine several switches. Each switch is introduced by a backslash (\) and a letter; the following table shows the letters capitalized for clarity, but they may be upper- or lowercase.

Controlling the Scope of an Index	
\B *bookmark*	Collects index entries only from the pages marked by *bookmark*.
\P *StartLetter-EndLetter*	Specifies the range of a partial index; the index is compiled only for entries beginning with the letters from *StartLetter* to *EndLetter*.
The default, with neither switch, is to collect entries from the entire document.	

Letter Group Separator Style

\H *"letter-group separator"*   Specifies the format of the paragraph separating groups of letters in the index.

For example, \h" " specifies a blank paragraph, \h"A" specifies heading letters, while \h"--A--" includes hyphens before and after the letters. \h"" (two quotes with nothing between them) specifies that letter groups should not be separated; this is the default.

Run-In Index

\R   Specifies a "run-in" index, in which a topic and its subtopics are combined into a single paragraph. A colon separates the topic and the subtopics, and a semicolon separates multiple subtopics.

Page Number Formatting

\E *"page number separator"*   Specifies the characters separating the index item and its page numbers. There can be no more than three separator characters. A comma and space are used by default.

\G *page range separator*   Specifies the character used as a page range separator (for example, \g: specifies a colon as the separator, so that 5:99 in the index signifies a range from page 5 to 99). A hyphen is used by default.

\L *"page number separator"*   Specifies the character or characters separating page numbers, when an index entry appears on multiple pages. If the pages are contiguous, Word uses the page range format set by the \g switch. The default separator is a comma followed by a space.

Chapter Numbering and Sequence Fields

\S *sequence*   Uses sequence fields to form the page number; that is, Word finds the value of the sequence field *sequence* on the page where it collects the index entry, and makes a page number consisting of the value of *sequence*, a hyphen, and the page number. This is most useful for collecting index entry page numbers when your document uses chapter numbering (for example, "8-3").

\D *"character"*   Specifies a separator other than a hyphen to separate sequence numbers from page numbers. This separator may be up the three characters long.

Indexing Long Documents

So far we've described putting an index inside the document it's indexing. You can also put an index in a separate file, with a list of other document files from which it will compile the index.

The list of external files is a series of RD (Referenced Document) fields. Each RD field identifies a file to include in the index. If the file specification includes the path, you must double each backslash (for example: d:\\SYBEX\\REF). Here's an example of a list of RD fields, followed by an INDEX field:

> {RD D:\\SYBEX\\REF\\INDEXES.DOC}{RD
> D:\\SYBEX\\REF\\FIELDS-1.DOC}{INDEX}

This sequence of fields tells Word to scan INDEXES.DOC and FIELDS-1.DOC for index entries, and insert the compiled index into the current document. The order of the RD fields doesn't matter, because Word sorts index entries after it's compiled them.

It's possible to create very long indexes this way. Microsoft recommends that if an index is longer than about 4000 entries, you should break the index up into separate segments. This means using the \p switch (see above) in an INDEX field to compile ranges of letters in several index segments.

See also: Bookmarks, Fields (the XE, INDEX, and RD fields in particular),
Pagination, Tables of Contents and Other Lists

LISTS

A *list* is a sequence of paragraphs related by a number series or related visually through the use of visual symbols (such as a "bullet"). See these topics for information about the lists you can create with Word for Windows:

- "Bulleted Lists" explains how to create lists designated with bullet symbols.
- "Numbered Lists" explains how to create sequences of numbered paragraphs.
- "Outlines" explains how to number headings in outline view.
- "Tables of Contents and Other Lists" explains how to have Word collect information from headings or fields in a document to create lists of various types.

MACROS

One way to look at Word is that it's a programmable text processing "engine" that's configured out of the box as a word processor. That is, the core of Word knows about documents, text, graphics, editing, and so on; the set of macros that come with Word make use of the built-in text processing functions to give you a word processor.

The implication of this is that you can reprogram Word to make it do just about anything you want with text and graphics.

Historically, the word "macro" has had a very limited meaning. More than anything, it referred to a record of actions taken by a user, that could be played back later to perform the same operation. Word does have a macro recorder facility, but what's really important is that Word's macros are really an implementation of the BASIC programming language, with extensions for text processing, called *WordBasic*. It's founded on Microsoft's QuickBASIC product. A typical WordBasic macro looks like this:

```
Sub MAIN
    Dim dlg As InsertPicture
    GetCurValues dlg
    dlg.Name = "D:\SYBEX\BITMAPS\*.BMP"
    Dialog dlg
    Super InsertPicture dlg
    CharLeft 1, 1
    FormatPicture .SetSize = 0, .ScaleX = "100",
    .ScaleY = "100", .CropTop = "-2pt", .CropBottom
    = "-2pt"
End Sub
```

Notice the commands `InsertPicture` and `FormatPicture`. Word has corresponding menu commands: Insert→Picture and Format→Picture, so, as you can guess, these WordBasic commands do the same thing as those menu commands. There are a number of options after `FormatPicture`, each of which corresponds to one of the items you can set in the Picture dialog box.

The various lines containing the word `dlg` set up and display a dialog box. Word includes a dialog box editor to let you design dialog boxes for use in WordBasic macros.

WordBasic programming covers an enormous scope, from simple macros you record to automate everyday tasks, to massive projects that change Word into something you'd never recognize as a word processor. Doing justice to the subject would require a book larger than this one, so here we'll address the basics of creating or recording macros, modifying them, and attaching them to keys and menus. The standard Word manuals are of only limited use, because they too couldn't cover the subject in any depth. Your best bet is actually the online help system, which has entries for each WordBasic command as well as categorical groupings and cross-references.

Recording a Macro

You can take advantage of Word's programmability without ever having to write a program in WordBasic. If all you want to do is automate a sequence of tasks, use Tools→Record Macro to have Word record every subsequent action you take, and when you're done store the record in a WordBasic macro.

1. Run the Tools→Record Macro command. It displays the Record Macro dialog box:

Word initially gives the macro it's about to create a generic name, of the form Macro*n,* where *n* is a number. The Record Macro Name box above shows **Macro4,** the fourth macro Word has recorded. You can enter another name.

In this box, you can also assign a key combination that will run this macro. This works like the Keyboard category of the Tools→Options command. You can (and should) enter a description for your macro, to help you later identify it.

2. Click OK to start recording. If you've configured Word to prompt for the storage location for macros and glossary entries, Word will display a dialog box asking whether to store the new macro in the global template (NORMAL.DOT) or the current document template.

   Your every action—commands and typing, but not mouse movements—from this point will be recorded by Word.

3. When you're done with the actions you want recorded, use the Tools→Stop Recorder command to store the macro. This command replaces Tools→Record Macro while you're recording.

   Tools→Stop Recorder immediately stores the macro. If you change your mind about recording it, use Tools→Macro to delete the macro.

The macro recorder stores its record of your actions as a series of WordBasic commands. This is quite useful as a shortcut when you're writing macros—you can have Word create a lot of the macro for you, by recording commands, and then you can add WordBasic commands of your own to complete the macro.

Suppose you start the recorder, and then use the Format→Character command to change some text to bold, and to select a new font. Here's what Word would record:

```
Sub MAIN
FormatCharacter .Font = "StoneSansSemibold",
   .Points = "13", .Bold = 1, .Italic = 0,
   .Strikeout = 0, .Hidden = 0, .SmallCaps = 0,
   .AllCaps = 0, .Underline = 0, .Color = 0,
   .Position = "0 pt", .Spacing = "0 pt"
End Sub
```

Notice that even though you only changed two items in the Character dialog box, the FormatCharacter command in the macro records every setting in the dialog box. In this example, the FormatCharacter command consists of one very long line. You may find that Word breaks the line at several points, and inserts a backslash (\) to signify that the lines logically make up one single command.

Writing Macros

Word provides a simple macro editor for creating and modifying macros. When the macro editor window is displayed, Word replaces the Ribbon with a series of buttons for running and testing your macro. To write a macro:

1. Run Tools→Macro to display the Macro dialog box:

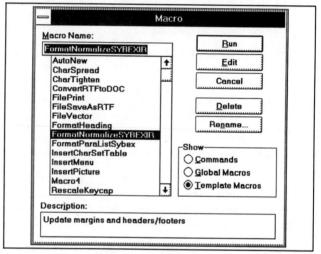

   The Show control group selects whether the Macro Name list shows macros from the global template (NORMAL.DOT) or the current document template; or whether it shows built-in commands.

   From this dialog box you can also run, delete, and rename macros with the corresponding buttons.

2. If you're editing an existing macro, select it from the Macro Name list. If you're creating a new macro, select Global Macros to store it in NORMAL.DOT, or Template Macros to store it in the current document template; and then enter the name in the Macro Name box.

3. Click ⌐Edit⌐. Word opens the macro editor window and replaces the Ribbon with macro debugging buttons.

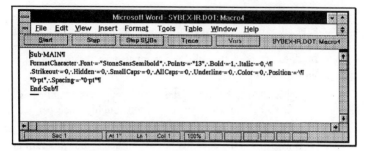

If you're editing an existing macro, the editor window shows it. If you're starting a new macro, the editor window will contain a template for starting a macro: the lines `Sub MAIN` and `End Sub`. Your macro goes between these lines.

4. Edit or enter the macro. The macro editor is a simplified editing tool, more like the Windows Notepad than a Word document window. You don't need formatting commands, and so they're not available while you're using the macro editor. You can display this window maximized, or you can reduce it to make it visible alongside other Word windows.

5. When you're done, double-click the macro editor's control menu box at its upper left corner. Word will display a dialog box asking if you want to save your edits; click ⟨Yes⟩, ⟨No⟩, or ⟨Cancel⟩ as appropriate.

Testing a Macro

While you have a macro displayed in the macro editor window, Word replaces the Ribbon with buttons to let you test your macro. These buttons do the following:

- ⟨Start⟩ runs the macro. After you use ⟨Step⟩ or ⟨Step SUBs⟩, or pause a running macro, this button changes to ⟨Continue⟩; it restarts an interrupted macro.

- ⟨Step⟩ executes the macro one instruction at a time. Word highlights the line it's executing. Click ⟨Step⟩ to advance a line at a time. If your macro contains subroutines, Word jumps to each subroutine as it's called and steps through it.

- Step SUBs works like Step, except that when it encounters a subroutine call it moves through it very rapidly, instead of stopping at each line. This is useful if you're sure the subroutines are correct, and don't want to take the time to step through them.

- Trace is a cross between Start and Step. Word "animates" the macro by executing an instruction roughly once per second, highlighting each line as it works.

- Vars... displays the contents of any variables your program is using.

You can pause the execution of a running macro at any time by pressing Esc. If you're stepping through the macro, Esc stops it. Word highlights the line where you paused or stopped the macro.

Some macros don't use commands specific to documents, and so you can run them from the macro editor window. However, most macros operate on documents, and they will fail to run if you try to execute them from the macro window—they use commands that aren't available in the macro window. To test these, reduce the size of the macro window, and place it alongside a document window with whatever test material you need. Click the mouse in the document window to make it the current window. The macro debugging buttons will still be displayed; when you use them, they execute the macro shown in the macro window, while the effects of the macro take place in the document window.

Modifying Built-In Commands

Most of Word's core functions are accessible through built-in commands. You can use built-in commands by name in macros; in that form, they're just like any other WordBasic command. For example, the core function for saving a file is represented by the Word-Basic/built-in command FileSave. You can also run built-in commands directly, from the Macro dialog box. The third option is to assign a built-in command to a menu, key combination, or a Toolbar button. When you first install Word, many built-in commands are already assigned; FileSave is assigned to the File→Save command, Shift+F12, and the ▣ Toolbar button, for example.

You can't directly modify a core function (that would involve modifying Word internally, generally a very bad idea). But you can *intercept* a built-in command, by creating a macro of the same name, so that menus, key combinations, and Toolbar buttons that reference that name run your macro instead. In a sense, you "wrap" the built-in command in a macro package.

When you intercept a built-in command, only menus and key combinations are affected. When you use the command name in a Word-Basic macro, it calls the built-in command directly.

For example, suppose you want to modify the built-in InsertPicture command. In many cases, the built-in InsertPicture function automatically expands or compresses the inserted picture to fill the current margins; you want to prevent that, so that your pictures are inserted at their original scale.

1. Use the Tools→Macro command, select Commands from the Show control group, and select InsertPicture from the list. Then click Edit. Word displays the macro editor window, containing these lines:

```
Sub MAIN
Dim dlg As InsertPicture
GetCurValues dlg
Dialog dlg
Super InsertPicture dlg
End Sub
```

Up until the moment you asked to edit InsertPicture, it didn't exist as a macro. Word created the above macro for you to use as a template for modifying InsertPicture. The word Super in front of the InsertPicture command means that you're calling the built-in version of InsertPicture, rather than this macro. You can add WordBasic commands before and after this line to modify how InsertPicture works, or you can delete the line entirely to substitute your own version of InsertPicture.

2. Rewrite InsertPicture, like this:

```
Sub MAIN
    Dim dlg As InsertPicture
    GetCurValues dlg
```

```
dlg.Name = "D:\SYBEX\BITMAPS\*.BMP"
Dialog dlg
Super InsertPicture dlg
CharLeft 1, 1
FormatPicture .SetSize = 0, .ScaleX =
"100", .ScaleY = "100", .CropTop = "-2pt",
.CropBottom = "-2pt"
End Sub
```

The first four lines illustrate in important concept in modifying built-in commands: you can "hijack" an existing dialog box for your own use. In this example, Dim dlg As Insert-Picture allocates memory for the predefined Insert Picture dialog box, creating a *variable,* and gives the variable the name dlg so that you can use it in your macro. GetCur-Values dlg retrieves whatever settings are currently in that dialog box (some dialog boxes show settings that Word stores internally; this is how you retrieve those settings).

Here, you want to set the default directory and file type that the Insert Picture dialog box shows, so you set the Name field of the dialog box by assigning the new path to the dlg.Name variable. Finally, Dialog dlg displays the dialog box.

After the user clicks OK in the Insert Picture dialog box, the macro continues. Super InsertPicture dlg calls the built-in version of InsertPicture, and passes it the results of displaying the dialog box in the dlg variable.

InsertPicture does its thing, and leaves the insertion point just after the inserted picture. CharLeft 1, 1 selects the picture, and the FormatPicture line restores its scaling to 100%, and adds a 2 pt border above and below the picture.

You're not limited to using predefined dialog boxes only with their associated built-in commands. Probably the most useful predefined dialog box is File Open, which you can take over and use any time you need a dialog box that selects a file. After you display it with the Dialog command, you can retrieve the name of the file the user selected from the Name field of the dialog variable.

spiff—Word's Secret Bonus Macro

Word's programming team has built into Word a hidden tribute to themselves. It's a rather peculiar macro called *spiff*, that doesn't exist in Word initially; you have to write it. At first, it was an inside joke at Microsoft. Then someone spilled the beans in the Microsoft forum on CompuServe, so now the story of *spiff* can be told.

When you create this little macro, it modifies the Help→About command to display a cute, animated...well, no sense spoiling it for you. Here's how to make it work:

1. Use the Tools→Macro command to start editing a new macro, giving it the name *spiff*.

2. The macro edit window contains the usual Sub Main and End Sub commands, and nothing else. Delete them. (That would cause an error in any other macro, but this is *spiff*.)

3. Close the macro window; be sure to tell Word to save *spiff*.

4. Run the Help→About command. In the About dialog box, click on the Word icon in the upper-left corner. Then watch the show. You can interrupt *spiff* before it's done by pressing ⟨Esc⟩.

Enjoy!

For Further Information...

- The topic "Customizing Word for Windows" explains how to assign macros to menus, keys, and Toolbar buttons.

- Word's online help system has complete, if terse, documentation about each WordBasic command. If you start from the Help→Help Index command, select the category WordBasic Programming Language. If you're in the macro editor window, select (or place the insertion point inside) a WordBasic command you'd like information about, then press ⟨F1⟩. Word will go directly to the help entry for that command.

- Some Word 2.0 packages include a mail-in card for a Word Developer's Kit, which includes a Technical Reference book on WordBasic. *Send in the card!* If the card didn't come with your copy of Word, contact Microsoft.

NAVIGATING THROUGH DOCUMENTS

Word relies on both standard Windows techniques, like scroll bars, and its own unique navigational systems, like bookmarks, to let you move around in a document.

A key point to remember is that the location of the insertion point or a text selection doesn't have to be visible on the display. You can move your view of a document (that part of it displayed in the document window) around, using mouse techniques like scroll bars, while the position of your last insertion point or selection remains unaffected. In general, some mouse navigation actions move the insertion point, and some don't, while changing the view; while keyboard navigation always moves the insertion point, and "drags along" the view to keep the insertion point visible.

Scrolling

You can configure whether each document window has scroll bars in the View category of the Tools→Options command. These scroll bars work like other Windows scroll bars: the arrow buttons move a line at a time, and you can drag the scroll bar button to move larger amounts. Clicking in a scroll bar gray area moves a screenfull at a time. How far that moves you through your document depends on the zoom factor currently in effect (how much text is currently shown in a single screen).

In Page Layout view, Word adds two paging buttons at the bottom of the vertical scroll bar. These paging buttons advance the display an entire page back (up) or forward (down).

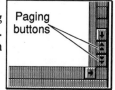

Moving the Insertion Point

Scrolling moves only the display, without moving the insertion point or changing a selection. When you move the insertion point off-screen, Word scrolls the display to keep the insertion point visible.

The most direct way to move the insertion point is to click the mouse at any location that's currently visible on the display.

Word has an extensive set of keyboard commands for moving the insertion point around the document. These commands move relative the current insertion point location; other commands, listed below in "Moving to Specific Parts of a Document" move the insertion point to specified places.

These keys...	Move the insertion point...	If text is selected, moves to...
⬆	Up one line.	One line up from the beginning of the selection; cancels selection.
⬇	Down one line.	One line down from the end of the selection; cancels selection.
⬅	Left one character.	The beginning of the selection; cancels selection.
➡	Right one character.	The end of the selection; cancels selection.
Ctrl + ⬅	Left one word.	The beginning of the first word in the selection; cancels selection.
Ctrl + ➡	Right one word.	The end of the last word in the selection, and cancels selection.
Home	To the beginning of the line.	The beginning of the first line in the selection; cancels selection.
End	To the end of the line.	The end of the last line in the selection; cancels selection.
Ctrl + ⬆	To the beginning of the current paragraph.	The beginning of the current paragraph; cancels selection.
Ctrl + ⬇	To the beginning of the next paragraph.	The beginning of the next paragraph; cancels selection.
PgUp	One screen up (back), at approximately the same relative position in the new screen.	One screen up, at approximately the same relative position in the new screen; cancels selection.
PgDn	One screen down (forward), at approximately the same relative position in the new screen.	One screen down, at approximately the same relative position in the new screen; cancels selection.

(continued)

These keys...	Move the insertion point...	If text is selected, moves to...
Ctrl + PgUp	To the top of the window (the first possible insertion point that's visible in the current view).	The top of the window; cancels selection.
Ctrl + PgDn	To the bottom of the window (the last possible insertion point visible in the current view).	The bottom of the window; cancels selection.
Ctrl + Home	To the beginning of the document.	The beginning of the document; cancels selection.
Ctrl + End	To the end of the document.	The end of the document; cancels selection.

Moving to Specific Parts of a Document

Word's Edit→Go To command is a comprehensive facility for moving the insertion point to a specified object in a document: a page, line, section, bookmark, footnote, and so on.

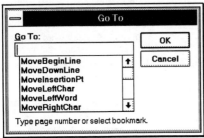

Edit→Go To displays the Go To dialog box. It has a list of bookmarks in the document, and a text box in which you can type the name of a bookmark or one of the other instructions described below. A variation of this command, the F5 key, prompts you in the status bar to enter a bookmark name or an instruction. These are the instruction sequences you can enter (the letters may be upper- or lowercase; they're shown uppercase here for clarity):

To move to:	Enter this instruction:
A specific section.	S*section number* Example: **S7** moves to section 7.
A specific page.	P*page number* Example: **P5** moves to page 5.
A specific line.	L*line number* Example: **L20** moves to line 20.

You can combine the above three instructions to pinpoint a location in a document. Put them together in order of increasing precision, so that you narrow in on the section+page+line you want; this is the order shown in this table. These are all valid compound instructions:

S3p10L33	section 3, page 10, line 33
P5L2	page 5, line 2
s3p5	section 3, page 5
S2L20	section 2, line 20

To move to:	Enter this instruction:
A bookmark.	Select the bookmark's name from the list in the Go To dialog box, or type it in the status bar after pressing ⌨F5⌨.
A footnote.	**F** Moves to the next footnote. **F***footnote number* Moves to the specified footnote number.
An annotation.	**A** Moves to the next annotation. **A***annotation number* Moves to the specified annotation.
A particular distance from the beginning of the document, expressed as a percentage of its total length.	*number*% Example: **75%** moves to a point three-quarters of the way through the document.

See also: Annotations; Footnotes; Text: Inserting, Selecting, and Editing

NUMBERED LISTS

Numbered lists are sequences of indented paragraphs introduced by a number; generally, numbered lists consist of a series of adjacent paragraphs with sequential numbers. Word provides an automatic facility for creating numbered paragraphs through the Tools→Bullets and Numbering command or the ▤ button on the Toolbar. You have other options for creating numbered lists if you use SEQ (sequence) fields, as described below.

If you use the Toolbar, Word formats the current paragraph according to its default list paragraph parameters (the following paragraphs are formatted with the defaults):

1. A .25-inch left indent

2. A hanging indent (first line indented -.25 inch relative to the left indent)

3. Numbers inserted as ordinary text

4. A tab between the number and the start of the text

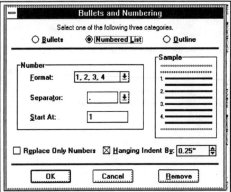

For more control, use the Tools→Bullets and Numbering command to display the Bullets and Numbering dialog box. Select the Numbered List category if it is not already selected.

The Number control group lets you control the appearance of the numbers that Word inserts in the numbered list. The Format drop-down list has these options, controlling the format of the numbers:

- **1. 2. 3. 4.**—arabic numerals

- **I. II. III. IV.**—uppercase roman numerals

- **i. ii. iii. iv.**—lowercase roman numerals

- **A. B. C. D.**—sequential uppercase letters

- **a. b. c. d.**—sequential uppercase letters

The Separator drop-down list lets you select the character that follows the number: nothing; a period (.); a left parenthesis,); a colon (:); a right square bracket (]); two underscores (__); or you can enclose the number in square brackets ([]).

The Start At box tells Word where to start numbering the selected paragraphs.

If the Hanging Indent By box is checked (the default), Word formats the paragraph with the left indent shown in the box, formats the first line with the negative value in the box (a hanging indent), and separates the number and text with a tab. You can change the value in the box if you want a different hanging indent distance.

If Hanging Indent By is not checked, Word doesn't indent the paragraph and separates the number from the text with one space.

The Replace Only Numbers option controls whether Word adds (or updates) numbers to all paragraphs, or only to those that already have numbers. This is useful if you've selected several paragraphs, some already formatted with numbers and some not, and you want to change the number or the indentation; with Replace Only Numbers checked, Word only formats paragraphs already starting with numbers.

Numbered Lists with the SEQ Field

Word's numbered paragraphs have several limitations: They follow a fixed format with the number at the left margin; and numbers are inserted as text, and you have to use the Tools→Bullets and Numbering command to have Word update the numbers. With a small amount of extra effort you can create numbered list paragraphs formatted any way you like, and use fields to automatically maintain numbering. Paragraph formatting is covered in the topic "Paragraphs"; we'll look at Word's SEQ automatic numbering field here.

The SEQ field has the following layout:

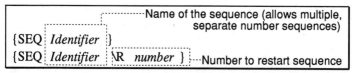

Each numbering sequence has a name (*Identifier*, above); the names allow you to set up several different sequences of numbers, and Word keeps track of each one separately through its name. You might want to have a sequence of figure numbers called *Figs*, and another sequence of table numbers called *Tables*. For numbered paragraphs, you might want to set up a sequence of list numbers called *L1*, for primary lists, and another called *L2*, for secondary numbers under numbers in L1. Using this system, you could set up the following paragraph numbering scheme:

With field code display turned on, you see this.	It produces this, with field code display turned off
→{seq L1 \R1}.→The \R1 switch restarts numbering of the L1 list.	1. The \R1 switch restarts numbering of the L1 list.
→{seq L1}.→Subsequent SEQ L1 fields need only the field name.	2. Subsequent SEQ L1 fields need only the field name.
→{seq L2 \R1}.→This secondary number sequence is called L2, and is restarted at 1.	1. This secondary number sequence is called L2, and is restarted at 1.
→{seq L2}.→Here's another secondary number.	2. Here's another secondary number.
→{seq L1}.→Another number in the primary sequence, L1. Notice that it hasn't been reset.	3. Another number in the primary sequence, L1. Notice that it hasn't been reset.

When you insert a SEQ field in the middle of an existing sequence of numbers, its number is one more than the most recent, previous SEQ field in the same sequence. Following SEQ fields aren't updated, so that you'll initially have two sequence numbers that are the same. Similarly, deleting a SEQ field doesn't update the remaining fields. You update SEQ fields, like other fields, with the [F9] key. Fields are also updated when you print a document, if you've turned on Update Fields in the Print category of Tools→Options.

See also: Paragraphs, Bulleted Lists, Fields

OUTLINES

Outlines can be a powerful tool for organizing documents. Word automatically integrates an outline into each document. That's right, automatically in each document—Word's outlines are based on heading paragraph styles, and you create an outline any time you use headings, whether you're conscious of it or not.

The best way to exploit outlines is to start a document as an outline. That is, plan each heading in advance, rearranging them as necessary to create a logical structure; then, when the outline is correct, start inserting text beneath each heading to write the document. Here's an example of an outline:

Annotations
    Inserting an Annotation
    Viewing Annotations
    Managing Annotations
Bookmarks
    Bookmark References
    Bookmarks in Linked and
        Inserted Files
    Bookmarks as Variables

Borders and Shading
    Paragraph and Frame
      Borders
    Picture Borders
    Table Borders
    Shading
Breaks
Bulleted Lists

This outline ought to look familiar—it's part of the outline by which this book was started. Each of the bold lines was a *heading 1* paragraph style, and each secondary line was a *heading 2* paragraph. From there, all we had to do was start writing (well, OK, it was a little tougher than that, but you get the idea).

Outline View

Because outlines are already implicit in each Word document, it's a matter of viewing the document differently to see the outline structure. That's what the View→Outline command does, when it changes the document window to outline view:

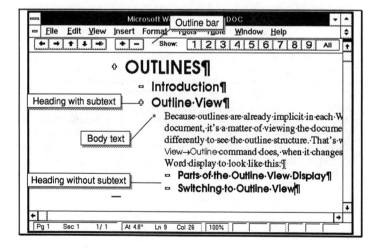

Word identifies headings with one of two symbols: ⊹, denoting a header that has additional lower-level headers or text below it; and □, denoting a heading with nothing below it. Body text—all paragraph styles except headings—are identified by the symbol □.

The outline bar provides a set of buttons for controlling outline view, and for manipulating outlines.

The outline view controls set the lowest level of heading displayed (higher numbers descend deeper into the outline). Initially, Word shows everything, headers and body text alike; this is selected with the [All] button (or press the asterisk key, ⊛ on the numeric keypad). The buttons [1] through [9] select the lowest heading level displayed, *heading 1* through *heading 9*. Click one of these buttons, or press the equivalent number (⬚ through ⑨) on the numeric keypad.

The number and All buttons control the entire outline at once. You can also selectively show subtext (expand a heading) or hide subtext (collapse a heading) several ways:

To:	Do this:
Expand all subtext below a heading	Double-click the outline symbol (⊹) next to the heading to toggle between full expansion and full collapse; select the entire heading and click the expand button ([+]); or press ⊞ on the numeric keypad.
Collapse all subtext below a heading	Double-click the outline symbol (⊹) next to the heading to toggle between full collapse and full expansion; select the entire heading and click the collapse button ([-]); or press ⊟ on the numeric keypad.
Expand subtext one level at a time	Position the insertion point in the header. Click the expand button ([+]); or press ⊞ on the numeric keypad.
Collapse subtext one level at a time	Position the insertion point in the header. Click the collapse button ([-]); or press ⊟ on the numeric keypad.
Expand or collapse several headings at once	Select the headings to expand or collapse. Click ([+]) or press ⊞ on the numeric keypad to expand the headings; click the collapse button ([-]) or press ⊟ on the numeric keypad to collapse the headings.

Rearranging Outlines

You can move parts of an outline around by dragging one of the outline symbols (✥, ▭, and ▫). When you position the pointer over one of these symbols, it changes to the outline drag pointer (✥). Hold down the mouse button over the outline symbol and start dragging. As you do so, Word displays a horizontal line between existing paragraphs, showing you where you can drop the selection to insert it.

When you drag a heading that has subtext (lower-level headings and body text), you drag the subtext along with the heading. In a single operation you can move an entire section of a document. This makes Outline view useful for editing a document, as well as planning it.

You can also use buttons on the outline bar to move body text and headings:

1. Select the paragraph or heading to move by clicking its outline symbol.
2. Move it up or down as required:
   - Click the move up button (↑) to move the paragraph up one position; or press Alt+Shift+↑.
   - Click the move down button (↓) to move the paragraph down one position; or press Alt+Shift+↓.

You'll often want to change the level of part of an outline. You *promote* a heading by giving it a higher heading style (going from *heading 2* to *heading 1*, for example), and you *demote* a heading to a lower level. You can also demote a heading all the way down to body text (the Normal style).

To:	Do this:
Demote a heading one level	Select the heading. Click →; or drag the outline symbol next to the heading to the right; or press Alt+Shift+→.
Promote a heading one level; or promote body text to a heading	Select the heading. Click ←; or drag the outline symbol next to the heading to the left; or press Alt+Shift+←.
Demote a heading to body text	Select the heading, and click ⇒.

Outline Numbering

Many outlines require each heading in a document to be numbered, for clarity or for legal reasons (for example, the U.S. Defense Department has a procurement specification requiring all manuals it buys to use numbered headings; and most contracts use numbered headings to identify sections of the document). In some situations you want every paragraph, both headings and body text, to be numbered. You can apply outline numbering in outline view; the numbers become part of the document (they're not just artifacts of outline view), and appear in the document.

Outline numbering is controlled by one section of the Tools→Bullets and Numbering command. Here's how to number an outline:

1. Select the part of the outline to number. This has two parts:

   · To apply outline numbering only to headings (down to a specified level) or avoid numbering body text paragraphs, click the appropriate number button in the outline bar. To apply outline numbering to all paragraphs, including body text, click the [All] button.

   · Select the paragraphs you want to number, or use Edit→ Select All to select the entire document.

2. Use the Tools→Bullets and Numbering command to display the Bullets and Numbering dialog box. It has three versions, selected by the controls at the top; select Outline if it isn't already selected.

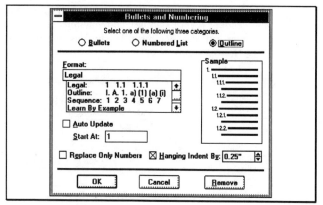

3. Select the number and formatting options you want to use (explained below).

4. Click |OK|.

The Format list lets you select the style of the numbers used in the outline:

- **Legal** uses only arabic numerals; each level is separated with a decimal point. Examples: 1.10, 1.10.9, 3.2.27, and so on.

- **Outline** uses a mixture of roman and arabic numerals with letters, and various separating punctuation (this is the numbering style many people are taught in school). First-level numbers use uppercase roman numerals; second-level numbers use capital letters; third-level numbers use arabic numerals; all separated with decimal points. Below that, Word uses lowercase letters, arabic numerals, and lowercase roman numerals; separated by parentheses.

- **Sequence** uses numbers in a simple numerical order.

- **Learn By Example** tells Word to look at sample number systems you've provided, figure out the pattern, and emulate it and apply it throughout the rest of the numbering. You must put a sample at the beginning of the first occurrence of each heading level, so Word knows which format to use at each level.

- **Outline All** is similar to Outline, except that it creates complete sequences of numbers (such as *II.A.7.g*), while Outline applies only the individual numbers for each level (for example, the first level header might be *II*, the second level header *A*, the third level header *7,* and the fourth level header *g).*

The Auto Update checkbox, if checked, tells Word to use AUTO-NUM fields to create outline numbers. If this option is turned off, Word inserts plain text. Also, when this option is turned on you can't enter a starting number in the Start At box, since AUTONUMOUT fields always start at 1.

If the Hanging Indent By box is checked (the default), Word formats the paragraph with the left indent shown in the box, formats the first line with the negative of the value in the box (a hanging indent, in which a value such as *.25* in the box corresponds to a -.25 first line indent), and separates the number and text with a tab. You can change the value in the box if you want a different hanging indent distance.

If Hanging Indent By is not checked, Word doesn't indent the paragraph and separates the number from the text with one space.

The Replace Only Numbers option controls whether Word adds (or updates) numbers to all paragraphs, or only to those that already have them. This is useful if you've selected several paragraphs, some already formatted with numbers and some not, and you want to change the number or the indentation; with Replace Only Numbers checked, Word only formats paragraphs already starting with outline numbers.

See also: Numbered Lists; Viewing Documents

PAGE FORMATTING

The layout of pages—page size and orientation, margins, and the paper source used when a document is printed—represent a document's most fundamental formatting. A major enhancement in Word 2.0 is the ability to have individual page formatting for each section of a document; you can even change the page orientation for separate sections.

You can control page margins with controls on the Ruler or in Print Preview mode, and all aspects of page formatting with the Format→ Page Setup command. We'll introduce the Page Setup dialog box, then cover each aspect of page formatting, with each of the available tools, separately.

The Format→Page Setup Command

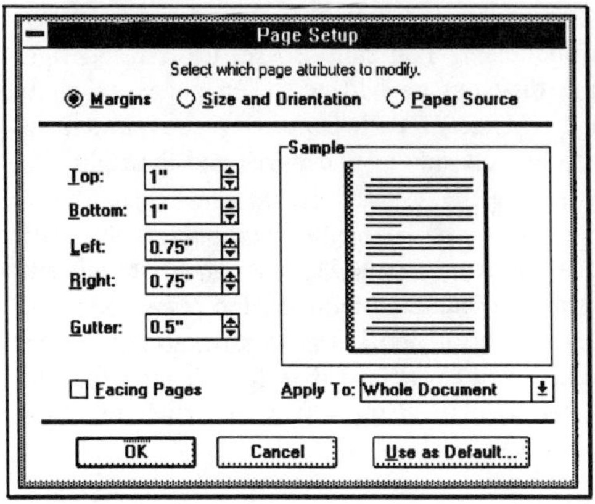

All page formatting begins with the Format→Page Setup command, with three associated dialog boxes. The first to be displayed shows the margin settings for the current section of the document.

Word 1.0/1.1 users: the old Format→Document command, with its massive jumble of page formatting settings and the template assignment control, has been replaced in Word 2.0 by the Format→Page Setup command. You now control a document's template with File→Template.

The Page Setup dialog box, like it's counterpart in earlier versions of Word, has a dangerous button labeled [Use as Default...]. This button lets you reflect the page setup you create in the Page Setup dialog box back to the current document template or to the global template NORMAL.DOT. It's intended as a convenient feature, when it is used carefully. Just be sure that you really intend to change page setup in the template for all future documents based on the template.

The three option buttons at the top of the Page Setup dialog box select which of the three variations on the dialog box to display. Each dialog box has the same sample page and the Apply To drop-down list controlling the scope of page formatting:

Whole Document — The selected page setup applies to all sections across the entire document.

This Section — The selected page setup applies only to the section currently containing the insertion point.

This Point Forward — The page setup applies to the current section, plus all sections after it, to the end of the document.

Selected Text — If text is selected, insert section breaks before and after the selection to create a new section; apply the page setup to the new section.

Selected Sections — If the selection spans more than one section, apply page setup to all sections "touched" by the selection.

Page Margins

You can control the size of the top, bottom, left, and right margins for each section in a document. You can also set up left and right margins so that they're different on odd and even pages, to allow room for binding on the inside of each page. (By convention, the "inside" of a page is on the left side of odd pages and the right side of even pages.)

You can use the Ruler in normal or page layout view to set left and right margins for the section containing the insertion point. Just drag the left or right bracket symbols ([and]) on the Ruler to the desired position. (The Ruler has several versions; if it doesn't look like the example below, click the symbol at the left of the ruler until the margin version is displayed.)

In print preview mode, you can drag lines representing the top, bottom, left, and right margins into place. You have the advantage, in print preview, of being able to see the entire page, so you can see how your margins interact with headers, footers, and page breaks. Use the File→Print Preview command to switch to print preview mode, and click the Margins button. Word displays four lines defining the margins (along with other indicators of text boundaries, page breaks, and so on). Each of the margin lines has a small square "handle"; position the pointer over a handle, hold down the mouse button, and drag the line to position the corresponding margin. Word doesn't immediately redraw the page, to allow you time to experiment or adjust your selection. Signal to Word that you're done by clicking the pointer in an empty space on the page, and Word will redraw the page according to the new margin setting.

The Page Setup dialog box gives you complete control over all margins. Simply enter a distance in the Top and Bottom text boxes.

The Left, Right, and Gutter text boxes, and the Facing Pages checkbox, interact to let you set up left and right margins that are different on odd and even pages. If you want the left and right margins to each be the same on all pages, enter zero in the Gutter text box, and leave Facing Pages unchecked.

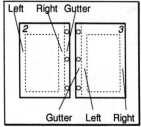

To specify an extra amount of space added to the left or right margins on odd or even pages, enter it into the Gutter text box. This amount is added to the left margin on odd pages, and to the right margin on even pages.

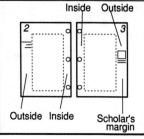

If you check Facing Pages, the names of the Left and Right text boxes change to Inside and Outside. This is an alternative to using a gutter setting with left and right margins. On odd pages, the outside margin is on the right, and the inside margin is on the left. On even pages, their positions are reversed. This allows you to set up a gutter on either side of the page, unlike the value you enter in the Gutter text box, which is always on the conventional inside of pages. The figure shows one situation where you'd want to have more white space on the outside than on the inside of pages—the fashionable textbook-style page layout with headings and art in the "scholar's margin" on the outside of each page. Material that appears in the scholar's margin must be in a frame formatted with the "outside" positioning style; see the topic "Frames" for more information.

Paper Size and Orientation

When you select Size & Orientation at the top of the Page Setup dialog box, Word changes the dialog box to show controls for paper size and orientation.

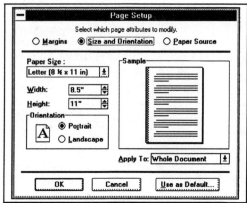

The Paper Size drop-down list shows several standard paper sizes currently in use: the legal and letter sizes used in the U.S., and the A and B metric sizes used in the rest of the world. (The available choices may depend on the currently selected printer.) It also has an option for Custom Size, which allows you to directly set the paper dimensions in the Width and Height text boxes.

The Orientation control group lets you select whether the page is printed in Portrait orientation (the paper's longest dimension oriented vertically), or Landscape (the paper's longest dimension oriented horizontally).

Selecting the Paper Source

A charming feature of Word 2.0 is the ability to select different paper sources (if you have a multiple-bin printer) for the first and subsequent pages of a document when it's printed. You can use letterhead for the first page of a letter, and blank paper for the rest of the letter, for example.

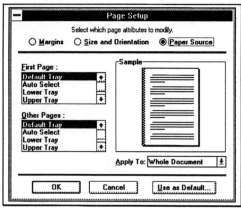

The choices shown in the two list boxes depends entirely on the capabilities reported to Word by the selected printer driver; the sample to the left shows a typical laser printer with two paper trays. The tray you select under First Page determines the paper source for the first page of a document; the tray you select under Other Pages selects the paper source for all the remaining pages of a document. Leave them both the same to use the same paper source for the entire document.

PAGINATION

Pagination is the process of determining where one page ends and another page begins when you print a document. Word can automatically paginate a document for you, or repaginate a document on command; you can use various paragraph settings or pagination settings in Tools→Options to influence automatic pagination; or you can insert manual page breaks where you want pages to end.

Automatic Pagination

Word documents are basically organized as a stream of text (and other objects) that flows from the upper-left corner of the first page, on through the document to its end. Word chops up the flow of text to make it fit within the margins of each printed page; this is automatic pagination.

In the General category of the Options dialog box (from the Tools→ Options command) is the Background Repagination checkbox. When this option is checked, Word automatically uses idle time to recalculate page breaks; it displays the result as a dotted line across the screen indicating where the page will break when printed. The page breaks computed by Word are called "soft" page breaks.

It's not entirely accurate to say that Word uses only idle time for background repagination. Often, with long documents, once Word starts repaginating, the process can temporarily take over your system and prevent you from doing anything else. If this is a problem, turn off background repagination. Then, when you want to see where page breaks will fall, use the Tools→Repaginate Now command to force Word to recompute page breaks.

You can influence how Word paginates a document by setting rules that modify pagination.

At the document level, the Print category in the Options dialog box
has the Widow/Orphan Control checkbox. When this option is turned
on, Word avoids breaking a paragraph across two pages when doing
so would leave the first line at the end of one page and the remainder
of the paragraph on the next (a widow), or would put just the last line
of a paragraph on the next page (an orphan). This setting is stored
with each document.

You can also influence automatic page breaks at the level of individual paragraphs, through these checkboxes in the Paragraph dialog
box (displayed with the Format→Paragraph command):

Page Break Before	Always starts this paragraph at the beginning of a page, regardless of the amount of white space left behind on the previous page (equivalent to putting a manual page break before the paragraph).
Keep With Next	If the paragraph after this one ends up on the next page, moves this paragraph also to the next page. This is useful for headings, for example, to make sure that they're not separated from the paragraph they introduce.
Keep Lines Together	Never breaks this paragraph across a page boundary; if any part of the paragraph would appear on the next page, moves the entire paragraph.

Manual Page Breaks

Manual page breaks are unequivocal instructions to Word to always
break a page where you indicate with a page break.

To insert a manual page break, press [Ctrl]+[↵], or select Page
Break (the default) in the Break dialog box displayed with the Insert
→Break command. Word displays a manual page break as a heavy
dotted line that's very similar to the dotted line that represents an
automatic page break. The definitive way to tell the difference is that
you can select a manual page break (in order to delete it, for example), while you can't select an automatic page break.

Another way to insert a page break is through a *section break*. You
can select a section break type either at the time you insert it (with
the Break dialog box), or with the Section Layout dialog box (displayed with the Format→Section Layout command) in an existing
section. Both methods give you five types of section breaks:

Continuous	No break; the section begins on a new page only if that's the natural breaking point.

New Column	Begins the section in a new column; equivalent to New Page in a single-column layout. (Not available with Insert→Break; use Format→Section Layout)
New Page	Begins the section on a new page, regardless of where the previous page ended.
Odd Page	Begins a section on the next odd page; doesn't break if the section is already on an odd page.
Even Page	Begins a section on the next even page.

Adjusting Page Breaks in Print Preview

You can drag page break symbols in Print Preview to adjust page breaks. Page breaks are represented by gray or dotted lines in print preview; move the cursor over the line until it changes to a plus symbol (+), then hold down the mouse button and drag the line.

You can adjust hard page breaks up or down (as far as the bottom of the page). Word actually moves the page break character within the document, so that material around the page break moves appropriately. Hard page breaks are represented in print preview with a darker or thicker line.

You can advance soft page breaks (those computed by Word) up the page; since soft page breaks represent the last possible place to break a page automatically, it wouldn't make sense to adjust them downward. However, advancing a soft page break turns it into a hard page break (logically enough, since it now signifies manual pagination), which you can then adjust up or down.

PARAGRAPHS

Back in the days of word processors that worked only with text, the definition of a paragraph was simple: a collection of text terminated by a carriage-return. Modern word processors, though, work with such a wide variety of objects—text, graphics, embedded objects, tables, footnote and annotation marks, and on and on—that we need a more general definition: a (modern) paragraph is a collection of objects grouped ahead of a paragraph marker.

Word's paragraph marker (displayed as ¶) is much more than a carriage return. The ¶ is a symbolic representation of all the formatting information associated with the paragraph; if you copy the paragraph marker to a new location, Word copies the formatting information it represents to the new location as well.

Word paragraphs have these formatting attributes, stored in the paragraph marker:

- *Alignment*—When a line in a paragraph is too long to fit between the page margins (plus the paragraph's indentations), Word automatically starts a new line in the paragraph; text that would have overrun one line is moved to the next line. A paragraph's alignment determines whether text in the paragraph "piles up" against the left margin ("flush left" and "ragged right"), or against the right margin ("flush right" and "ragged left"); is centered between the margins (ragged left and right); or whether each line is padded with a uniform amount of blank space ("justified") so that both the left and right edges of the paragraph are flush.

- *Indentation*—The amount of space between the left and right edges of the paragraph and the margins; as well as a separate indentation setting for the first line of the paragraph.

- *Interparagraph spacing*—The amount of space before and after the paragraph.

- *Line spacing*—The distance between lines in the paragraph.

- *Pagination*—Whether the paragraph can be split across pages, whether it must appear on the same page as the following paragraph, and whether it must always be the first paragraph on the page.

- *Line numbers*—For each section of a document, you can turn line numbering on and off (see the topic "Sections" for more information). You can suppress line numbering of individual paragraphs, if the section they're part of has line numbering turned on.

- *Tabs*—Each paragraph can have its own tab stops (the horizontal position to which text moves when you press the [⇥] key).

- *Border*—Each paragraph can have a border around it and shading in its interior. See "Borders and Shading" for more information.

(If you're a veteran of Word 1.0 or 1.1, you might be asking yourself, "What about positioning?" Word 2.0 has raised the concept of positioning to a new and useful level of abstraction by introducing the "frame" object for positioning things on the page. A frame can have its own border, can contain multiple paragraphs, and can be moved around and resized in Page Layout view. Information about frames is still stored in the paragraph markers, but since you work with frames as discrete entities, frames are covered separately in the topic "Frames").

The Format→Paragraph Command

You control all aspects of paragraph formatting in the Paragraph dialog box, which you display with the Format→Paragraph command, or by double-clicking in the top half of the Ruler.

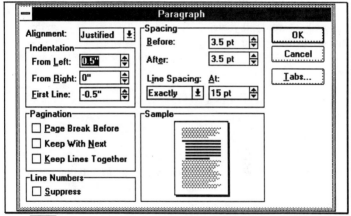

The Tabs button displays the Tabs dialog box to let you set the tab stops and types for the current paragraph. See the topic "Tabs" for more information about using that dialog box.

The Suppress checkbox under Line Numbers determines whether the current paragraph has line numbers, *if you've elected to print line numbers for the current section*. When this box is not checked, the paragraph conforms to the section's line numbers setting; when this box is checked, line numbers will not be printed regardless of the section's line numbers setting.

The Sample box shows a representation of the paragraph formatting you've selected. Use it for general guidance; it's too small to be an accurate picture of how the paragraph will be formatted.

Most of the remaining controls in the Paragraph dialog box have visual equivalents in the Toolbar, Ruler, and Ribbon. Below, we'll discuss each aspect of paragraph formatting separately, and describe all the related controls for each aspect.

Alignment

Word's paragraph alignment options come in four flavors:

Left alignment causes all text in the paragraph to be flush with the left margin. Lines end naturally at word or hyphen breaks on the right, giving the paragraph a "ragged right" appearance.

Right alignment is the mirror-image of left alignment: flush on the right, ragged on the left.

Center alignment causes all text in the paragraph to be centered between the margins.

Justified alignment means that Word will add a uniform amount of blank space between each word in a line so that both the left and right ends are flush with their respective margins.

To set paragraph alignment from the Paragraph dialog box, drop down the Alignment list box and select one of the four options.

To set paragraph alignment from the Ribbon, click on one of the paragraph alignment buttons:

Indentation

The *indentation* of a paragraph is the distance between its left and right edges and the page (or column) margins. A justified paragraph with zero indentation would be flush against the left and right margins (like most paragraphs in this book). Word lets you control three paragraph indents:

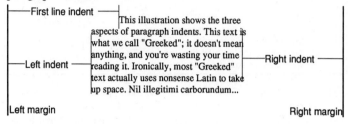

You can set the indentation to negative values. In the case of the left and right indents this causes the paragraph edges to protrude beyond the corresponding left and right margins. A negative first line indent is known as a "hanging indent":

This paragraph has a left indent of 0.5 inches, and a first line indent of -0.5 inches. Thus, the first line is flush with the left margin, while the rest of the paragraph is indented 0.5 inches.

To set paragraph indents in the Paragraph dialog box, enter the appropriate values in the From Left, From Right, and First Line boxes.

To set paragraph indents with the Ruler, drag the left and right indent indicators into position.

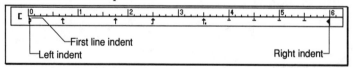

You can drag the first line indent marker (the top triangle) independently of the left indent marker. However, the left indent marker (the bottom marker) is locked to the first line indent marker and normally moves in tandem with it. You can move it independently by holding down ⌷Shift⌷ while you drag the marker.

Interparagraph Spacing

Word lets you directly specify the amount of space before and after a paragraph. The actual space between paragraphs on the printed page is a function of those two settings and line spacing, as shown here:

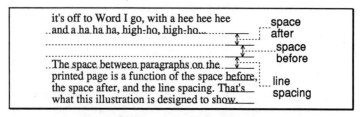

Typesetters generally specify interparagraph spacing in terms of a "baseline-to-baseline" distance—the distance from the bottom of text in the preceding paragraph to the bottom of the first line of text in the next paragraph. That's almost, but not quite, how Word does it:

Baseline-to-Baseline = Space after + Space before + Line Spacing

To set interparagraph spacing in the Paragraph dialog box, enter the appropriate values in the Before and After boxes.

Word 1.0 and 1.1 veterans might be looking for the Ribbon buttons that used to allow you to set the space between paragraphs to zero or one line. They're not available on the Ribbon any longer, but if you really want them you can use the Toolbar section of Tools→Options to assign the CloseUpPara or OpenUpPara commands to Toolbar buttons.

Line Spacing

Word gives you six methods of controlling the spacing between lines in a paragraph. The line spacing is measured from the baseline (bottom of characters that don't descend below the line, such as "n") of one line of text to the baseline of the next line. Select the line spacing method in the Line Spacing box in the Paragraph dialog box.

Auto   The line spacing is allowed to "float" to accommodate the largest character on each line, plus two points of leading (a typographer's term for additional space between the top of the highest character and the baseline of the line above). Notice how, in the next line, the very tall X forces this line's spacing to be greater than the other lines in the paragraph.

Single   The line spacing is exactly one line (12 points, as defined by Word) plus two points leading, for a total of 14 points.

1.5 Lines The line spacing is 1.5 lines (18 points) plus two points leading, for a total of 20 points.

Double   The line spacing is two lines (24 points) plus two points leading, for a total of 26 points.

At least   Specifies a minimum line spacing (in the At box); taller characters or graphics can force a larger line spacing, but the line spacing can't be less than the amount specified in the At box.

Exactly   Specifies an exact line spacing in the At box. Characters or graphics in lines that are larger than this amount are clipped, like the large X in this line.

(Word 1.0 and 1.1 veterans: Yes, the Ribbon buttons that used to set single, 1.5, or double line spacing have been removed. You can add equivalent buttons to the Toolbar by associating Toolbar buttons with the SpacePara1, SpacePara15, or SpacePara2 commands.)

Controlling the Behavior of Paragraphs at Page or Column Breaks

By default, Word is free to split a paragraph in half if a page or column break falls in the middle of a paragraph (subject to the limitations of widow/orphan control during printing; see the topic "Printing"). There are many situations in which that isn't appropriate; for example, you'd never want a heading to be separated from the text that follows it, nor, by the same token, would you want to let a heading split across a page break. You can control how Word splits, or doesn't split, paragraphs at page/column boundaries with the Pagination options in the Paragraph dialog box.

Option	When checked...	When not checked...
Page Break Before	Forces the paragraph to begin at the top of the next page.	No page break.
Keep With Next	If the next paragraph after the current paragraph moves to the next page, Word moves this paragraph to keep them together.	If the next paragraph after the current paragraph moves to the next page, Word leaves this paragraph on the current page.
Keep Lines Together	Does not split the paragraph if a page break falls in the middle of it; moves the entire paragraph to the next page.	Allows this paragraph to be split by a page break.

Reusing Paragraph Formatting

It would be tedious beyond endurance to have to manually format each paragraph in your document. Luckily, Word provides three mechanisms for leveraging your efforts:

- You can record paragraph formatting in a *style*. Each style has a unique name, and the information about the style is stored in the document's "style sheet" or in a template. You can then apply the style to other paragraphs, and the paragraphs will take on all the formatting associated with the style. See the topic "Styles" for more information.

- You can copy formatting from one paragraph to another:

  1. Position the insertion point inside the paragraph to *receive* the formatting.

  2. Move the pointer into the style area (the empty area to the left of text) next to the paragraph that will *supply* the formatting.

  3. Hold down [Ctrl]+[Shift] and click the mouse button.

- Once you've set up the formatting in a paragraph, pressing [↵] "clones" a new paragraph with the same formatting; you can do this repeatedly to create a sequence of paragraphs with the same formatting. Exception: If the paragraph has a style that specifies a different style for the next paragraph, then that setting takes precedence.

See also: Borders and Shading, Bulleted Lists, Character Formatting, Frames, Headers and Footers, Numbered Lists, Ribbon, Ruler, Styles, Tabs, Toolbar

PICTURES

"What is the use of a book," thought Alice, "without pictures or conversations?"
—From *Alice in Wonderland*, by Lewis Carroll

The combination of text with graphics is your most powerful tool for communicating your ideas. Word recognizes the importance of graphics, and makes using them as natural as using text. At the most basic level, you insert pictures into the document from the Clipboard or from a file. Word offers further refinements, such as linking and embedding, that let you create automatically updated and managed graphics within your Word documents.

Of Bitmaps and Metafiles

Word's *picture* can be either of the two types of graphics supported by Microsoft Windows:

Bitmaps Images you obtain from scanners, screen captures, and clip art PCX files, and images you create with Windows Paintbrush or other painting programs, are all bitmaps. Bitmaps consist of a series of dots, or *pixels*, much like a television picture. In a monochrome bitmap, each dot is either black or white; in a color bitmap, each dot can assume a color. (The number of available colors can vary, depending on the type of device that produced the bitmap; captures from a standard VGA screen, for example, have sixteen colors.)

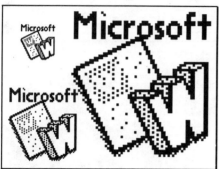

The most important thing to know about bitmaps is that they have a fixed *resolution*—the number of dots horizontally and vertically can't change once the picture is created. This means that when you *scale* a bitmap (enlarge or reduce it), you don't get any more or less picture inform-ation. When you enlarge a bitmap, it simply becomes "coarser," as each dot is enlarged.

Windows bitmaps are stored in files with the .BMP extension. You can insert BMP files directly into a document with the Insert→Picture command. You can also exchange bitmaps through the Clipboard with other Windows applications.

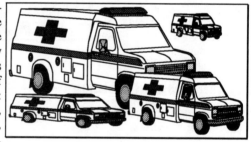

Metafiles Windows metafiles are true drawings. The information they contain is stored as descriptions of geometric objects: lines, rectangles, circles, curves, text, and so on.

The dimensions of each object are stored as numbers, so that metafiles can be scaled freely without introducing distortion into the picture. In addition, if you scale a picture differently in the horizontal and vertical dimensions, you can distort a metafile, as shown by the lower left ambulance in the figure above.

Converting File Formats

Word 2.0 comes with a set of *graphic filters* that convert graphic files from several file formats produced by popular applications into one of the two standard Windows formats; the converted results are

what Word inserts into your document when you use the Insert→
Picture command.

The file formats listed in the Picture dialog box depend on the
choices you made when you installed Word 2.0.

Bitmap File Formats	Drawing File Formats
Windows BMP	Windows Metafile (WMF)
PC Paintbrush (PCX)	Encapsulated PostScript (EPS)
Tagged Image File Format (TIFF)	AutoCAD Data Exchange (DXF); two dimensions only.
	AutoCAD Plotter Format (PLT)
	Computer Graphics Metafile (CGM)
	HP Graphic Language (HPGL)
	DrawPerfect (WPG)
	Micrografx Designer (DRW)
	Lotus 1-2-3 Graphics (PIC)

Your copy of Word may offer other formats; see the file GRAPH-
ICS.DOC that came with Word for information about specific filters.

Only the Windows BMP and WMF formats guarantee that nothing
will be lost in the converted image, since they're the "official" Windows formats. Any other conversion has the potential for omission
and distortion, because other applications, even Windows applications, may use graphic features that aren't supported by BMP or
WMF. For example, the Micrografx Designer 3.0 filter supplied with
Word omits Designer's gradient fills, as shown in this test drawing:

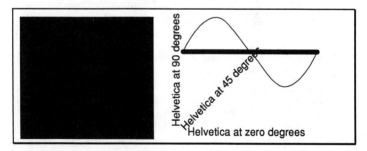

Yet the filter does a good job on text, thick lines, and Bezier curves.
Meanwhile, here's the same picture copied through the Clipboard
from Designer and pasted into a Word document:

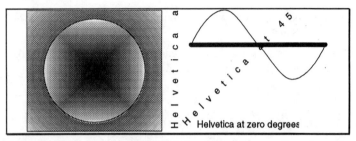

Helvetica at zero degrees

Gradient fills come through fairly cleanly, but the spacing of text is off. The lesson: In most cases if you want to include pictures from a Windows application, and you have a copy of the application, transferring the picture through the Clipboard will work better. When it doesn't, you should try the filter.

Inserting Pictures

To transfer a picture through the Clipboard into a document, start the application that created the drawing (the "source"). In the source, use that program's method for copying something to the Clipboard (usually selecting all or part of the drawing, and using the Edit→Copy command). Return to Word, position the insertion point where you want the picture to be inserted, and use the Edit→Paste command or press ⌈Ctrl⌉+⌈V⌉ or ⌈Shift⌉+⌈Ins⌉. You can also select a picture in Word and copy it to the Clipboard.

To insert a picture from a file into a document, position the insertion point where you want to insert the picture, and select the Insert→Picture command. Word displays the Picture dialog box.

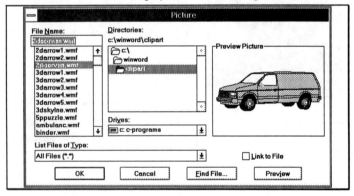

Part of this dialog box is a standard set of file selection controls; use them to pick a file to insert.

The List Files of Type drop-down list shows the file types recognized by the installed graphic filters. The default type shows any file name (*.*); when you pick a file, Word relies on the file's extension to determine which filter to use. If you pick a specific graphic file type, the file list changes to show only files of that type. If you want to insert a graphic file that has a nonstandard extension (for example, some graphic programs produce HPGL output to files with the extension .PLT, rather than the conventional .PGL), first select the correct file type for the file, then type in either the complete name of the file, or a wildcard with the extension you're looking for ("*.PLT" for example).

Once you've selected a file, you can click the Preview button to see a sample of the graphic in the Preview Picture box. Word will convert the graphic if it has to, to be able to display it. When you're ready to insert the picture, click OK.

The Find File... button displays the Find File dialog box to let you search for the file you want. Use this if you're having trouble locating a file.

The Link to File checkbox, when checked, tells Word to insert an IMPORT field referring to the file containing the picture, rather than the picture itself. Linking to a graphic file means that each time the IMPORT field is updated, Word will read in the linked file and update your document; if the linked file has changed, the picture will change with it. See the topic "Embedding and Linking" for more information.

Word has an irritating habit of automatically scaling pictures you insert to fill all of the available space (expanding it to fill the width between margins, for example), whether you want it to or not. You'll often have to use the Format→Picture command immediately after inserting a picture to get the scaling you want (see "Formatting Pictures" below for more information). If you'd like to override Word's rescaling of pictures, see the topic "Macros"; it provides a sample macro that redefines the Insert→Picture command to restore a picture to 100% after inserting it.

Formatting Pictures

You can put a border around a picture by selecting it and using the Format→Border command. See the topic "Borders and Shading" for more information. You can position a picture by enclosing it in a frame, and positioning the frame; see the topic "Frames."

The Format→Picture command displays the Picture dialog box, which you use to scale and crop pictures. (This command is only available when you have a picture selected.)

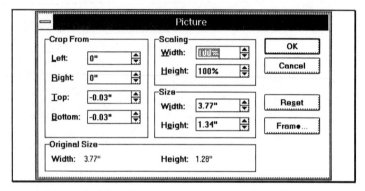

Scaling a picture means adjusting its height and width. The bottom of the Picture dialog box shows the selected picture's original dimensions. You can change the size of the picture in terms of percentage by entering scaling factors in the Width and Height boxes in the Scaling control group; or you can specify the picture's exact finished size (after scaling) by entering dimensions into the Size group's Width and Height boxes. In either case, you can enter different values for height and width to resize a picture differently in the horizontal and vertical dimensions.

A note about scaling bitmaps: Bitmaps don't resize well, because their resolution is fixed: Making a bitmap larger merely makes its dots larger and the picture "grainy" overall; while reducing the size of a bitmap forces Word to decide which dots to discard or merge together. You get the best results when you enlarge a bitmap by an integer amount (200%, 300%, and so on) because Word simply has to double or triple the dots in the bitmap.

Cropping means adjusting the size of the rectangle containing the picture, without changing the size of the picture itself (just like cropping a photograph). You might want to do this if the picture has unnecessary white space around its edges, or if you want to focus on one part of the image and leave out parts near the edges. When you apply a border style to a picture, the border is applied to the rectangle containing the picture, so that cropping a picture affects the size of its border.

The Picture dialog box has text boxes in the Crop From control group for Left, Right, Top, and Bottom crop dimensions.

Positive crop values move the picture's boundary inward; negative values move the boundary away from the picture, as shown here:

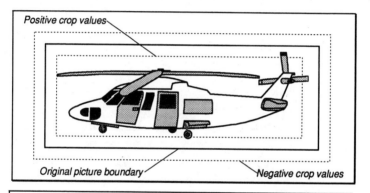

See also: Borders and Shading; Draw (Microsoft Draw); Embedding and Linking; Fields; Frames

PRINTING

Most Word documents ultimately end up printed, usually more than once. Word relies on the Windows printing facilities (printer drivers and the Print Manager) to print your document, so that, as long as your printer is supported by Windows, you can print any document.

If all you want to do is print all of the current document, click the 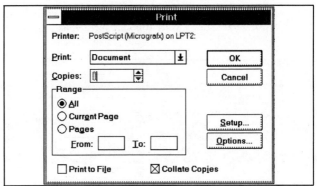⬚ (Print) button on the Toolbar; this tells Word to send the entire document to the currently selected printer.

Here's the general procedure for printing a document:

1. Select a printer using the File→Print Setup command. If you need to adjust the printer's setup, click the ⎡Setup⎤ button to display the printer's settings dialog box (this dialog box is different for each printer, because it shows options specific to that printer).

2. Use the File→Print command to display the Print dialog box.

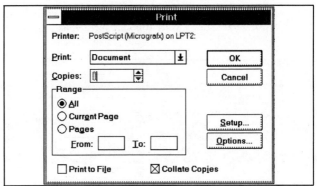

3. Select the printing options you want to use (discussed in detail below), then click ⎡OK⎤; Word starts sending the document to the printer.

Step one presupposes that you've formatted your document the way you'd like it to print. You can (and should) review page formatting using the File→Print Preview command to switch Word to print preview display mode. See the topic "Pagination" for instructions on using print preview mode.

Print Dialog Box Options

To control what part of your document is printed, select options from the Range control group in the Print dialog box:

- **All** tells Word to print the entire document.

- The second option is different depending on whether or not you have anything currently selected in the document:

  · **Current Page** is an option with nothing selected; it tells Word to print only the page containing the insertion point.

  · **Selection** appears when you have something selected; it tells Word to print only what is selected.

- **Pages,** and its associated From and To text boxes, lets you specify an inclusive range of pages to print. If you move the cursor directly to the From or To boxes and enter something, Word automatically selects the Pages option. Note that the page numbers you enter here are the page numbers set within the document; if your document starts on page 5, enter **5** to print the first page rather than **1**. If page numbers are restarted in your document, Word will print all the pages that have page numbers within the range you specify (for example, if you restart page numbering at 1 in the middle of your document and specify a page range of 1 to 5, Word will print both page 1s, both page 2s, through both page 5s).

To print more than one copy of a document, enter the number of copies to print in the Copies text box. If the Collate Copies checkbox is checked, Word sends the entire document to the printer once for each copy selected. If Collate Copies is turned off, Word sends each page to the printer the selected number of times before proceeding to the next page.

To send print output to a file instead of to a printer, check the Print to File checkbox. This option causes Word to tell the selected printer driver to print to a file instead of the printer, and the printer driver will prompt you for a file name. Most printer drivers support this feature. You can use this option to prepare print files for output on a printer you don't have direct access to (such as a printer connected to somebody else's computer), or to transfer them to a service bureau, for example to get typeset output.

Most of the time, you'll be printing just the current document. The Print drop-down list lets you select other things to print besides the default Document:

- **Summary Info** prints the document's summary information (author, title, keywords, date, and so on). You can edit some of this information with the File→Summary Info command.

- **Annotations** prints just the annotations in a document.
- **Styles** prints a catalog of the paragraph styles defined for the current document.
- **Glossary** prints a catalog of the glossary entries.
- **Key Assignments** prints a catalog of the commands and macros assigned to keys.

Selecting an option from the Print drop-down list prints that item separately. You can also choose to print summary information and annotations along with a document by selecting those options in the Print category of the Options dialog box (explained below).

Clicking Setup... displays the setup dialog box for the currently selected printer. The setup dialog box is different for each printer driver. Clicking Options... displays the Options dialog box (from the Tools→Options command) with the Print category selected. These options are explained next.

The Print Category in the Options Dialog Box

Word has several printing options that apply to all documents (not just the current document) that are part of the customizations available with the Tools→Options command. When the Options dialog box is displayed, select the Print category (the 🖨 icon in the Category list). This dialog box also appears when you click the Options... button in the Print dialog box.

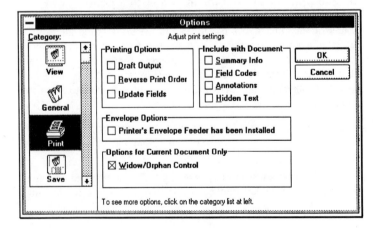

The *Printing Options* Control Group

Draft Output, when on, causes Word to print your document without formatting. The exact results depend on your printer; at one extreme the printed output may be analogous to the Draft view mode, in which characters are all one font, and bold, italic, and so on are shown underlined; in other cases, such as with a PostScript laser printer, Word may show correct fonts and character formatting.

Reverse Print Order, when on, causes Word to print your document starting at the last page and printing toward the first page. This is handy if your document delivers output face-up.

Update Fields, if on, causes Word to first update a document's fields before printing the document.

The *Include with Document* Control Group

These options control what's printed *in addition to* your document. You can also elect to print summary info and annotations separately through the Print list box on the Print dialog box.

Summary Info, when on, prints the information from the Summary Info dialog box on a separate page after the document.

Field Codes, when on, causes Word to print the codes inside fields, rather than field results.

Annotations prints a document's annotations on separate pages after the document.

Hidden Text, when on, causes Word to print hidden text. Normally, hidden text does not appear when a document is printed (that's why you use hidden text).

The *Envelope Options* Control Group

There's currently just one envelope option: Printer's Envelope Feeder Has Been Installed. This simply means that the selected Windows printer driver has told Word that the printer has an envelope feeder.

The *Options for Current Document Only* Control Group

These options are stored with the document, and may be set individually for each document.

Widow/Orphan Control, when off, lets Word break paragraphs wherever necessary from one page to the next. When this option is on, Word is prohibited from leaving behind just a single line at the end of a page (a "widow") when it breaks a paragraph onto the next page, or from moving just the the paragraph's last line onto the next page (an "orphan"). Word must, instead, move at least the last two lines of a paragraph onto the next page to prevent an orphan, or move the entire paragraph to the next page to prevent a widow.

A second option, **Use TrueType Fonts As Defaults**, appears in the dialog box only if you're using Windows 3.1 (or later). TrueType is a font manager similar to Adobe Type Manager, and was developed jointly by Microsoft and Apple as an alternative to Adobe PostScript.

> **See also:** Annotations; Breaks; Customizing Word for Windows; Glossaries; Headers and Footers; Page Formatting; Pagination; Sections.

PRINT MERGE

Decades of junk mail have demonstrated how print merge works: it allows you to create customized versions of documents based on information in some kind of database. You often see examples like the above, in which the database is a mailing list. Everybody on the mailing list gets a "personalized" post card with his or her name, city, and state, and often other "personal" information. Print merge has many other uses: sending memos to distribution lists, business form letters, address books, catalogs, directories, and on and on. It can be a tremendous time saver.

Print Merge Concepts

Print merge got its name from what it does: it *merges* a *data file,* containing the information that's different for each document printed, with a *merge document,* a master "template" containing the parts of the document that are the same each time it's printed.

A data file is organized into *records* and *fields.* Each record contains all the information required for each document that's printed; Word prints the document once for each record. Records, in turn, are organized as a series of fields; each field is a single item of information that's inserted into the merge document. Records and fields are analogous to the rows and columns of a table; in fact, one kind of data file that Word works with is a table in a Word document.

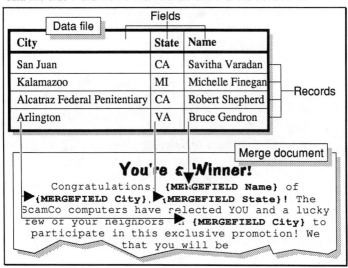

Each field in the data file has a name. You can include the names as the first record of the data file, called the *header record* (each name goes in its corresponding field), or you can put the field names in a separate file called a *header file*. Each field name corresponds to one or more of Word's fields embedded in the merge document. These are MERGEFIELD fields, and each contains the name of the corresponding field in the data file. In our ScamCo example, their mailing list has a field called *Name*. Everywhere that the lucky recipient's name should appear, there's a field like this:

{MERGEFIELD Name}

That's what you'd see if you had field code display turned on (the View→Field Codes command). With field code display turned off, Word shows the name of the field enclosed in the left and right guillemet characters: « and ». The Name field would look like this with field code display off:

«Name»

When the document is print merged (not printed), Word substitutes a name from the data file.

Word can print merge from many kinds of data files:

- A Word document consisting solely of a table; each row in the table is a record, and each column is a field. Field names make up the first row of the table.

- A Word document or a plain text file in which each record is a paragraph (ends in a carriage return), and each field is separated by either a comma or a tab (you must use one or the other consistently; you can't mix them).

- A file created by one of the database or spreadsheet programs for which Word has a file conversion filter. Word 2.0 includes filters for Microsoft Excel and Lotus 1-2-3 spreadsheets, dBASE database files, and WordPerfect data files.

Data files based on Word tables can have no more than 31 fields (columns). If you need more fields in each record, you must use a text file delimited with commas or tabs. The filters convert database and spreadsheet files with fewer than 32 fields to tables; otherwise, they're converted to comma- or tab-delimited text files.

Basic Print Merge

Word 2.0 has a helpful facility that walks you through the process of print merging a document. You can use this basic print merge for the majority of your print merge projects.

You can use this system to work with existing data files, or to create new one. We will go through the full scenario here, and note where you could have done things another way. These are the steps for a basic print merge operation:

1. Start or open the merge document. This can be based on any template.

2. Use the File→Print Merge command. Word displays the Print Merge Setup dialog box:

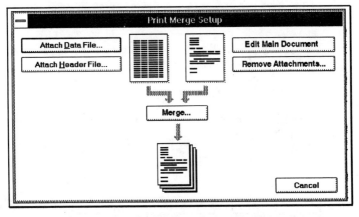

This is the "control panel" for Word's many print merge options. Edit Main Document would move you to the window containing your merge document. Remove Attachments... removes the information Word embeds in the Merge document associating it with a data file, and converts it to an ordinary Word document; in other words, this breaks the connection between the document and the data or header file.

3. Click Attach Data File.... Word displays the Attach Data File dialog box.

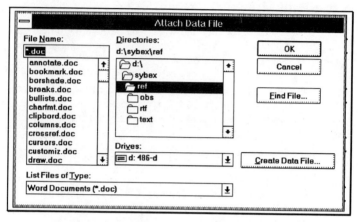

This dialog box attaches a data file to the merge document. If you already had a data and/or header file, you would select it and attach it to the document by clicking $\boxed{OK}$. The List Files of Type drop-down list shows text formats Word can read; if you want to import a database or spreadsheet file, select All Files (*.*) to view every kind of file, select the file you want, and Word will convert it with the installed filters.

4. Click $\boxed{\text{Create Data File...}}$. Word displays the Create Data File dialog box.

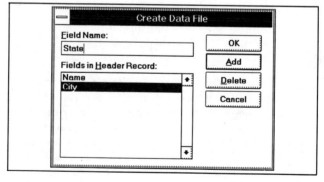

5. Use this dialog box to design the data file. You can enter the field names in any order. Enter a name in the Field Name box, and click $\boxed{\text{Add}}$ to add it to the Fields in Header Record list.

Continue entering names and adding them until you're done. If you change your mind about a field, select it in the Fields in Header Record list and click [Delete].

6. When you've entered all the field names for the data file, click [OK]. Word will display the Save As dialog box so that you can give your data file a name and save it.

Word now starts a new document with the file name you entered, based on the DATAFILE.DOT template included with Word 2.0. It creates a table with two rows: the top row contains the field names, and forms the *header record*; the second row is blank.

7. Start entering data into the table. Press the tab ([→]) key to advance from one cell to the next. When you reach the end of the last row in the table, press [→] to start a new, blank row.

Each row in this table is a record; each column is a field. Enter as much data as you need in each cell, even if it takes several lines. You can insert paragraph markers by pressing [↵], and line breaks with [Shift]+[↵].

If you intend to leave a field (cell) blank (and print nothing in the merged document), be sure you don't type a space, since the space would appear in the merged document.

Word changes the middle part of the Toolbar, adding several buttons that run DATAFILE.DOT's data file management macros. These macros are also attached to the Tools menu, through the items Database Management Tools and Record Management Tools. Each button has a letter on it.

A Add record	**G** Goto record number
D Delete record	**F** add Field
E Edit record	**S** Sort data file
C Check (run several diagnostic tests)	**L** Link (create a DDE link in a cell to an external file)
N Insert record number field, or update existing record numbers	**M** go to the Merge document

8. When you're done entering data into the data file, do one of these things:

   · Close the datafile. You can open it later to enter new data or edit data. Make sure the insertion point is in the merge document after the data file's document window closes.

   · Move the merge document by clicking the M button in the Toolbar. This leaves your data file open.

9. Create the merge document. Most of the work is ordinary word processing, like any other document.

   Word adds a print merge toolbar to the merge document's window:

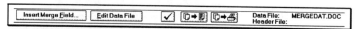

   Click Edit Data File to open or switch to the data file associated with the merge document.

   Position the insertion point wherever you want a merge field to be printed in your document, and click Insert Merge Field... to display the Insert Merge Field dialog box. It has two lists: One shows the merge fields assigned in the data file; the other shows Word field types that you might want to use in a merge document (you can use other Word fields; these are just the field types most often used in merge documents). Select a merge field or Word field, and click OK to insert it into your document.

10. Click ✓ to have Word perform a dry-run of the print merge. It tests the data file and the merge document to see if they'll print merge correctly.

11. Print merge the document. There are two kinds of print merge you can use:

    · Click ⟦□→🖨⟧ to print merge to the printer.

    · Click ⟦□→🗎⟧ to print merge to a file. This creates a new Word document containing multiple copies of the merge document. Word fills in the appropriate information from the data file into the merge fields in each copy (the MERGEFIELD fields are replaced by the data).

Both buttons begin the print merge immediately, and don't give you the chance to set any print merge options (although merging to a printer does let you set print options).

If you would like to set up print merge options, such as record selection and the technique for handling blank fields, click Merge in the Print Merge Setup dialog box to display the Print Merge dialog box, which gives you access to print merge options. These options are covered briefly in "Advanced Print Merge" below.

Advanced Print Merge

Word has a cornucopia of print merge options and advanced techniques. We have the space here to only skim the surface, to point you in the right direction and suggest what you can do. Use Word's online help for more information, or crack the manual.

Print Merge Options

When you use the File→Print Merge command in a merge document, and click Merge in the Print Merge Setup dialog box, Word displays the Print Merge dialog box:

The Merge Results control group corresponds to the three buttons on the print merge toolbar in a merge document. You can elect to send output to the printer or to a file; or you can have Word do a dry run to check for errors.

The Print Records control group lets you print either all the records in a data file, or a range of record numbers.

The options in Treatment of Blank Lines Caused by Empty Fields select how Word will deal with the case of a merge field all by itself in a paragraph, when the merge field produces no result. A common example is the second line of an address, usually used for a suite or apartment number; if that information is not present, should Word print a blank line or not?

The Record Selection button lets you select specific records from the data file to print, based on various comparison criteria. It displays the Record Selection dialog box:

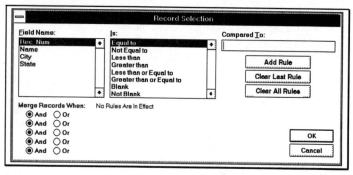

This dialog box sets up rules that determine whether a particular record is printed. Select the name of a merge field from the Field Name list, a comparison method from the Is box (is Equal to, is Blank, and so on), and then enter what the field is being compared against in the Compared To box: a number or a text string.

As you define rules, they're listed in the bottom half of the dialog box. You control how the rules are combined with the Merge Records When options: And means that this rule *and* the preceding one must both be satisfied; Or means that if this rule *or* the preceding rule, or both, are true, then the record is printed.

Clear Last Rule and Clear All Rules let you remove any or all rules from the list.

Other Word Fields Used in Print Merge Documents

Several of Word's field types affect how print merge works. See the entries for these field types in the topic "Fields":

- ASK and FILLIN fields prompt the user for information at the time you perform the print merge; the information they obtain is stored in bookmarks, which may be referenced by bookmark fields to produce results in the merge document.

- The SET field defines a bookmark. Bookmark fields can be used in the merge document to reproduce the text of the bookmark.

- MERGEREC inserts the current record number during a print merge.

- The NEXT field advances to the next data file record, without starting a new document. This is useful in a catalog, for example, when you want to print several records in tabular format on a single page, in a single document.

- The SKIPIF field lets you set up criteria by which Word decides whether or not to print a data record; if the condition is true, the record is skipped and no document is printed. The NEXTIF field is similar, but like NEXT you use it in situations where you don't want to start a new document, but rather to skip to the next record to be printed within the document.

- IF fields can be used to print individual merge fields, or any other text, based on conditions specified in the field.

Miscellaneous Advanced Print Merge Techniques

If you're working with a data file that's a Word table, you can add fields to the table by adding a column to the table. Be sure to include a name for the field in the header record (the first row in the table).

If you add a field to a plain text data file (one whose records are marked by carriage returns, and fields are separated by tabs or commas), be sure that you add space for the field to each record. Add an extra tab or comma where necessary to allocate room for blank fields.

In data files in Word documents, where the records and fields are defined by a table, you can use DDE and link fields in cells to get information for the print merge from external sources. You treat the data file table as a sort of staging area, which collects the information from linked files and then passes it in to the print merge operation.

Header files aren't normally required when you use a Word table or a plain text data file. They can come in handy when you're importing a spreadsheet or database file, because the header file can hold the names you've assigned to fields.

You can change the data file associated with a merge document; the only requirement is that the new data file must have the same field layout as the old one. With the File→Print Merge command, click the ⌗Attach Data File⌗ button and select the new file.

If you're a speed typist, you might find it easier to insert merge fields by typing them rather than selecting them from a dialog box. Press ⌗Ctrl⌗+⌗F9⌗ to insert empty field markers, then type **MERGEFIELD**, a space, and the name of the merge field.

You can set up templates as merge documents. When you do so, you store the data file association, merge field names, and so on in the template. New documents based on the template will inherit this framework, allowing you to concentrate on the contents of the merge document. For example, if you frequently send out form letters to people on a specific mailing list, create a template attached to the mailing list data file. Then, when you write a form letter based on that template, you'll have all the merge field names ready for you to insert into the document.

Word 2.0 includes a template called MAILLABL.DOT that sets up a print merge for mailing labels. It has macros to set up data files, select label size and sheet layout, and also to print individual labels.

See also: Exchanging Documents with Other Programs; Fields; Printing; Tables

REVISION MARKS

Revision marks are useful when a document undergoes repeated cycles of editing and review, because they identify those areas of a document that have been changed. You can turn revision marking on and off while you work, and you can remove the markings when you're ready to finalize the document.

<u>In this paragraph, this text has been added</u>, and ~~this text has been deleted~~. Notice that the deleted text remains and is formatted with overstriking, while the new text is underlined. Notice also that there is a revision bar beside this paragraph. These three features of revision marking give reviewers complete information about changes that have been made (<u>obviously, this sentence was added after revision marking was turned on</u>).

Use the command Tools→Revision Marks to display the Revision Marks dialog box.

To turn on revision marking, click the Mark Revisions checkbox. From now until you turn off revision marking, all edits will be marked. After you turn off revision marking, the revision marks remain, but any new edits will not be marked. The legend "MRK" is displayed in the status bar while revision marking is in effect.

Choose the revision bar style by selecting an option from the Revision Bars group. None means no revision bars; Left and Right position the revision bars at those positions in the margin, outside text; and Outside positions the revision bars in the outside margin when you have set up your pages with a gutter for odd/even alternation.

Choose how new text is marked by selecting an option from the Mark New Text With group. Note that deleted text is always marked with strike-through characters.

Click Search to look for revisions. The search proceeds forward from the insertion point; at the end of the document you will be prompted to continue searching from the beginning of the document.

To incorporate revisions:

- Click Accept Revisions to have Word delete all text marked with strike-throughs and remove underlining from new text. If you've selected text, only that text is affected; if no text is selected then Word accepts revisions for the entire document.

- Click Undo Revisions to have Word delete all new text marked with underlining, and remove strike-through from the text marked for deletion. The operation applies either to selected text, or the whole document if no text is selected.

To compare two versions of a file and mark the differences between them, select Tools→Compare Versions while you have the newer version of the document open. Then select the older version in the dialog box. Word will use the older version as a reference to mark the new document where it's different from the old document.

See also: Annotations, Printing

THE RIBBON

The Ribbon is a series of buttons that gives you quick access to various formatting features. The Ribbon and each of its buttons are identified below.

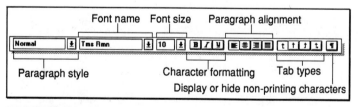

Font name   Font size   Paragraph alignment

| Normal | Tms Rmn | 10 | B I U | ≡ ≡ ≡ ≡ | t t t t | ¶ |

Paragraph style   Character formatting   Tab types
                    Display or hide non-printing characters

| Normal ± |
| Paragraph style |

Clicking the arrow on this box drops down a list of paragraph styles. Select from the list to apply a style. If the style you select has the same name as the style of the current paragraph, and you've manually changed the paragraph's formatting, Word asks you if you'd like to redefine that style according to the manual formatting (this is sometimes called "formatting by example").

The left box lists the names of the fonts available on your system (a function of the selected printer and the screen fonts you've installed in Windows). The right box lets you select a point size.

These buttons apply bold (the B button), italic (*I*) or underlining (u) to selected text.

These buttons control whether the selected paragraph is aligned to the left, center, right, or is justified.

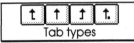

These buttons select a tab type that you can apply to the ruler by clicking at the appropriate location on the ruler. The buttons signify (in order): left, center, right, and decimal tabs.

Causes Word to display or hide non-printing characters (paragraph marks, tab and space symbols, and so on).

THE RULER

The Ruler is displayed (or not displayed) individually in each document window. As the name implies, it shows dimensions across the width of the printed page. You can select the unit of measure with the Tools→Options command, in the General options category.

The View→Ruler command controls whether the Ruler is displayed in a particular window. There are actually several rulers, each of which provides a visual way to set some aspect of a document's formatting. Sometimes Word switches automatically to a particular ruler; for example, when you move into a table Word displays the table ruler. You can switch to another ruler yourself by clicking on the symbol at the far left of the ruler.

The Paragraph Ruler

The Paragraph Ruler lets you set the indentations of a paragraph and its tab stops.

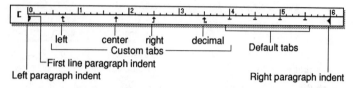

To set paragraph indents, drag the triangle symbols into position. The top symbol, showing the first line indent, can be dragged freely. The bottom symbol, left indent, is normally locked to the top symbol, and moves in tandem with it. You can move the left indent marker independently by holding down [Shift] while you drag the symbol.

To move a tab stop, drag its symbol left or right. **To remove a tab stop,** drag its symbol off the Ruler.

To set a tab stop, select the desired tab type from the Ribbon, then click in the bottom half of the Ruler to set the tab stop.

The Table Ruler

When the insertion point is inside a table, the Table Ruler lets you adjust the table's left margin and its column spacing.

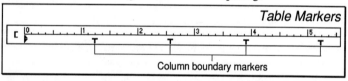

Dragging one of the Table Ruler symbols adjusts the corresponding column boundary for the entire table. Use Table→Column Width to set column widths individually.

The Margin Ruler

The Margin Ruler lets you adjust the left and right margins of the current section.

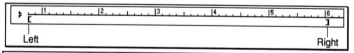

See also: Page Formatting, Paragraphs, The Ribbon, Sections, Tables, Tabs

SECTIONS

A *section* is a subdivision of your document. Each section has a number of formatting attributes, each of which can be set differently in different sections:

- Margins, paper size, and orientation. (Prior to Word 2.0, you could only set these for an entire document; with Word 2.0 you can have different margins in each section, and you can even intermix different paper orientations and page sizes in the same document.)

- Page numbering (start number, formatting, number style).

- Number of columns.

- Headers and footers (different contents, formatting, and position in each section).

- Line numbering.

- Presence of footnotes (whether footnotes are printed or suppressed).

Creating a Section

Each new document has the same number and format of sections as are defined by the template you base the document on. (Microsoft's manual tells you that each new document starts with one section, but that's incorrect—you can define as many sections in a template as you like, and each new document will inherit the template's sections.) The beginning and end of a section are defined by *section breaks*. Like paragraph formatting, which is stored in the paragraph marker, formatting for a section is stored in the section marker at the end of the section. Word displays section markers as dotted lines on your computer screen. Section markers, like paragraph markers, are not printed.

To insert a section break, use the Insert→Break command to display the Break dialog box. Select one of the options in the Section Break control group and click OK. These options control the pagination of the new section, and are explained below under "Section Formatting."

Inserting a section break splits the current section in two, divided by the section break. Both resulting sections start out with the same formatting.

To delete a section break and join two adjacent sections, select the section marker and delete it. This deletes the formatting of the section above the deleted marker, causing it to take on the formatting of the section below it.

Section Layout

The primary formatting attributes of a section are available in the Section Layout dialog box, displayed with the Format→Section Layout command. Options in this dialog box affect the current section, unless you've selected text that crosses a section marker; then, the formatting applies to all sections touched by the selection.

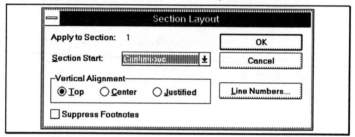

Items in the Section Start drop-down list control how the beginning of the section is paginated:

Continuous	No break; the section begins on a new page only if that's the natural breaking point.
New Column	Begins the section in a new column; equivalent to New Page in a single-column layout.
New Page	Begins the section on a new page, regardless of where the previous page ended.
Odd Page	Begins a new page on an odd page; doesn't break if the section is already on an odd page.
Even Page	Begins a new page on an even page.

Four of these options—Continuous, New Page, Odd Page, and Even Page—are also options in the Break dialog box.

The Vertical Alignment control group sets how Word positions material on each page of the section:

Top	The default; material starts at the top margin, and any blank space is at the bottom of the page.
Center	Word centers material vertically on the page; any required blank space is divided equally before and after the material.

Justified   Word aligns the top of the material at the top margin, and the bottom of the material at the bottom margin; any blank space required to do so is distributed between paragraphs.

If you've formatted footnotes to print at the end of a section, the Suppress Footnotes checkbox controls whether footnotes are printed; when checked, Word doesn't print footnotes. This checkbox is grayed-out when footnotes are formatted to print at the end of the document, beneath text, or on each page.

1   The Line Numbers... button displays the Line Numbers dialog box,
2   which controls whether Word prints line numbers in the margins or
3   between columns. Word doesn't display line numbers in normal or
4   page layout view, but does display them in print preview. This para-
5   graph is contained within its own section, with line numbering turned
6   on.

```
┌─────────────────────────────────────────────────────────────┐
│ ▄  ▓▓▓▓▓▓▓▓▓▓▓▓      Line Numbers      ▓▓▓▓▓▓▓▓▓▓▓▓▓▓▓▓▓▓▓▓▓▓ │
├─────────────────────────────────────────────────────────────┤
│                                                             │
│  ☒ Add Line Numbering                          ┌──────────┐ │
│                                                │    OK    │ │
│                            ┌─Restart at──────┐ └──────────┘ │
│  Start at #:   [1    ] ▲▼  │ ◉ Every New Page │ ┌──────────┐ │
│                            │ ○ Every New Section│ Cancel   │ │
│  From Text:    [Auto ] ▲▼  │                  │ └──────────┘ │
│                            │ ○ Continue       │              │
│  Count By:     [1    ] ▲▼  └──────────────────┘              │
│                                                             │
└─────────────────────────────────────────────────────────────┘
```

Add Line Numbering is initially unchecked, and all the dialog box controls are grayed out; the section will not have line numbers. Check Add Line Numbering to turn on line numbers for the section.

The Restart at options control whether line numbers are restarted at the beginning of every new page or the beginning of every new section, or whether line numbers continue from the previous section. When line numbers restart, they start at the number entered into the Start at # text box.

The From Text box controls the distance between line numbers and the text. The default, Auto, puts line numbers .25 inches from text in single-column layouts, and .13 inches from text in multiple-column layouts.

The Count By text box should have been named "Print Every," because it controls how often Word prints line numbers, and doesn't affect how line numbers are counted. For example, a Count By value of 5 means that Word will print line numbers 5, 10, 15, and so on, and won't print a number next to lines 1, 2, 3, 4, 6, 7, and so on.

You can exclude paragraphs from line numbering with the Format→ Paragraph command. In the Paragraph dialog box, check Suppress (it's the only item in the Line Numbers control group) if you want the current paragraph to be exempt from line numbering (if line numbering is turned on for the section containing the paragraph).

Section Formatting

You can set the following formatting options individually for each section in a document:

To Set up:	Use the command:	For more information, see:
Margins, paper size and orientation	Format→Page Setup	"Page Formatting"
Number and spacing of columns	Format→Columns	"Columns"
Headers and footers	View→Header/Footer	"Headers and Footers"

THE SPELLING CHECKER

Word's spelling checker compares the words in your document against a "dictionary" containing standard spellings. All spelling checkers have limitations and blind spots that you have to keep in mind (they can't read your mind, and tell you that "there" should really have been "their"). On balance, though, everyone can benefit from checking the spelling in a document.

Word's spelling checker is a powerful collection of tools. It's based on a main dictionary, with several hundred thousand words in your primary language, and special-purpose dictionaries you create as you work containing the specialized vocabulary you need for various kinds of writing. You can check individual words, part of a document, or an entire document. The spelling checker also detects simple grammatical errors like repeated words.

Checking Spelling

There are several ways to start Word's spelling checker. First, select a single word or a range of words; or leave the cursor as an insertion point to check the entire document forward from the insertion point. Then, press 🄵🟋, use the Tools→Spelling command, or click 🔽 in the Toolbar.

Word checks the spelling of selected words, or checks from the insertion point forward. (If the insertion point wasn't at the beginning of the document, Word asks you if you want it to continue checking from the beginning of the document.) If the spelling checker doesn't find any misspellings, it tells you so. If you selected just a word or range of words, Word also gives you the option of checking the rest of the document.

If Word finds a spelling error, it displays the Spelling dialog box.

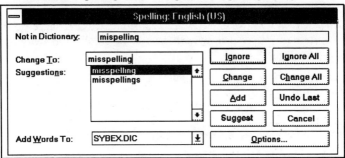

The Spelling dialog box remains on the screen as long as you're checking spelling. In fact, unlike other Word dialog boxes, you can click in the document to edit something without putting away the dialog box, and then return to it. You can move the dialog box if it's obscuring something in the document you want to see.

Because the Spelling dialog box hangs around, checking spelling is an ongoing process:

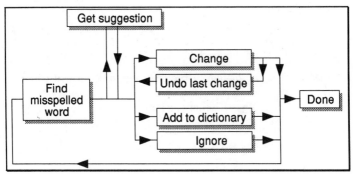

Click [Ignore] to leave the word alone. This is useful for one-of-a-kind words, like the last name of an addressee in a letter, that aren't worth adding to a dictionary. Click [Ignore All] to have the spelling checker ignore all future occurrences of the word; otherwise, it will stop each time it finds the same word.

If you turned on the Always Suggest option (discussed below in "Spelling Options"), the Suggestions list will display the spelling checker's best guess about what you meant to type. It's often correct, since it considers common typing errors like transposed or repeated letters (when it's wrong, the results can be hilarious). If suggestions are turned off, you can always ask the spelling checker for advice by clicking [Suggest].

To correct the word, you can either select a word from the list of suggestions, or you can enter new text in the Change To box. Then click [Change], to make the correction and advance to the next misspelling. Click [Change All] to have the spelling checker make the same correction to all future occurrences of the word.

Word remembers your last change; if you change your mind about a correction before you do another one, click [Undo Last] to return to the location of your previous correction, and restore it to its previous spelling.

Note that each time you click [Change], Word makes an edit in your document. Clicking [Cancel] doesn't undo your changes; you can use the Undo command immediately after running the spelling checker to reverse all of the edits it made.

When the spelling checker encounters a properly spelled word that isn't in its dictionary, you can add that word to the current dictionary by clicking [Add]. You can add the word to another dictionary by selecting a dictionary from the Add Words To drop-down list.

The larger a custom dictionary becomes, the longer it will take the spelling checker to look up words. Add only words that you're confident you'll be using in the future; ignore one-shot words.

The [Options] button displays the Spelling category of the Options dialog box; that's discussed next.

Spelling Options

When you click the |Options| button in the Spelling dialog box, Word displays the Spelling category of the Options dialog box from the Tools→Options command. If you use Tools→Options directly, select the Spelling category by clicking the Spelling (▣) icon in the category list. These options control Word's spelling checker.

Options in the Ignore control group select types of words that the spelling checker will not try to proof: Words In UPPERCASE, and Words with Numbers.

Custom Dictionaries controls the dictionaries involved in the spelling check. You can select up to four dictionary files in the list box. The |Add| button lets you create a new custom dictionary; all dictionaries are stored in the directory containing Word's program files.

Always Suggest, when checked, causes the spelling checker to look at misspelled words and try to guess what the word should be. The spelling checker automatically presents a list of one or more words that closely resemble the misspelling, if it can find any.

Click |OK| to make the changes and put away the dialog box, or |Cancel| to cancel your changes.

See also: Grammar Checker, Hyphenation, Thesaurus, Undo

STYLES

A *style* is a record of paragraph formatting stored under an assigned name; you can apply a style to any number of paragraphs in a document, saving yourself an enormous amount of effort. A list of styles is called a *style sheet*, and every template and document contains a style sheet.

Each style defines the following:

- Paragraph formatting
- Character formatting

- Tab stops and tab styles
- Border style
- Frame (positioning information)
- Language (the default dictionary to be used on the paragraph during a spelling check)

Word for DOS users: The way style sheets work in Word for Windows differs from the way they work in Word for DOS. In Word for DOS, each style sheet is a separate file with the .STY extension, while in Word for Windows the style sheet is one component in a template. More dramatically, each Word document gets a complete copy of its template style sheet; changing templates doesn't change the document's style sheet, unlike in Word for DOS, where changing the .STY file associated with a document completely changes the document's style sheet. Also, Word for Windows only allows you to define paragraph styles; you can't define character styles as you can with DOS Word.

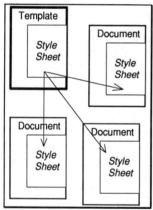

Styles are stored in style sheets, which are in turn stored in templates. When you create a new template, it contains just a handful of standard styles (the Normal paragraph, basic headings, and a few others). You can add or delete styles to the new template, and redefine the styles it started with.

Next, when you start a new document based on a template, the document begins with a copy of the style sheet it inherited from the template. Within the document you can add, delete, or redefine styles, so that the document can have a unique style sheet of its own.

Applying Styles

Word gives you two methods for applying an existing style to selected paragraphs.

To apply a style using the Ribbon, click the arrow on the left drop-down list; this list displays all the available styles for the current document. When you select a style from this list it's applied to the selected paragraph (or paragraphs). If you want to use the keyboard for this, press ⌈Ctrl⌋+⌈S⌋; Word positions the cursor in the drop-down style list for you. You can then type the name of the style you want. However, be careful—if you misspell the name of the style, you'll end up defining a new style using the style-by-example feature (explained later in "Defining a Style").

To apply a style using menus, use the command Format→Style to display the Style dialog box.

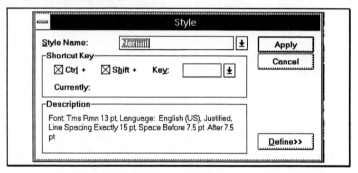

The Style Name drop-down list shows the available styles. Select a style name from this list and click Apply. The Description box contains a brief description of how the selected style is formatted. The other controls in this dialog box relate to defining styles, and are described later.

You can manually override the style's formatting in selected paragraphs with the various items on the Format menu. If you want to remove manual formatting and restore a paragraph to the formatting defined by its style, press ⌈Ctrl⌋+⌈X⌋.

Defining a Style

There are two ways to define a style: explicitly, through the Style dialog box; and using "style by example" to tell Word to define a style based on an existing paragraph.

Style By Example

When you define a style by example, you tell Word to examine the paragraph containing the insertion point, and use its paragraph, character, frame, border, language, and tab formatting to define or redefine a style.

To create a new style from an example:

1. Format a paragraph exactly as you want the new style to be formatted.

2. With the insertion point inside the paragraph to be used as the example, click the mouse in the style drop-down list in the Ribbon, or press `Ctrl`+`X`.

3. Type the name for the new style, and press `↵`.

   If the name that you type already exists (and it's not the same as the paragraph's current style), Word assumes that you want to format the paragraph with that style, rather than defining a new one, and removes your manual formatting.

The new style you define this way is based on the style with which the paragraph was formatted before you gave the style a new name, and Word records how the new style differs from the old style. Thus, the new style automatically becomes the child of the previous style.

To redefine an existing style by example:

1. Apply the style you want to redefine to a paragraph in the current document.

2. Change any aspects of the paragraph's formatting that you want to redefine.

3. The style drop-down list in the Ribbon will still show the name of the style; drop down the list and select the name of the style again. Word will display a dialog box asking you to confirm that you intend to redefine the style:

   · Click `Yes` to redefine the style.

   · Click `No` to reapply the style and remove the manual formatting you've applied.

   · Click `Cancel` to do nothing.

Style-by-example formatting lets you define every aspect of a style except its shortcut key, and its Based On and Next Style attributes. If those settings are relevant to the new style you'll have to use the Format→Style command to set them (but you've still saved a great deal of work).

The Format→Style Command

To define everything about a style from the Style dialog box, display it with the Format→Style command, then click Define>>. This causes the Style dialog box to expand to show its style definition controls.

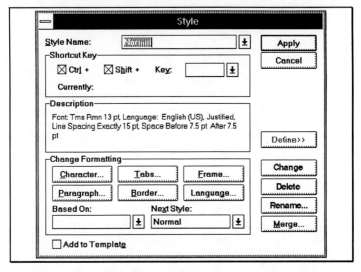

As before, choose a style to work with from the Style Name drop-down list. When you first display this dialog box, it shows the name of the style of the paragraph containing the cursor.

You can assign a shortcut key combination to the current style with the controls in the Shortcut Key control group. Check or uncheck Ctrl and Shift, and select a key, or enter one, in the Key box.

The six buttons in the Change Formatting control group display the same dialog boxes displayed when you choose the corresponding command from the Format menu. Clicking Tabs, for example, is equivalent to the Format→Tabs command. Set up the various format options in these dialog boxes, then click OK in them to return to the Style dialog box.

As you make changes to the style, you'll see its description change to reflect the new formatting. There's a limited amount of space in this box, and so Word may truncate the description. The description lists the style on which the current style is based, and shows how the current style differs from its parent.

The Based On drop-down list shows the parent of the current style. You can select a new parent from this list; if you do, the description changes to show how the current style differs from its new parent.

The Next Style setting is very handy indeed. It lets you specify the style of the next paragraph, when you press ⏎ at the end of a paragraph. For example, if Normal always follows a heading (such as the heading 1 style), then set the heading's Next Style to Normal. You'll save yourself a lot of work. Subtle wrinkle: This feature only works when you press ⏎ at the end of a paragraph (when the insertion point is just before the paragraph marker); in the middle of a paragraph, pressing ⏎ simply creates two paragraphs with the same (original) style.

Check Add to Template to have Word copy the new style, or changes to an existing style, back to the document's template. With Add to Template unchecked, the style is defined only in the document's style sheet. This setting applies to individual styles, allowing you to selectively update the template; the Merge... button, described later in "Managing Styles," updates the entire style sheet.

When you're done defining a style, click Change to store the changes. At this point the Cancel button changes to Close, but Word continues to display the Style dialog box, so that you can make further changes to the current style, or to another style. Up until the time you click Change you can click Cancel to put away the Style dialog box without making any changes to the style sheet; once you click Change the style definition is stored in the style sheet, and you can't undo changes without resetting each formatting option.

Click Delete to remove the current style from the style sheet. Word displays a message box asking you to confirm that you really want to delete the style.

Click Rename... to give the current style a new name.

Managing Styles

People generally master creating and applying styles quickly. You'll find yourself creating new styles, or variations on old styles, at the drop of a hat to respond to an immediate need. Word certainly encourages this. However, the day will come when you fill up a style sheet, or when you find you have too many styles to remember what they're all for, or you find you have dozens of templates for special needs, or you find you've created so many custom styles within individual documents that no two documents look the same. That's when you'll have to confront taming the Style Monster.

Managing Individual Styles

Each style sheet can contain up to 250 styles. Of these, 230 are available for your use; the others are standard styles used in every document:

heading 1	annotation text	index 1...6
heading 2	annotation reference	toc 1...6
heading 3	footnote text	heading 4 through heading 9
Normal	footnote reference	

Styles in the left column are always present in a style sheet. Styles in the remaining two columns are created on demand, when you create one of the associated document features (annotations, footnotes, indexes, or tables of contents); or when you add heading levels in outline view.

Two hundred and fifty styles may seem like a lot, but Word's paradigm for creating new child styles based on parent styles encourages you to create a lot of styles; and you *should* do this, to maximize your productivity by predefining the styles you use. However, when Word displays a message box telling you the style sheet is full, you'll have to prune back the style sheet, deciding what you must keep and what you can do without. Use the Delete button in the Styles dialog box to clear out the underbrush in a style sheet.

One way to fill up the style sheet is to insert one document into another. Word merges their style sheets, so that paragraphs in the inserted file that have corresponding styles in the destination file assume the styles of the destination, while styles in the inserted file that have no counterpart in the destination are added to the destination's style sheet. Styles that overflow the style sheet are discarded, and paragraphs in the inserted document with the discarded style are converted to Normal.

When you prune a style sheet, look first for styles you haven't used in a while. Often, you'll create a style that seems like a good idea at the time, or that addresses some special need, and that you later stop using. Look also for styles that have crept into your document when you've inserted another document. Then look for ways to reduce the number of styles in a family. Or, if you have things like a variant of Normal that's right aligned, consider deleting the right-aligned style and manually applying right alignment to a Normal paragraph.

Managing Style Sheets

Many people learning Word for Windows assume that it manages style sheets the same way as its DOS ancestor. They believe that style sheets are in a separate file (assumed to be the template), and that switching templates automatically (and often dramatically) re-defines the styles associated with a document. Alas, that's not so with WinWord: Each time you start a new document it contains its own style sheet, a copy of the template's style sheet. If the template becomes unavailable, the document formatting survives in its own style sheet. If you make changes to styles in a template, those changes are *not* automatically reflected in existing documents based on the template. Each style sheet exists in regal isolation from its parent and peers.

To compensate, Word lets you merge style sheets from documents, between documents and templates, and between templates. For simplicity we'll call a document or template involved in the merge either the *source* or *destination*. The term *merge* is used because the process works like this:

- If a style exists in both the source and destination, the style in the source replaces the style in the destination.

- If a style exists in the source but not the destination, the source style is copied into the destination.

- If a style exists in the destination but not the source, the destination style is unchanged.

To merge style sheets:

1. Open either the source or the destination to be used in the merge (merges can go either way).

2. Use the Format→Style command to display the Style dialog box.

3. Click Merge.... Word displays the Merge Styles dialog box. This dialog box is like most of Word's file selection dialog boxes, with two additional buttons.

4. Select the other file involved in the merge from the File Name drop-down list. The dialog box at first shows templates in your WINWORD directory; use the Directories, Drives, and List Files of Type controls to select other files, if necessary. If you select a document file, the To Template button is grayed out, because you can only merge a style sheet from a document; you can't merge into it.

5. Perform the merge:

   · Click From Template to merge a style sheet *from* the selected template (or document) into the current document.

   · Click To Template to merge the style sheet in the current document *into* the selected template.

See also: Borders and Shading, Character Formatting, Frames, Paragraphs, Tabs, Templates

---

SUMMARY INFORMATION

You can include information in a document, about the document, in its summary information section. You can configure Word to prompt you for this information when you save a new document (this feature is enabled, by default), and you can edit this information with the File →Summary Info command. It displays the Summary Info dialog box.

The five text boxes in this dialog box are pretty straightforward. The Author field is taken from the Name entry in the User Info category of Tools→Options by default; you can enter another name. The Key-words information is used by the file find function (described later) to search for documents about specified subjects.

You can insert the information from Summary Info into your docu-ment with various INFO fields. There's an AUTHOR field that inserts the author's name; a KEYWORDS field that inserts the key-words, and so on. By the way, the meaning of each of these entries is arbitrary (although the Keywords field does have a use in the find file function), and you can use these fields to store other kinds of information. You might use Title as a title, and then redefine the Subject information as a section title; or use the Comments field to store the issue date of a magazine article.

The | Statistics... | button displays a dialog box showing information Word has compiled about the current document. Most of these items are self-explanatory. The Revision number is simply the number of times you've saved the document since it was created, while Total editing time is the amount of time you've had the document open (whether you were actually editing or not).

SYMBOLS

A symbol in broad terms is any special character you can't type di-rectly at the keyboard. Word provides two methods of inserting sym-bols into your document.

SYMBOL Fields and the Insert→Symbol Command

SYMBOL fields are a field type that lets you specify the numeric code, font and font size necessary to produce a given symbol in your document. An example of a SYMBOL field might look like this:

{SYMBOL 169 \f "Symbol"} *produces the symbol* ♥

While the Symbol font is common on PostScript laser printers, it's not always available on other printers, so Microsoft includes its own

Symbol font with Word for Windows. That way you can print symbols on any printer.

The Insert→Symbol command is the simplest way to insert a SYMBOL field. It displays the Symbol dialog box:

The Symbol dialog box initially shows the characters produced by the Symbol font. Click on the symbol you want, highlighting it, then click OK. Word inserts a SYMBOL field in your document to produce the selected character.

The Symbols From list box shows at least three items:

- **(Normal Text)** produces an ANSI character in the current font; most printer fonts use the ANSI character set, as shown in the ANSI character table at the back of this book. *When you select (Normal Text), Word does not use a SYMBOL field—the character is inserted as simple text.* (The Microsoft documentation says that holding down [Shift] while selecting a character causes it to be enclosed in a SYMBOL field; it doesn't seem to work this way in practice). You can specify a particular font by typing its name into the Symbols From box.

- **MS LineDraw** is a font included with Word for Windows, and produces the line drawing symbols shown in the table at the back of this book. It's a small character set, but very useful: It reproduces characters 177 through 223 from the IBM PC character set. These are mostly the line drawing and shading characters used to draw boxes by DOS character-mode applications.

- **Symbol**

- Other non-ANSI fonts that your printer may provide. (With a PostScript printer you may see "Zapf Dingbats," for example.)

You can also create a SYMBOL field manually, by inserting field characters with (Ctrl)+(F9) and typing the contents of the field; or by using the Insert→Field command. The general SYMBOL field is laid out like this:

the numeric code identifying the character to print

{SYMBOL*code* \f *FontName*\s *FontSize*}

the name of the font in which to print the character   the size of the character

The numeric code is a decimal number identifying the character in the specified font. If you want to use hexadecimal notation, preface the number with *0x*(zero, x). Preface the name of the font (spelled exactly as shown in the various font list boxes used by Word) with \f and the size of the font, in points, with \s.

Inserting Special Characters the Old-Fashioned Way

Prior to Word for Windows 2.0, with its nifty SYMBOL field, you had to use the general Windows procedure for specifying a character using its numeric code. You did this by activating (NumLock), typing a zero, and then typing the numeric decimal code for the character, all on the numeric keypad. This method is still available if you want to use it.

See also: Character Formatting, Fields

TABLES

Word's *tables* are rectangular arrangements of *cells* containing text and graphics, arranged in rows and columns. Tables are analogous to spreadsheets, so experience with spreadsheets will help you understand Word's tables.

The table below shows off various features of Word's tables.

← Tables can have borders...	of various styles...	applied to different parts of the table.
The height of a row in a table can be set to automatically accommodate the tallest cell in the row.	↑ or no border at all (here, what looks like a single L-shaped cell spanning two rows is really two cells with no border between them).	
Or, you can fix the height of a row.	Microsoft	
	You can control the width of individual cells.	
You can have different numbers of cells in each row.		
You can treat text in a table just like text anywhere else...	with different paragraph styles...	or **character** *formatting*.
Tables don't have to be strictly rectangular.	Individual rows can have different lengths.	

You're free to put anything in a table cell that you'd put elsewhere on the page. You can treat a cell as a miniature document, one whose margins are defined by the size of the cell. When a table straddles a page break, Word splits the table at a row boundary; it never breaks up the contents of a row.

Creating a Table

Word offers two ways to create a table, each of which can create an empty table or enclose existing material with a table.

Creating a Table around Existing Material

The idea of enclosing existing material in a table needs some explanation. If you have material selected when you insert a table (explained later), Word assumes that you want that material inside the table. Word looks at the nature of the material, and tries to figure out how many rows and columns the table should have.

- The table will have as many rows as there are paragraphs in the selection. Each paragraph will become one row in the table.

- If Word finds *delimiters,* tabs or commas within the material (but not both), it breaks the material into columns at the delimiters. The table will have as many columns as the largest number of delimiters in all selected paragraphs, and each paragraph will be split at the location of the delimiter and the parts put into separate cells.

If the material has both tabs and commas, or there's some other reason Word isn't sure where to break columns, it will display a dialog box asking you to tell it whether to use paragraph breaks, tabs, or commas, to carve up the material for the table.

Suppose you select the text

Write the vision, and make it plain upon tables¶
that he may run that readeth it.¶
—from Habbakuk 2:2, the Old Testament¶

and insert a table around it, telling Word to use commas as delimiters. Word will key on the commas to create a two-column table with three rows, one for each paragraph.

Write the vision	*and make it plain upon tables*
that he may run that readeth it.	
—from Habbakuk 2:2	the Old Testament

Notice that Word preserved, in each cell, the .5" left indent of the original paragraphs. Those lines that had commas were split into cells, while the middle line, with no comma, was put entirely into the first cell in its row.

To enclose selected material in a table:

- Use the Table→Insert Table command. If Word can figure out how many rows and columns to insert, it inserts the table immediately. If it needs your advice, it will display a small dialog box asking you to choose paragraphs, commas, or tabs, as the table's delimiters.

  or

- Click the ▦ (Table) icon in the Toolbar. Word will ask for your help if it needs it, before enclosing the selection in a table.

Inserting a Blank Table

When nothing is selected in the document (the cursor is an insertion point), you must tell Word exactly how many rows and columns the new table should have. You can use the Toolbar or the Table menu to do this.

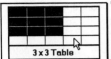

To insert a blank table using the Toolbar, move the pointer over the ▥ (Table) icon in the Toolbar, and press and hold down the mouse button. Word displays a small control like the example to the left, that lets you visually set the number of rows and columns in the new table. Drag the pointer down and to the right to increase the number of rows and columns. The text at the bottom of the control confirms your selection. When you're ready, release the mouse button. To cancel without inserting a table, move the pointer left or up, outside the table.

To insert a blank table using menus, select the Table→Insert Table command. Word displays the Insert Table dialog box, which asks you for the number of rows and columns in the new table, and for the initial column spacing. The initial column spacing applies to all columns in the table. Leaving it set to Auto tells Word to divide the space between the margins by the number of columns, to come up with the column spacing. Note: Column width is fixed until you explicitly change it; column width, unlike row height, doesn't change dynamically to accommodate material in the cells.

Formatting Tables

Word offers a plethora of ways to format tables. You can change its basic layout (number and size of rows or columns), change its appearance with borders, and rearrange the material in the table.

Selecting Parts of a Table

There are three levels of table selection:

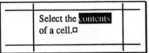

You can select the contents of a cell (text or graphics) using standard selection techniques, as long as you don't select the cell marker (the ¤ symbol). The cell marker works like a paragraph marker, in that it stores the formatting of the last paragraph in the cell; but it's also the handle by which you select the entire cell.

To select a cell, select the cell marker (¤). Word highlights the entire cell. If that proves awkward, move the pointer into the left area of the cell until it

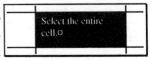

changes to an arrow; this is easiest if the cell's paragraph has a large left indent.

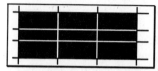 **To select multiple adjacent cells,** extend the selection; you select a rectangular subset of the table by putting the insertion point in the cell at one corner of the selection, holding down the mouse button, and dragging to the opposite corner.

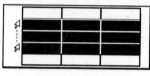 **To select an entire row in a table,** position the mouse in the style area at the left of the screen, so that the pointer changes to a right arrow (⟂). Click next to the row you want to select. Hold the mouse button and drag to select several rows. You can also use the Table→Select Row command to select the row containing the insertion point.

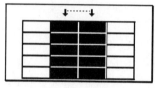 **To select an entire column in a table,** position the mouse at the top border above the column you want to select, so that the pointer changes to a column selection arrow (↓). Click to select the column; drag the selection to select several adjacent columns. Click somewhere else to cancel the selection if you change your mind. You can also use the Table→Select Column command to select the column containing the insertion point.

To select the entire table, use the Table→Select Table command. Or, you can select all the cells, rows, or columns in a table using one of the above methods.

Table Borders

You can apply any of Word's border styles to any boundary of a cell and to groups of cells with the Format→Borders command (see the topic "Borders and Shading" for complete information). The way that you apply border formatting depends on what part of the table you've selected, and is reflected in the options you're given by the border selection control in the Border Table (or Border Cell) dialog box:

If you've selected...	The border control shows...	You can...
a single cell		Apply a border to the four sides of the cell. The pre-defined box style applies a thin line to all four sides.
cells in a single column		Apply a border to the four sides of the selection; and to the sides common to cells in the selection, as represented by center horizontal line in the border control.
cells in a single row		Apply a border to the four sides of the selection; and to the sides common to cells in the selection, represented by the interior vertical line in the border control.
a region containing cells in multiple rows and columns		Apply a border to the sides of the selection; and to the common sides between cells, represented by the interior horizontal and vertical lines in the border control. This is also the sort of selection you'd use for an entire table.

Column Width

You can change the width of an entire column of cells, a group of cells selected vertically, or a single cell; and there are three ways to set column width.

The Ruler Usually, when the selection is inside a table, Word changes the Ruler to show column size dragging controls, represented by T symbols for each column. If the Ruler doesn't display these symbols, click on the symbol at the left of the rule until it does. You can use the Ruler to adjust the width of entire columns, not individual cells.

To change the width of an entire column, without changing the width of adjacent columns, just drag the T marker for the right edge of the column to the left or right. Word doesn't change the width of other columns, so that the overall width of the table changes by the amount you increase or decrease the width of a column.

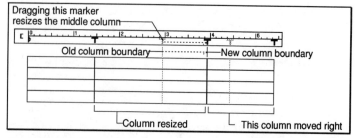

To adjust the boundary between two columns, hold down [Shift] while you drag the marker representing the boundary between two columns. Word adds space to one column and subtracts it from the other as you drag. The total width of the two columns is kept the same while you move the boundary between them right or left.

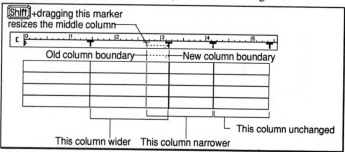

To resize a column and maintain the overall table width, and distribute the change among columns to the right, hold down [Ctrl] while you drag a T marker. Word changes the width of the columns to the right proportionately, to ensure that the overall width of the table doesn't change. If you make a column wider this way, Word decreases the width of columns to the right; if you make a column narrower, Word adds width to the columns to the right.

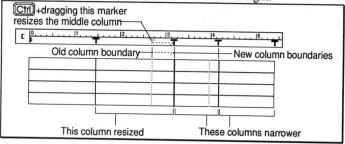

The Column-Dragging Tool When you move the pointer over a vertical cell boundary, it changes to the column-dragging cursor (◂╫▸). Its effect depends on the selection within the table:

- If there are no cells selected (but the insertion point is in a cell), or all the cells in a column are selected, the tool adjusts the width of the entire column.

- If one or more cells are selected, and the tool is applied to the border of the selected cells, the tool adjusts only the width of those cells.

Like the Ruler column-width adjustment method, the column-dragging tool's effect is modified by [Shift] or [Ctrl] keys:

- Without a shift key, columns to the right of the column being adjusted are moved, and remain the same size.

- Holding down [Shift] while dragging a column boundary adjusts the boundary between two columns; the total width of the two columns remains the same, and remaining columns to the right are moved.

- Holding down [Ctrl] while dragging a column boundary resizes the column, and keeps the overall width of the table (or selected rows) the same by distributing the changed width among the remaining columns.

The example below shows a table after using each of the above three methods.

	This cell widened by dragging.		These two cells keep the same size...	...but they're moved to the right.
	This cell widened by [Shift]+dragging		This cell narrowed.	This cell stays the same.
	This cell widened by [Ctrl]+dragging		These cells narrowed...	...equally and proportionately.

The Table→Column Width Command When you use this command, Word displays the Column Width dialog box. In this dialog box, you can specify a measurement for the width of the currently selected cells; the rules for what cells are affected are the same as those for the column-dragging tool. This dialog box also has a setting for column spacing; that will be covered in the next section.

The Next Column and Previous Column buttons let you move the selection right or left in the table to set the width of other cells. Word moves the entire selection with these buttons; for example, in a table with five rows and three columns, if you've selected three cells vertically in the second column in rows two, three, and four, pressing Next Column moves the entire selection so that the cells in column three at rows two, three, and four, are selected.

Column Spacing

The Column Spacing setting in the Column Width dialog box sets the spacing between columns for all the cells in each selected row (if you select one cell in a row, the spacing for all cells in that row is set). Use Table→Select Table to select the entire table, to set column spacing for the entire table.

The default spacing for a newly created table is .15 inches.

What is column spacing? For most purposes you can look at it as the left and right margins *within* a cell: Larger column spacings reduce the usable horizontal space within the cell.

A quirk of column spacing is that its origin (the zero-point for figuring how to allocate the column spacing) is the left margin of the page. With non-zero column-spacing values, this means that the left edge of the table will extend to the left, beyond the left margin. If you can't allow your tables to stick out into the left margin, set the column-spacing to zero, and then add left and right indent settings to the paragraphs in the table to allow for space between text and any table borders.

The figure below shows the effect of a fairly large column spacing. Word divides the amount of column spacing equally on either side of cells in the table. In the left cells, it puts half the column spacing beyond the left margin. Word puts half the column spacing at the right side of the right cells, but doesn't extend the right edge of the table past the right margin.

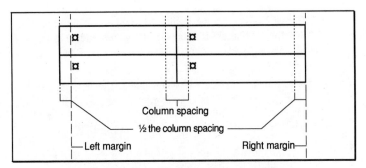

Column spacing
½ the column spacing
Left margin   Right margin

Row Height, Indent, Alignment, and Spacing

The Table→Row Height command displays the Row Height dialog box, in which you control the height of selected rows in a table, and control the entire table's horizontal alignment and left indent.

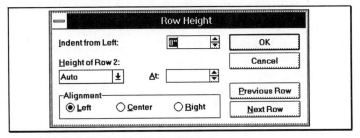

The Previous Row button moves the selection up one row in the table, and the Next Row button moves the selection down.

Row Height· You can specify that each row in a table will adjust its height automatically to accommodate the tallest material in the row (the default); set a minimum height for a row; or set a fixed row height.

The Height of Row x (where x shows the currently-selected row) drop-down list contains three selections controlling how row height is determined:

- **Auto** means that Word will adjust the row height up or down to accommodate the tallest cell in the row.

- **Exactly** forces the row height to always be the height you enter in the At box. The part of material that's taller than the row, if any, is clipped and doesn't print.

- **At Least** lets you set the minimum row height. Word will increase the row height if necessary to accommodate taller material, but will never decrease row height below the value in the At box.

Row Indent Indent from Left lets you indent the left edge of the row from the left margin. This is analogous to a paragraph's left indent, in that it shifts the entire row to the right. If the entire table is selected, this setting shifts the entire table to the right.

You can also indent rows using the Ruler. When the Ruler is showing column-width drag marks (T), you can drag the two triangle symbols at the left edge of the Ruler to set the row indent, as shown below.

Table left indent drag markers

Row Alignment Table rows, like paragraphs, can be aligned left, center, or right between the margins. You can align individual rows, or the entire table if it's selected, by choosing an option in the Alignment control group.

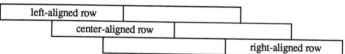

left-aligned row

center-aligned row

right-aligned row

Row Spacing Word has no explicit setting for the space between rows, as it has for the space between columns. Rather, you set the Space Before and Space After of paragraphs in the table to control the amount of vertical space between material in a cell and the cell's upper and lower boundaries.

Changing Tables

This section is about changing the number of rows and columns in a table: inserting rows, columns, or cells; copying and moving that material; and removing tables and converting their contents to text.

Inserting Rows

To extend a table (add a row at the end of the table), position the insertion point in the last cell in the table (the right cell in the bottom row), and press ⬛. Word automatically adds another row to the table and positions the insertion point in its first cell. The new row takes on the paragraph and border formatting of the previous row, along with its column-width and row-height settings.

To insert a row into a table, the easiest way is to select one or more rows of the table, and then use the Table→Insert Rows command. Word inserts as many new rows into the table, above the selection, as there are rows currently selected. If you have three rows selected, Word inserts three empty rows.

If you have less than an entire row selected, Table→Insert Row will be unavailable. In its place, you'll find the Table→Insert Cells command. When it displays its dialog box, select the Insert Entire Row option, and click OK.

Deleting Rows

Select one or more rows and use the Table→Delete Rows command. If you have less than an entire row selected, Table→Delete Rows will be unavailable; instead, use the Table→Delete Cells command. In its dialog box, select the Delete Entire Row option and click OK. Deleting a row deletes the contents of the cells in the row.

Note that pressing ⬛ with part of a table selected doesn't delete the table itself, but rather the contents of all the selected cells. The only way to delete part of a table this way is to include something outside the table, like a paragraph marker before the table, in the selection. In that case, Word assumes you really mean to delete part of the table (and its contents).

Inserting Columns

To insert a column in a table, select the column *to the right* of where you want the new column to go, and use the Table→Insert Column command. Word inserts the new column to the left of the selection. If you select more than one column, Word will insert the same number of columns. Each new column will have a column width equal to that of the column you first selected (the one that's now to its right). If your table was already the width of the margins, the new column will push the table into the right margin and you'll have to adjust column widths to bring the table back within the margins.

If you want to add a column to the right of the table, select all the end-of-row marks (¤) at the right edge of the table. Word knows that this means you want to add a column. The new column will have the same width as the column to its left (the column that used to be the last column in the table).

If you don't have an entire column selected, Table→Insert Columns won't be available. Instead, use the Table→Insert Cells command, choose the Insert Entire Column option, and click OK.

Deleting Columns

To delete a column in a table, select the column and use the Table →Delete Columns command. You can select several columns and delete them at once. Word moves the remaining columns to the left. If you don't have an entire column selected, use the Table→Delete Cells command, choose the Delete Entire Column option, and click OK.

The ⌦Del key won't remove a selected column; rather, it deletes the contents of the selected cells.

Inserting Individual Cells

You can add cells to a table by positioning the insertion point in a cell and using the Table→Insert Cells command. Its dialog box has two options for inserting cells (Insert Entire Row and Insert Entire Column were covered earlier):

- **Shift Cells Right** tells Word to insert a new cell to the left of the cell containing the insertion point, and shift the remaining cells in the row to the right. The new cell has the same width and paragraph formatting as the cell that contained the insertion point.

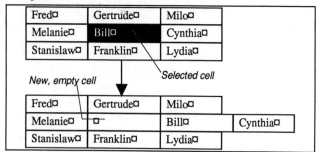

- **Shift Cells Down** moves the contents of the selected cells, and all those below them, down by the number of rows in the selection, and adds new rows to the table to contain the selected cells. It leaves behind blank cells where the selection was.

A1◻	A2◻	A3◻
B1◻	B2◻	B3◻
C1◻	C2◻	C4◻
D1◻	D2◻	D4◻

New, empty cells   *Selected cell*

A1◻	A2◻	A3◻
B1◻	◻	B3◻
C1◻	◻	C4◻
D1◻	B2◻	D4◻
◻	C2◻	◻
◻	D2◻	◻

New rows added to table

Deleting Individual Cells

Select the cells you want to delete, and use the Table→Delete Cells command. The Delete Cells dialog box has four options; two of them, Delete Entire Row and Delete Entire Column, were covered earlier. Use one of the remaining two options to control how Word deletes the selected cells:

- **Shift Cells Left** removes the selected cells and shifts the remaining cells on the row to the left.

- **Shift Cells Up** is the mirror-image of the Shift Cells Down option you would use when inserting cells (described in the previous section): Word deletes the selected cells, and then moves cells below the selection up to occupy the position of the deleted cells.

Merging and Splitting Cells Within a Row

You can merge two or more cells together, horizontally, to create larger cells. Word doesn't let you merge cells vertically. If you have several cells selected vertically, as well as horizontally, Word merges the cells within their respective rows. You can also split previously-merged cells back into their original cells.

To merge cells, select the cells you want to merge and use the Table →Merge Cells command.

Fred¤	Gertrude¤	Milo¤	Ichabod¤
Melanie¤	Bob¤	Joanne¤	Melissa¤
Stanislaw¤	Franklin¤	Lydia¤	Cynthia¤

Selected cells

↓

Merged cell

Fred¤	Gertrude¤	Milo¤	Ichabod¤
Melanie¤	Bob¶ Joanne¤		Melissa¤
Stanislaw¤	Franklin¤	Lydia¤	Cynthia¤

Word converts every end-of-cell marker (except the rightmost marker) into a paragraph marker, and combines the material in the selected cells into one cell.

To split a previously merged cell, position the insertion point inside the merged cell and use Table→Split Cells. Word keeps track of how many cells made up the merged cells, but it doesn't remember their individual column widths. When you split a merged cell, Word just divides the width of the merged cell among the component cells into which it splits it.

Moving Rows, Columns, and Cells Within a Table

To move a row within a table, just select the row and drag it (see the topic "Text: Inserting, Selecting, and Editing" for information about dragging objects). At the destination of the move, position the insertion point in the first cell of the row; if you position it somewhere else in the row, Word will think that you intend to move the selected cells, and insert them into the target row without creating a new row, rather than moving an entire row.

To move a column within a table, select the column and drag.

Converting a Table to Text

We earlier described how you can enclose text with a table, so it shouldn't be surprising that Word has a complementary function to turn a table into text.

1. Select the entire table, or a group of rows. If you select partial rows, Word won't be able to convert the table to text.

2. Use the Table→Convert Table to Text command.

3. In the small dialog box that appears, select whether to you want Word to separate each cell into paragraphs, or whether Word should make each row a paragraph, with the material in cells separated either by commas or tabs.

4. Click OK.

Splitting a Table

You can split a table into two parts, separated by an empty paragraph marker. The first step is to position the insertion point within the row below where you want to split the table. That row will become the top row of the second table created by splitting. Then use one of two methods:

- Run the Table→Split Table command.

- Press Ctrl + Shift + ↵. This key combination, used outside of a table, inserts a column break; inside a table, it doesn't actually insert a column break, but just splits the table.

If a table is the first item in a document (no text or anything else before it), you'll need to use this method in the first row of the table to insert a paragraph before the table.

See also: Borders and Shading; Text: Inserting, Selecting, and Editing

TABLES OF CONTENTS AND OTHER LISTS

Word lets you create various kinds of lists of things that appear in your document. Tables of contents are a specific kind of list, consisting of heading text and page numbers. Word's list facility is generalized, so that you can compile other kinds of lists as well. All of Word's lists consist of some kind of text and a page number.

Generally, these lists are used in the front matter of a document to create tables of contents (in other words, headings that appear in a document), tables of figures and tables of tables, and so on. However, you don't have to place these lists at the front of a document; you can also use this facility to create cross-reference tables, interior (section) tables of contents, and many other things.

A Word index is similar in concept to a list, with the big difference that Word sorts indexes alphabetically. Word doesn't sort lists, but compiles their entries in the page-number order they appear in a document. You're free to sort a compiled list yourself, or to do other kinds of rearranging and formatting. The important thing is that Word automatically compiles the list for you.

Word actually has two facilities for compiling lists. It can create a table of contents by collecting all text formatted with one of the standard heading styles. That's specifically a table of contents. The more general facility uses fields to create list entries (including tables of contents).

Compiling a Table of Contents from Headings

Word has predefined heading paragraph styles, named *heading 1* through *heading 9*. When you use these styles to format headings, Word can collect all the heading text to create a table of contents.

Note: Word only recognizes those specific heading style names. If you create variants of these names (such as *heading 1-Top* for a heading at the top of the page with no space before), Word *will not recognize these variants as headings*. It will collect only the predefined styles.

You don't have to do anything special to prepare for creating a table of contents from headings; just format the headings with the predefined styles as you normally would. When you're ready to create the table of contents,

1. Position the insertion point where you want to put the table of contents.

2. Use the Insert→Table of Contents command to display the Table of Contents dialog box. The Use Heading Paragraphs option is selected by default.

3. Select the range of headings from which Word will compile the table:

   · **All** (the default) collects entries from all headings.

   · **From** and its two text boxes let you specify a range of heading styles from which to collect entries. Enter numbers in the text boxes corresponding to the heading level (**1** signifies *heading 1*, for example).

4. Click OK. Word will repaginate the document, if necessary, then scan through it to collect the text of all heading paragraphs. When it's done, Word inserts a TOC field at the insertion point; its result is a table of contents. (TOC fields have several options for customizing the appearance of the list; those options are discussed later.)

With field code display turned off, the TOC field produces the table of contents. Later, if pagination in your document changes, select the field and update it with the ▦ key. This causes Word to recompile the table produced by the field. Note that inserting a table of contents at the front of your document may change the document's pagination. You may have to update the TOC field immediately after inserting it to get correct page numbers.

Word formats the collected entries with a series of predefined table of contents styles called *toc 1* through *toc 8*. As you can probably guess, each numbered *toc* style corresponds to the same numbered level in *heading* styles. Thus, Word puts text collected from *heading 1* paragraphs in *toc 1* paragraphs, text from *heading 2* paragraphs in *toc 2* paragraphs, and so on. There's no *toc 9* (unless you create one), so Word lists *heading 9* paragraphs in *toc 8*.

You can format and edit the table of contents produced by the TOC field. However, any changes you make are lost the next time you update the field. If you find an error in the table of contents, it's better to edit the source of the material in the document, and recompile the table, than to edit the table.

If you don't anticipate changes in the table of contents (your document's finished), you can convert the field results to text. This eliminates the TOC field (and any possibility of updating it), and inserts the table of contents as text. To do this, select the field, then press ⌘ + ⇧ + 🄵🄵, or run the UnlinkFields built-in command from the Tools→Macro menu command.

Creating Lists with Fields

You can use two fields together, the TC field for entries and TOC for compiled lists, to create lists of any kind. Each entry in the list that's produced consists of some text followed by a page number. Each field has options to vary the appearance of the entries in the compiled list.

A key feature of lists compiled from fields is that you can create several *independent* lists. For example, you might want a separate list of headings, figures, and tables, in a complete table of contents. Word keeps track of lists by identifying each list with a single letter. Typical letter assignments are *C* for headings (contents), *F* for figures, *T* for tables, and so on.

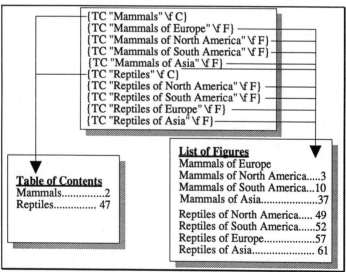

List Entries—The TC Field

The TC field marks table entries. Put TC fields as close as possible to the material they identify (you want to make sure that the page numbers shown in the compiled table are accurate). This often means putting a TC field for a contents list in the heading paragraph that it identifies.

To insert a TC field, position the insertion point at the location of the entry. Insert the field one of two ways:

- Use the Insert→Field command. Select the TC field from the list, type the text of the entry enclosed in quotes, and add options as described below.
- Insert empty field markers by pressing ⌈Ctrl⌉+⌈F9⌉. Type **TC**, a space, the text of the entry inside quotes (regular straight quotes, not fancy "typographer's" quotes), another space, and any options.

Word formats TC fields as hidden text. You must have hidden text display turned on to see TC fields.

The TC field has two options. You can use both in the field.

\F*character*	*character* is a single letter identifying the table of which this entry will be a member. Examples: \f C for contents; \f F for figures. If you omit this option, Word assumes **C**.
\L*number*	*number* identifies the level of the entry, from 1 to 9. The entry will be formatted with the corresponding *toc* paragraph style (*toc 1* through *toc 9*).

The options may be upper- or lowercase. The **\L** switch must come after the **\F** switch.

Compiling Lists with the TOC Field

A TOC field with no options compiles a table from headings. You can add TOC field options to compile a table from fields, and to customize the range and appearance of the table.

These are the TOC field options:

\B *bookmark*	Compiles a partial list only from entries covered by *bookmark*.
\F *character*	Compiles a list from TC fields that specify table identifier *character*. Corresponds to the single letter used in the TC fields.

\F	Compiles a list from TC fields that don't have a table identifier or that use the default "c" identifier. If you omit this switch entirely, Word compiles a table of contents from headings.
\O *first level-last level*	Compiles a table of contents from paragraphs whose heading level is within the range *first level-last level*. (For example, if you specify \o2-3, Word collects entries only from *heading 2* and *heading 3* paragraphs.) To specify a single level, use the same number for *first level* and *last level*.
\s *chapter*	Preface the page numbers in the list with the sequence number identified by *chapter*. This is commonly used when a document is organized by chapter page numbers (for example, "2-12" is page 12 in chapter 2). Sequence numbers are generated by SEQ fields; like the table identifier in lists, SEQ fields have an identifier that separates different numbering sequences. *chapter* specifies that identifier, and has Word use the latest number in that sequence, nearest the TC entry, as part of the page number. See the topic "Numbered Lists" for more information.
\d *separator*	Use *separator* to separate the page numbers in a chapter-style table (see the previous entry for the \s switch). *Separator* can be from one to three characters long. The default separator is a hyphen.

Lists for Long Documents

The procedures so far assume you're putting the list inside the document it refers to. You can also put a list in a separate file, with a list of other document files from which it will compile the list.

The list of external files is a series of RD (Referenced Document) fields. Each RD field identifies the file to include in the list. If the file specification includes the path, you must double each backslash. Here's an example of a list of RD fields, followed by a TOC field:

> {RD D:\\SYBEX\\REF\\TABLISTS.DOC}{RD
> D:\\SYBEX\\REF\\FIELDS-1.DOC}{TOC}

This sequence of fields tells Word to scan TABLISTS.DOC and FIELDS-1.DOC for TC entries, and insert the compiled list into the current document. The order of the RD fields is important, since Word puts entries into the list in the order that it finds them.

See also: Bookmarks; Indexes; Outlines; Pagination; Printing; Styles

TABS

Tab stops are predefined horizontal positions, against which Word will align text when you insert a *tab* character. Word's tabs have three characteristics:

- *Position*, the distance from the left margin at which the tab stop occurs.

- *Alignment*, which determines how Word aligns text with the tab stop.

- *Leader,* the pattern of spaces, dashes, dots, or underscores that leads from the end of the text before the tab, up to the text aligned with the tab stop.

To insert a tab,

- In text, press the tab key: ⎆.

- In a table, press ⎈+⎆ (in a table, you use the ordinary tab key to advance to the next cell).

Tab Formatting

Tab formatting is stored along with paragraph formatting in paragraph markers. You can include tab formatting in the definition of a paragraph style.

If you don't manually format tabs, Word uses these defaults:

- Tab stops every 0.5 inches (you can also specify a different default tab increment, that will be used in any situation when there are no custom tab stops).

- Left alignment.

- No leader.

Word gives you four choices for tab alignment:

- **Left** alignment is the default. Text following the tab character is inserted after the tab.

- **Center** alignment centers the text following the tab character horizontally around the tab stop.

- **Right** alignment causes the right edge of text inserted after the tab character to be aligned with the tab stop; text "piles up" to the left of the tab stop. Inserting another tab character moves beyond the tab stop.

- **Decimal** alignment is used primarily for numbers. It aligns the decimal point in a number with the tab stop; text to the left of the decimal point behaves like the tab stop is right-aligned, and fills to the left; text after the decimal point fills to the right.

The tab leader is a series of characters that Word uses to fill the space taken up by the tab character (the space between the end of the text before the tab, up to the beginning of text after the tab). If there is no tab leader, the space is blank. The other leader options are:

Dotted .... Leader
Dashed --------------- Leader
Solid _____ Leader

You can format tab position, alignment, and leader with the Tabs dialog box. You can use the Ruler and the Ribbon to set tab position and alignment; for leader formatting you must use the Tabs dialog box.

Formatting Tabs with the Tabs Dialog Box

You set up manual tab formatting with the Format→Tabs command, which displays the Tabs dialog box. You can also display this dialog box from within the Paragraph dialog box and the Style dialog box.

You can use this dialog box to set up a default tab interval that's used throughout the current document. Enter an interval in the Default Tab Stops box; this interval starts at the left margin, and results in a default tab at multiples of the interval. For example, the default 0.5 inches results in default tabs at 0.5", 1.0", 1.5", and so on.

You can also set up multiple custom tabs with the Tabs dialog box. The general procedure is:

1. Enter a tab stop measurement in the Tab Stop Position text box; or select an existing tab stop from the list to reformat.

   The default unit of measure is whatever you've set in the General category of Tools→Options. You can add suffixes, such as "in" or "pt," to override the default.

2. Select an alignment and leader for the tab.

3. Click ⎡Set⎤. If you're setting up a new tab, this adds it to the list at the left.

To clear a tab stop, select the tab stop to clear from the Tab Stop Position list, and click ⎡Clear⎤. Click ⎡Clear All⎤ to clear all tab stops.

When you're done, click ⎡OK⎤ to put away the dialog box.

Formatting Tabs with the Ribbon and Ruler

The Ruler shows tab stops for the paragraph currently containing the insertion point, allows you to drag markers around to adjust tab positions, and lets you define new tab stops. The Ruler uses these symbols for tabs:

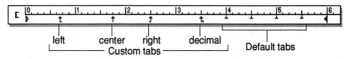

To move a tab stop, drag its symbol left or right. **To remove a tab stop,** drag its symbol off the Ruler.

To set a tab stop, first select the tab alignment type from the Ribbon:

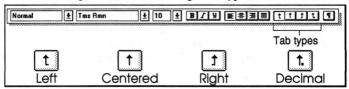

Then click in the bottom half of the Ruler to set the tab stop.

See also: Paragraphs; Styles

TEMPLATES

Word templates, as the name implies, form a foundation upon which new documents are based. If that were all, you could use an ordinary document and copy it as needed. Templates go further than that, though, in their role as the central repository for glossaries, macros, and key, menu, and Toolbar assignments.

When you create a document based on a template, Word bases the initial page formatting in the document on that in the template, and copies the paragraph style sheet from the template into the new document. If the template also contains text or other material, Word copies that also.

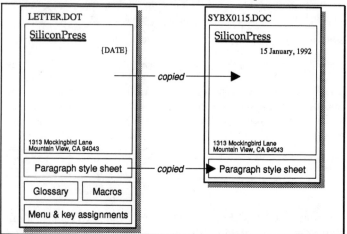

You can modify the paragraph style sheet, page formatting, and inherited text in the document; you're working with copies, and you can change them as you wish. The changes apply only to the document. However, macros and glossaries aren't copied, but are stored centrally in the template; any changes you make to those items are stored in the template, and affect all documents based on the template.

Word templates always have the file extension .DOT; documents usually have a .DOC extension.

Word has a master template named NORMAL.DOT, that establishes a "baseline" for your entire Word system; it's often called the *global template,* for that reason. To keep things straight, other templates are therefore called *document templates,* because they apply only to the specific documents based on them.

NORMAL.DOT contains macros and glossaries that you can use no matter what document (based on whatever template) you're working in. The global template also contains key, menu, and Toolbar assignments that apply wherever you are, except when you're working in a document whose template has redefined them. In other words, what shows up on menus and the Toolbar, and how keys work, can change from document to document. This is very useful: you can add items like Address, Date, Logo, and so on to the Insert menu associated with a letter template, so that you have those features available when you're working on a letter; but they don't clutter up your menus when you're working on other documents.

Creating Templates

By default, Word stores all templates in the same directory as that which contains Word's program files (usually C:\WINWORD). When you start a new document or template, the New dialog box lists only the templates it finds in that directory, and it doesn't provide controls to let you change the drive or directory to look for new ones. However, that doesn't prevent you from typing in a file name specifying a different drive or directory. The File→Template command's Template dialog box has the same lack of drive and directory controls, but there also you can type in a different drive and path if you need to do so.

If you'd like to use another default directory for templates, you can change this line in the [Microsoft Word 2.0] section of your WIN.INI file:

```
DOT-PATH=C:\WINWORD\TEMPLATE
```

By default this line doesn't exist, telling Word to look in its own program directory; adding the line tells Word to look somewhere else. You can use the Win.ini category in Tools→Options to add this line.

Word comes with a number of sample templates. You can modify those templates for your use, or you can derive new templates based on existing templates (including NORMAL.DOT).

To start a new template, based on an existing template, use File→ New, and select Template in the New control group; select the existing template on which you want to base the new one. The new template inherits everything from the old template; it's essentially a copy of it.

To save a document as a template, use File→Save As and select *Document Template (*.dot)* from the Save File As drop-down list. The new template contains only the paragraph style sheet and any text or other material that was in the document. It has nothing in its glossary, no macros, and no key, menu, or Toolbar assignments. Initially, it's a template in name only. Note that just changing the file suffix to DOT doesn't make the file a template; you must use File→Save As to change the file's internal format to that of a template.

Modifying Templates

You can open and directly modify templates, the same way you'd work with a document. Just use File→Open and select *Document Template (*.dot)* from the List Files of Type drop-down list. Any changes you make to the template become part of it when you save the file.

You can also modify a template when you're working on a document based on that template. Doing so is sometimes a little indirect, as this table shows.

To modify the template's:	Do this in a document:
Paragraph style sheet	Create or modify styles in the document's style sheet. In the Styles dialog box (Format→Styles), update the template one of these ways:
	· Update individual styles by checking the Add to Template option.
	· Update the entire style sheet by clicking the Merge... button.
Page formatting	Use Format→Page Setup to format margins, paper size, and so on. In the Page Setup dialog box, click Use as Default... to reflect the changes back to the template.
Default character formatting	Use Format→Character; in the Character dialog box, select the character formatting to use as the default. Click Use as Default... to reflect the changes back to the template.
Default language	Use Format→Language; in the language dialog box select the language to use as the default. Click Use as Default... to reflect the changes back to the template.
Menu, key, Toolbar assignments; macros and glossary entries	Do nothing special; when you work with one of these items, they're stored in the template automatically, after you choose a global context (NORMAL.DOT) or the current document template.

You'll find more detailed instructions in the topics for each of the above subjects.

Changing a Document's Template Assignment

When you create a new document, it receives a copy of its parent template's text, page formatting, and style sheet. They're copies, stored in the document, and so have no further relationship to the template. However, things like macros and glossaries, and key, menu, and Toolbar assignments, remain in the template; in any given document, these things depend on the document's template assignment. The template assignment specifies a *current* relationship between the document and a template, and only by default does it specify the original template on which the document was based.

To change the template associated with a document, use the File→ Template command to display the Template dialog box. Select the new template from the Attach Document To drop-down list. This list shows templates stored in the default template directory; you can also type the complete path and file name for a template stored elsewhere.

The dialog box also lets you set the default location in which new glossary entries are stored:

- **Global (Available to All Documents)** means that new or redefined glossary entries are automatically stored in NOR-MAL.DOT (the global template).

- **With Document Template** means that new or redefined glossary entries are stored in the current document template.

- **Prompt for Each New** tells Word to make no assumptions; Word asks you where to store new glossary entries.

Although the control group is labeled "Store New Macros and Glossaries as," these settings have a meaningful effect only on glossary entries. In dialog boxes referring to macros, such as the Menu, Keyboard, and Toolbar categories of Tools→Options, and the Tools→ Macro command, you must always explicitly select a global or template list of macros, so there's rarely any question about where they're located.

See also: Borders and Shading; Character Formatting; Columns; Customizing Word for Windows; Frames; Glossaries; Page Formatting; Paragraphs; Sections; Tabs; The Toolbar

TEXT: INSERTING, SELECTING, AND EDITING

Text is fundamental to Word, and text must first exist in a document before you can deal with it at the higher levels discussed in the topics "Character Formatting" and "Paragraphs." This topic deals with putting text in a document and manipulating it once it's there.

Inserting Text

The *insertion point* is where Word inserts new text. It's usually represented by a blinking vertical bar. When you're using a mouse, the insertion point moves to wherever (in text) you click the mouse button. The insertion point also moves when you press one of the directional arrow keys on your keyboard, or [Home], [End], [PgUp], or [PgDn].

Word is set to *insert mode* by default, so that any text you type or insert from the Clipboard is inserted at the insertion point, and existing text is pushed to the right or down to make room.

The other typing mode is *overwrite*. In this typing mode, any text you type overwrites existing text to the right of the insertion point. That is, for each character you type, Word deletes one character to the right of the insertion point and substitutes what you typed. However, Word stops deleting characters when it encounters a paragraph marker, so that additional text pushes the paragraph marker to the right. Also, anything pasted from the Clipboard doesn't overwrite existing text; Word behaves as if it's still in insert mode, in this case.

Press [Ins] to toggle between insert and overwrite mode. When Word is in overwrite mode, it displays the legend *OVR* in the status bar at the bottom of the screen.

Another option that affects how text is inserted is the Typing Replaces Selection checkbox in the General category of the Options dialog box (displayed with the Tools→Options command). This feature controls how Word will behave if you have text (or anything else) selected in a document, and type text or paste something from the Clipboard (selecting text is covered below). If this option is off (the default condition), Word inserts the next text (or whatever) to the left of the selection and moves what was formerly selected to the right. It also clears the highlighting from the selection. If this option is on, Word deletes whatever was highlighted before inserting the new material.

While the typing-replaces-selection option may take some getting used to, most people find it to be very natural. Among other things, it allows you to replace material in a document in a single fluid step, by highlighting the old material and then simply inserting the new material at the same location.

Selecting Text

You must *select* text before you can manipulate it. This means highlighting it so that you can see what you've selected, and so that Word knows what you want to work with. Word offers a wide array of text selection methods.

Selecting Text with the Mouse

The primary mouse selection method is simply to hold down the left mouse button where you want to begin selecting text, drag the cursor to the end of your selection, and release the button. You might think of it as "painting" your selection on the computer screen. This method selects text and other objects in a linear sequence as they appear in the document. Word reverses the color of anything you've highlighted, like this:

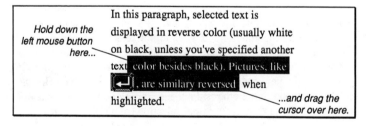

If you use the right mouse button to select text, Word lets you select rectangular regions of text with a *column selection*, like this:

Hold down the
right mouse button
here...

This is an example of column selection. You use the right mouse button
to define a rectangular region of the
display, by defining two opposite
corners of the rectangle.

...and drag the
cursor over here.

Word also gives you methods for selecting varying amounts of text in one operation:

To select...	Do this...
A single word	Double click anywhere in the word.
A sentence	Hold down [Ctrl] and click anywhere in the sentence.
A single line of text	Move the pointer into the selection bar (the region at the left of the screen past any text) until the pointer changes to an arrow ($\nearrow$), and click.
A whole paragraph	Double click in the selection bar next to the paragraph you want to select.
The entire document	Hold down [Ctrl] and click in the selection bar.

Another method you can use to select a large area of the document is to move the insertion point to one end of what you want to select, then hold down [Shift] and click the mouse somewhere else to define the other end of the selection. Word highlights and selects everything between these two points.

A variation of this method allows you to adjust an existing selection, by moving the *second* point of the selection (in all cases the start of the selection remains at the same location). With the selection already highlighted, hold down [Shift] and click where you want the end of the selection to move to. If your initial selection proceeds from left to right, and you move the end point somewhere to the right of the start of the selection, you can expand or contract the selection. If you move the new end point to the left of the selection, you flip the selection around to the other side of the starting point. This behavior is reversed if you made your initial selection from right to left.

Yet another method of selecting a region in a document is to use the *extend selection key,* [F8]. When you press this key once, Word displays the legend *EXT* in the status bar. Wherever the insertion point is located at this time becomes the beginning of a selection; the next place you click the mouse defines the other end of a selection. As long as extend-selection is in effect, you can keep moving the selection endpoint to adjust the selection. This mode is canceled when you do something to the text, or when you press ⟨Esc⟩. The ⟨F8⟩ key has several more uses during keyboard selection, as explained below.

At any time you can cancel a selection by moving the insertion point (unless extend-selection mode is in effect).

Selecting Text with the Keyboard

Even though most people use a mouse with Word, there are times when the keyboard shortcuts for selecting text can save you time and effort. Each of these keyboard selection methods assume that the current location of the insertion point marks one end of a selection; these methods, therefore, all act to extend a selection.

Press...	To extend the selection...
⟨Shift⟩ + ⟨→⟩	One character to the right.
⟨Shift⟩ + ⟨←⟩	One character to the left.
⟨Ctrl⟩ + ⟨Shift⟩ + ⟨→⟩	To the end of the word containing the insertion point.
⟨Ctrl⟩ + ⟨Shift⟩ + ⟨←⟩	To the beginning of the word containing the insertion point.
⟨Shift⟩ + ⟨End⟩	To the end of the line (that is, one row on the screen, not necessarily a sentence).
⟨Shift⟩ + ⟨Home⟩	To the beginning of the line.
⟨Shift⟩ + ⟨↓⟩	To the corresponding horizontal position one line down.
⟨Shift⟩ + ⟨↑⟩	To the corresponding horizontal position one line up.
⟨Ctrl⟩ + ⟨Shift⟩ + ⟨↓⟩	To the end of the current paragraph.
⟨Ctrl⟩ + ⟨Shift⟩ + ⟨↑⟩	To the beginning of the current paragraph.
⟨Shift⟩ + ⟨PgDn⟩	One screen down. (The exact distance depends on the current display zoom factor and the type of display; it's an amount equal to whatever fits on the screen with the current settings.)
⟨Shift⟩ + ⟨PgUp⟩	One screen up.
⟨Ctrl⟩ + ⟨Shift⟩ + ⟨End⟩	To the end of the document.
⟨Ctrl⟩ + ⟨Shift⟩ + ⟨Home⟩	To the beginning of the document.
⟨Ctrl⟩ + ⟨5⟩ (on the numeric keypad)	The entire document. (Alternatively, use Edit→Select All.)
⟨Alt⟩ + ⟨5⟩ (on the numeric keypad)	The entire table containing the insertion point. (Alternatively, use Table→Select Table.)

You can also use the ex-
tend-selection key, [F8],
to select ever larger units
of text. That is, starting
with the insertion point
as a thin bar (nothing
highlighted), press [F8]
once to turn on extend-

> Pressing [F8] repeatedly selects:
> [F8] [F8] a word
> [F8] [F8] [F8] a sentence
> [F8] [F8] [F8] [F8] a paragraph
> [F8] [F8] [F8] [F8] [F8] an entire section
> [F8] [F8] [F8] [F8] [F8] [F8] the entire document.

selection mode; thereafter, each time you press [F8], you'll select the
next larger unit of text, as shown in the list above. Press [Esc] to cancel extend-selection mode.

Moving, Copying, and Deleting Text

Once you've selected text, you can work with it. The three methods
that Word offers are discussed below.

Moving and Copying Using Drag and Drop

Drag-and-drop is one of Word 2.0's most innovative features. You
simply highlight the material you want to copy or move, press and hold
down the mouse button with the pointer inside the selection, drag it to
the desired location, and release the mouse button. In more detail:

1. Highlight the material you want to copy or move.

2. Position the pointer over the highlighted material until the
    pointer changes to an arrow (↖). Then,

    · **To move the selection**, press and hold down the mouse
       button.

    · **To copy the selection**, hold down [Ctrl] while you press
       and hold down the mouse button.

3. While you're holding down the mouse button, Word changes
    the pointer to the drag-and-drop cursor (↖). Keeping the but-
    ton depressed, move the pointer to the destination for the copy
    or move operation. (You don't have to hold down [Ctrl] if
    you're using it.) While you drag, a standard vertical bar
    pointer accompanies the drag-and-drop cursor, showing you
    potential destinations. (Although you can move the ↖ pointer
    anywhere on the screen, the only "legal" destinations are inside

existing text, as indicated by the moving insertion point.) If you move the pointer to the top or bottom of the screen, Word starts to scroll the display in the appropriate destination.

4. When you've reached your destination, release the mouse button.

To cancel a drag-and-drop operation, move the ▨ pointer back inside the highlighted selection and release the mouse button. If it's too late for that, you can always use Undo (Edit→Undo or `Ctrl`+`Z`).

Copying and Moving through the Clipboard

Like all Windows applications, Word supports the use of the Clipboard to copy or move material.

To copy something through the Clipboard, select the material and use the Edit→Copy command or press `Ctrl`+`Ins` or `Ctrl`+`C` to put a copy of the selection on the Clipboard. Paste the material back into the document at another location with the Edit→Paste command or with `Shift`+`Ins` or `Ctrl`+`V`. You can paste multiple copies of the material this way, and of course other applications can paste what you put on the Clipboard.

To move something through the Clipboard, select the material and use the Edit→Cut command or press `Shift`+`Del` or `Ctrl`+`X` to remove the selection from your document and put it on the Clipboard. Then paste the material as described above.

Copying and Moving with the `F2` Key

All versions of Word for Windows have allowed you to copy and move with the `F2` key. This method has certain advantages over both drag-and-drop or using the Clipboard:

- You can make the destination a selection, so that whatever you're copying or moving overwrites the destination. Drag-and-drop can only insert the copied or moved material.

- The operation doesn't go through the Clipboard, so that you won't lose material already on the Clipboard that you might want to use later. This means that you can combine the `F2` key method described below with Clipboard operations when you have a complicated rearrangement to perform.

Here's how you use the ▣ key:

1. Select the material to copy or move.

2. Depending on whether you want to copy or move the selection:

    · Press ▣ to copy the selection. Word displays the prompt *Copy to where?* in the status bar.

    · Press ▣+▣ to move the selection. Word displays the prompt *Move to where?* in the status bar.

3. Set up the destination. Unlike drag-and-drop, you can reposition the destination insertion point (even if you release the mouse button) until it's in the correct position, and you can highlight material at the destination. You're also free to release the mouse button to use the scroll bars to move the display. Word uses a dotted-underline to show a destination selection, rather than reversing the colors as it does for a normal selection. When the destination is set up, press ▣ to tell Word to execute the operation. If you decide not to carry through with the operation, just press ▣.

Deleting

To delete a selection from a document, select it and press ▣. You can also cut the material to the Clipboard (Edit→Cut or ▣+▣) to remove it from the document and leave a copy in the Clipboard.

To delete the character to the right of the insertion point, also use ▣. This deletes a single character at a time; Word won't delete fields or graphics from the insertion point (you must select and highlight them).

To back up and delete text to the left of the insertion point, use the Backspace key (▣). You can backspace only over text; Word refuses to backspace over graphics and fields.

There is also an EditClear command that deletes material. You can assign it to a menu (typically Edit→Clear) using the Menus category of Tools→Options. EditClear is not initially assigned to a menu in Word's default configuration.

Special Characters

Many characters have a special meaning to Word; they're not printed text (unless noted below), but rather are embedded in the document. The tables below list these special characters and the keys you press to insert them.

Hyphens		
Display	**Key(s)**	**Usage**
-	⊟	Simple hyphen; always displayed and printed, the word containing it is broken at the end of a line.
¬	Ctrl + ⊟	"Soft" hyphen; display controlled by the Optional hyphens check box in the View category of Tools→Options; printed as a simple hyphen only if it falls at the end of a line and is used to break a word.
-	Ctrl + Shift + ⊟	Non-breaking hyphen; not used to break a line (treated like any other character); the character printed is an "en-dash."

Tabs and Spaces		
Display	**Key(s)**	**Usage**
•	Space	Whether the symbol is displayed or not depends on settings in the View category of Tools→Options.
→	⊡ (tab)	

Breaks		
Display	**Key(s)**	**Usage**
¶	⏎	Paragraph break; ends the current paragraph and starts a new one.
↵	Shift + ⏎	Line break; ends the current line and starts remaining text at the beginning of the next line, within a paragraph.
————	Ctrl + ⏎	Page break; starts a new page.
············	Ctrl + Shift + ⏎	Column break; starts a new column in a multi-column format; equivalent to a page break in a single-column layout.

See also: Breaks, Character Formatting, Paragraphs, Revision Marks, Symbols, Tabs

THE THESAURUS

A *thesaurus* is a list of synonyms for words—alternative words that have the same or similar meaning as the word you're looking up. Word's thesaurus is an automated facility for looking up synonyms.

To look up a word in the thesaurus, position the insertion point within or next to the word to look up, or select it. Start the thesaurus with the Tools→Thesaurus command, or press Shift + F7.

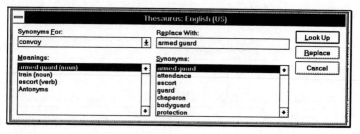

If you want to replace the word you're looking up with Word's first suggestion, click Replace.

Many words have different meanings; some words can be both nouns and verbs. The thesaurus takes this into account by showing alternative meanings for the selected word in the Meanings list. For each word you select in that list, Word displays a list of synonyms in the Synonyms list. The thesaurus can also display antonyms—words opposite in meaning from the selected word.

The sample above shows the word "convoy" as the word being looked up. The following figure summarizes the results produced by the thesaurus:

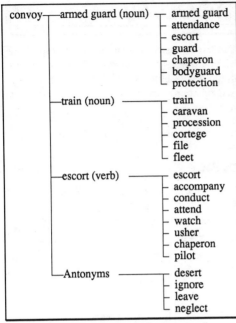

When you double-click on a word in the Synonyms box, or select it and click Look Up, Word puts it into the Synonyms For box, and looks up further synonyms for the new word. Word keeps track of the words you've looked up in the drop-down part of Synonyms For, so that you can back up through the trail of synonyms to a prior word.

When Word can't find an entry in its thesaurus file for the word you want to look up, it changes the caption of the Synonyms For box to Word Not Found, and displays a list of the words it found that are adjacent alphabetically to your word. This gives you a chance to correct misspellings, or pick an alternate word.

Word may show the item Related Words in the Meanings box. If you select Related Words, the thesaurus will display variations on the selected word.

See also: Grammar Checker; Spelling Checker

TOOLBAR

Word for Windows' Toolbar is a strip of buttons at the top of the Word display that gives you quick access to many Word functions. The Toolbar is preconfigured with buttons corresponding to many of the most commonly-used functions, and you can add your own custom buttons, as explained later.

To control display of the Toolbar, use the View→Toolbar command.

The Standard Toolbar

The Toolbar comes configured as shown below. The definition of each standard button is listed after the figure.

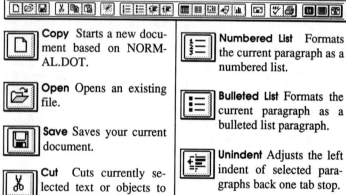

Copy Starts a new document based on NORMAL.DOT.

Open Opens an existing file.

Save Saves your current document.

Cut Cuts currently selected text or objects to the Clipboard.

Copy Copies currently selected text or objects to the Clipboard.

Paste Pastes the Clipboard contents into the document.

Undo Reverses your most recent action.

Numbered List Formats the current paragraph as a numbered list.

Bulleted List Formats the current paragraph as a bulleted list paragraph.

Unindent Adjusts the left indent of selected paragraphs back one tab stop.

Indent Adjusts the left indent of selected paragraphs forward to the next tab stop.

Insert Table When you click this button, a grid drops down below it; drag the pointer over the grid to visually define the number of rows and columns in the table.

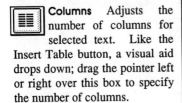 **Columns** Adjusts the number of columns for selected text. Like the Insert Table button, a visual aid drops down; drag the pointer left or right over this box to specify the number of columns.

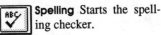 **Frame** Places a frame around selected text, tables, or graphics, or inserts an empty frame if nothing is selected.

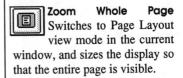 **Draw** Starts Microsoft Draw with an empty picture frame. Does *not* edit a picture, if one is selected; you must double-click existing graphics to edit them with Draw.

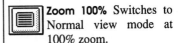 **Graph** Starts Microsoft Graph with the default graph. Does *not* edit an existing graph, if one is selected; you must double-click an existing graph to edit it.

Envelope Displays the Create Envelope dialog box to let you address and print an envelope.

Spelling Starts the spelling checker.

Print Prints all of the current document.

Zoom Whole Page Switches to Page Layout view mode in the current window, and sizes the display so that the entire page is visible.

Zoom 100% Switches to Normal view mode at 100% zoom.

Zoom Page Width Sets the zoom so that the width of the document fills up the width of the document window.

Customizing the Toolbar

Word for Windows 2.0 comes with a preconfigured Toolbar that represents Microsoft's best guess as to the functions people use most often. To change the Toolbar to suit yourself, display the Options dialog box with the command Tools→Options. If the Toolbar category is not already displayed, select the ⛰ icon in the Category list box.

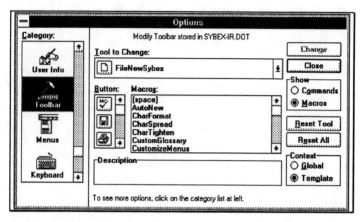

There are 30 positions (or "slots") for icons in the Toolbar, and their current assignments are shown in the Tool to Change list box (click the arrow on the right of the box to see the rest of the list). To change an assignment:

1. Decide whether you want to customize the Toolbar for all documents (globally) or only for documents using the current template; then check the appropriate option under Context.

2. Select the Toolbar slot to customize with the Tool to Change list box. Unassigned positions show the legend *(space)*.

3. You can associate either a command or a macro with the selected Toolbar slot. Which one depends on the option you select in the Show group:

   · *Macros* makes the list box in the center of the Options dialog box display the macros defined in both the document template and the global context (macros in NORMAL.DOT).

   · *Commands* makes the list box show the Word commands you can associate with buttons. You'll recognize many of these as a form of menu items; for example, *EditFind* in the list box is the same as the Edit→Find menu command.

   After selecting a Show type, select a macro or command from the list box.

4. Select a button from the Buttons list.

5. Click Change to assign the selected button and command or macro to the current Toolbar position.

To restore the selected Toolbar position to its default, click Reset Tool. Click Reset All to restore the entire Toolbar to the default assignments.

When you're all done, click Close to put away the Options dialog box.

See also: Customizing Word for Windows, Macros, The Ribbon, The Ruler

---

UNDO

Word has a built-in safety net to save you (most of the time) from making irrevocable mistakes.

When you modify a document, Word remembers what you did. When you're typing, Word remembers the last character you inserted, or, if you're replacing a block of text, what was there before you replaced it. Word remembers what you cut or delete, and how characters or paragraphs were formatted before you made changes with Format menu commands. When you insert something (a picture, a draw or chart object, another document), Word remembers what your document looked like before the insertion. When you use the Edit→Replace command, Word records every changed location.

In every case, this recorded information allows Word to reverse your most recent action. There are two ways to undo a change:

- Use the Edit→Undo command. This command is always the first item on the Edit menu; its text may change to reflect your last operation. For example, if you've just made selected text bold, the menu item reads "Undo Formatting."

   When Word can't undo a change, it grays-out this menu item. Quite a few changes are irrevocable: changes in Tools→Options, all File and View menu commands, every action taken by the macro except its last action, and several others. These are generally changes that Word can't logically undo, such as saving a file or changing the view, or changes that are stored in an external configuration file.

- Use the Undo key. By default it's `Ctrl`+`Z`. Word also recognizes `Alt`+`←Back` because that's the Windows standard.

- Click ▨ on the Toolbar.

What happens when you undo twice? You get Undo-Undo, which literally means that you undo the act of undoing. Whatever change you undid is restored. In fact, immediately after an undo, the first item on the Edit menu reads "Undo Undo." You can use this feature to experiment with changes, switching between the "before" and the "after" until you're satisfied with your change.

As soon as you save a document, Word clears its record of changes, and you can't undo whatever you did just before saving. Logical, because saving a file "commits" its changes to your disk. Painful, if you realize too late that you made a mistake. You should save often, but you should also get into the habit of pausing briefly before saving, and reviewing what you've just done to be sure that you want to make it permanent.

VIEWING DOCUMENTS

Word gives you a great deal of control over how it displays your documents. You have an ordinary word-processing view, a page layout view, and a print preview; and you can have your document displayed with no formatting for quick editing. You can magnify or reduce a document on the screen, to see more of it less clearly, or less of it more clearly.

Word's ability to magnify, or "zoom," the display, new in version 2.0, can be of some help to vision-impaired people. It makes the document easier to read, although text in menus. dialog boxes, and buttons is still the same size. In general, using the largest zoom you can will help reduce eyestrain.

Normal View

Word's *normal view* is the traditional word-processor display of a document. Everything consists of a linear stream of text and other material, and you move up or down through this stream by scrolling the display. Any objects that are positioned on the page (that aren't "inline") aren't shown positioned; they're shown at the location they were inserted into the document. In multicolumn layouts, you see only one column at a time.

To switch to normal view from another view, use one of these methods:

- Use the View→Normal command. Word restores the display to normal view, preserving the zoom factor in effect in the last viewing mode.

- Click the normal view button (■) on the Toolbar. This button also sets the zoom to 100%, regardless of the zoom you had selected the last time you used normal view.

Draft Mode

Draft mode uses the Windows System font to display all text, regardless of the font the document actually uses. This applies only to how the document is displayed, and has no effect on how it's printed. (On most systems, the System font is a variation on Helvetica.) The System font is usually faster to display, so Word can write and scroll the document display much faster than it can without draft view.

In draft mode, Word indicates character formatting (bold, italic, and so on) by underlining the formatted text. It shows empty boxes at the location of pictures and other embedded objects. Word still displays borders and shading in draft mode,

Draft mode is a variation of normal view, so if you're in page layout view or print preview when you turn on draft, Word switches to normal view.

Use View→Draft to toggle draft mode on or off. ("Toggling" means that each time you use the command, it changes to the opposite of its current state: if draft mode is on, it's turned off; if it's turned off, draft mode is turned on.)

Page Layout View

If you could use Word only in normal view, it would be terribly difficult to use positioning to design pages. In fact, designing pages at all would be difficult, since you'd have to put a lot of energy into imagining what pages will look like printed. While normal view is most convenient for typing new material and most formatting, switch to page layout view when you need to see what the printed page will look like.

Note that you can edit in page layout view just as you can in normal view, and you can position things on the page. You can directly edit footnotes, headers, and footers, rather than having to open a separate pane as you do in normal view. Word displays multiple columns as they'd print (side by side). Depending on the speed of your computer, you may find that page layout view is slower than normal view, because Word spends more time making page layout decisions.

Print preview is similar to page layout view, but you can't edit in print preview. (Print preview has its own advantages, as described below.)

Use View→Page Layout to switch to page layout view. When you use this command, Word sets up page layout view at the zoom factor you used last time you used page layout view.

The Toolbar's page layout view button, 🔳, switches to page layout view, but it also selects a zoom factor that fits the entire page on the display. You can use the zoom-width button, 🔳 or the View→Zoom command (described later) to set a different zoom.

In page layout view, Word adds two paging buttons at the bottom of the vertical scroll bar. These paging buttons advance the display an entire page back (up) or forward (down). The regular scroll bar controls move you up and down on the current page; if you move far enough, Word will automatically move to the previous or next page.

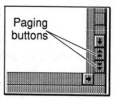

Paging buttons

Outline View

The View→Outline command switches the display to outline view. See the topic "Outlines" for detailed information about this view.

Zooming

In normal view (with or without draft mode), outline view, and page layout view, you can have Word magnify or reduce the size of your document as displayed on the screen. As noted at the beginning of this topic, you might want to use the largest magnification you're comfortable with, most of the time; but at other times you'll want to "get the big picture" by zooming out to see more of the document.

The View→Zoom Command

The View→Zoom command displays the Zoom dialog box, which controls the magnification of the display. It has controls to select standard zooms of 50%, 75%, 100%, and 200%, and an option to enter a custom zoom factor.

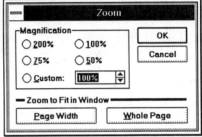

100% is "actual size." Zoom factors greater than 100% magnify the display, making everything larger, while smaller zoom factors pack more on to the screen by making everything smaller.

The two buttons at the bottom of the dialog box automatically compute zoom factors to fit the document into the display in two ways:

- Page Width tells Word to compute the zoom factor necessary to fit the document's current margins between the left and right sides of the document window. It doesn't consider the effect on the height of the display.

- Whole Page makes the view of the document fit both horizontally and vertically into the document window. This is really only meaningful in page layout view, where Word can identify a top and bottom to the current page. In normal view, Word makes the same calculation as if you're in page layout view, but remains in normal view.

Zooming with the Toolbar

Three buttons at the right of the Toolbar control the display, and they all affect the zoom factor.

 Switches to page layout view in the current window, and sizes the display so that the entire page is visible. The zoom factor is the same as that computed by the Whole Page button in the Zoom dialog box.

Switches to normal view mode at 100% zoom.

 Sets the zoom so that the width of the document (the distance between the current margins) fills up the width of the window. Works in page layout, outline, and normal view.

Print Preview

Print preview displays an approximation of how your document will look when printed. It emphasizes accurate margins and positioning over displaying text clearly, and you may find the print preview display a little hard to read. You can't edit in print preview, but you can adjust margins and header and footer position. Print preview is useful for just what its name implies: previewing a document's layout prior to printing it.

You can display one or two pages in print preview. If your document's page setup uses a gutter or the Facing Pages option is checked, Word assumes that you want even pages on the left and odd pages on the right, and sets up the two-page mode of print preview accordingly.

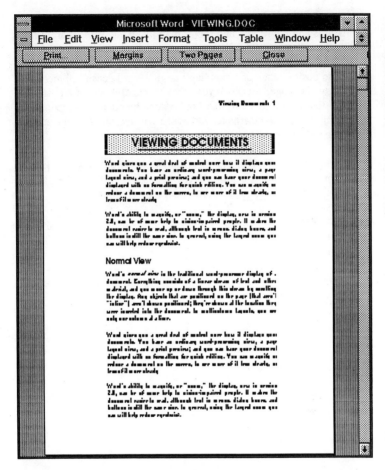

The scroll bar at the right of the display moves the display forward or backward one page at a time in one-page mode, or two pages at a time in two-page mode. You can drag the scroll control to move several pages at a time.

Clicking the Print... button displays the Print dialog box so that you can print the document.

Clicking ⟮Margins⟯ displays a series of guidelines showing the text margins and the header and footer margins. Each of the margin lines has a small square "handle"; position the pointer over a handle until it turns into the $+$ cursor, hold down the mouse button, and drag the line to position the corresponding margin. Word doesn't immediately redraw the page, to allow you time to experiment or adjust your selection. Signal to Word that you're done by clicking the pointer in an empty space on the page, and Word will redraw the page according to the new margin setting.

In single-page display, the third button is ⟮Two Pages⟯; click it to display two pages at a time. If you're already in two-page display, the button is ⟮One Page⟯; clicking it does the obvious thing.

The fourth button sometimes is ⟮Close⟯, and sometimes ⟮Cancel⟯, but either button ends print preview and returns you to your previous display mode.

See also: Frames, Headers and Footers, Navigating through Documents, Outlines

Index

Help Yourself with Another Quality Sybex Book

Mastering Windows 3.1
Robert Cowart

The complete guide to installing, using, and making the most of Windows on IBM PCs and compatibles now in an up-to-date new edition. Part I provides detailed, hands-on coverage of major Windows features that are essential for day-to-day use. Part II offers complete tutorials on the accessory programs. Part III explores a selection of advanced topics.

600pp; 7 1/2" x 9"
ISBN: 0-89588-842-4

**Available
at Better
Bookstores
Everywhere**

Sybex Inc.
2021 Challenger Drive
Alameda, CA 94501
Telephone (800) 227-2346
Fax (510) 523-2373

Sybex. Help Yourself.

The ANSI Character Set

	0	1	2	3	4	5	6	7	8	9
30+				!	"	#	$	%	&	'
40+	(	)	*	+	,	-	.	/	0	1
50+	2	3	4	5	6	7	8	9	:	;
60+	<	=	>	?	@	A	B	C	D	E
70+	F	G	H	I	J	K	L	M	N	O
80+	P	Q	R	S	T	U	V	W	X	Y
90+	Z	[	\	]	^	_	`	a	b	c
100+	d	e	f	g	h	i	j	k	l	m
110+	n	o	p	q	r	s	t	u	v	w
120+	x	y	z	{	|	}	~			
130+										
140+						'	'	"	"	•
150+	–	—								
160+		¡	¢	£	¤	¥	¦	§	¨	©
170+	ª	«	¬	–	®	¯	°	±	²	³
180+	´	µ	¶	·	¸	¹	º	»	¼	½
190+	¾	¿	À	Á	Â	Ã	Ä	Å	Æ	Ç
200+	È	É	Ê	Ë	Ì	Í	Î	Ï	Ð	Ñ
210+	Ò	Ó	Ô	Õ	Ö	^	Ø	Ù	Ú	Û
220+	Ü	Ý	Þ	ß	à	á	â	ã	ä	å
230+	æ	ç	è	é	ê	ë	ì	í	î	ï
240+	ð	ñ	ò	ó	ô	õ	ö	~	ø	ù
250+	ú	û	ü	ý	þ	ÿ				

Note: This table shows the ANSI character set as printed. You may notice that certain characters are different on your display, due to inconsistencies in the display font.